PSYCHIATRIC MALPRACTICE

PSYCHIATRIC MALPRACTICE

Stories of Patients, Psychiatrists, and the Law

▼▼▼▼▼▼▼▼▼▼▼▼▼▼▼▼▼▼

JAMES L. KELLEY

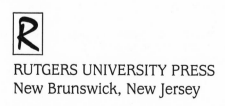

RUTGERS UNIVERSITY PRESS
New Brunswick, New Jersey

Excerpt from *The Cocktail Party*, copyright 1950 by T. S. Eliot and renewed 1978 by Esme Valerie Eliot, reprinted by permission of Harcourt Brace & Company.

Library of Congress Cataloging-in-Publication Data

Kelley, James L., 1935–
    Psychiatric malpractice : stories of patients, psychiatrists, and
the law / James L. Kelley.
        p.   cm.
    Includes bibliographical references (p.)
    ISBN 0-8135-2323-0 (alk. paper)
    1. Psychiatrists—Malpractice—United States.   I. Title.
KF2910.P753K45   1996
346.7303'32—dc20
[347.306332]   95-52270
                                                                    CIP

British Cataloging-in-Publication information available

For my mother

CONTENTS
▼ ▼ ▼

ACKNOWLEDGMENTS
▼ ▼ ▼

I could not have written this book without the generous help of three forensic psychiatrists, Professors Thomas G. Gutheil, Seymour L. Halleck, and Robert L. Sadoff. They reviewed parts of the text, submitted to interviews, and saved me from many errors. They have my thanks and gratitude. Paul Chodoff and Joseph Tarantolo, practicing psychiatrists in Washington, D.C., provided helpful insights on standard-of-care issues.

As a lawyer, I felt more comfortable with the legal than the medical issues but sensed, correctly, that my manuscript would benefit from review by a specialist in this area. My thanks to Professor Ralph Slovenko for his comments on the law. Dr. Steven Bisbing gave me the benefit of his extensive research on relevant judicial decisions. Gary Chefetz provided helpful assistance in reviewing the *Bean-Bayog* case (chapter 10) for factual accuracy.

I'm grateful to my agent, Jane Dystel, for showing me how to write a book proposal, for her continuing support, and for her persistence in finding a publisher. Karen Reeds, my editor at Rutgers University Press, brought her considerable skills and patience to this project and was a pleasure to work with. I also benefited greatly from readings of drafts by my writer friends, Margaret Anderson and David Riley.

The logistics of obtaining copies of court records were formidable in some cases. In that regard, I appreciate the cooperation of lawyers G. Eugene Boyce, Wade Boyd, Ann Loflin, and Paul Sugarman, and of Dr. Raphael J. Osheroff. Professor J. Peter Byrne facilitated access to the Georgetown University Law School Library.

My informal education in mental illness and treatment came largely from the mental health professionals who have treated me over the past twenty years. Norman E. Rosenthal, M.D., diagnosed my manic depression; psychotherapists Isaiah M. Zimmerman, Ph.D., and Lora Price, L.C.S.W., helped to put that illness (among other things) in perspective, and Naomi B. Heller, M.D., my psychopharmacologist, helps me keep the beast at bay. I owe them more than I can say.

Finally, thanks to my friends Joyce and Bill Tager for their hospitality and encouragement on repeated trips to Boston, and to the Morris and Gwendolyn Cafritz Foundation and Virginia Center for the Creative Arts for giving me a friendly and stimulating place to finish this book.

PSYCHIATRIC MALPRACTICE

CHAPTER 1
▼ ▼ ▼

Introduction

> To restore the human subject at the centre—the suffering,
> afflicted, fighting human subject—we must deepen a case
> history to a narrative or tale.
> —OLIVER SACKS, *The Man Who Mistook His Wife for a Hat*

This is a collection of true stories about people in pain who went to psychiatrists for help and ended up suing them for malpractice. Based on actual court cases, the stories are compelling, tragic, and sometimes bizarre. Betrayal and violence are recurring themes.

Psychiatric malpractice is a problem of uncertain dimensions. In the torrent of medical malpractice litigation—obstetricians and orthopedists are frequent defendants—one might expect to find a roughly proportional number of suits against psychiatrists and other mental health professionals. Professions associated with hefty fees, uncertain results, and release of repressed hostilities should have a high potential for driving dissatisfied customers to the law courts.

Until the 1980s, however, the volume of lawsuits against healers of the mind was a trickle compared with suits against healers of the body. Psychiatrists comprise about 6 percent of all medical doctors. A nationwide study by the National Association of Insurance Commissioners found that of 71,778 malpractice claims filed against all medical doctors between 1974 and 1978, only 217 (.3 percent) were against psychiatrists. But in 1985 one insurance underwriter reported that "the number of lawsuits filed against mental health professionals has skyrocketed in recent years."

Although sexual misconduct cases attract the most attention, in fact suicide cases rank first in the number of malpractice suits brought against psychiatrists. About 20 percent of all such suits arise out of patient suicide or attempted suicide. Sexual misconduct cases rank second. Cases where a psychiatrist is sued for failure to prevent a patient's violence—for example, the malpractice suit against John W. Hinckley, Jr.'s psychiatrist following Hinckley's attempt to assassinate President Ronald Reagan—are less common but not infrequent.

In any event, the number of lawsuits alleging psychiatric malpractice isn't an accurate measure of the malpractice that occurs—particularly sexual misconduct. No one knows how many therapists have sex with their patients. Not surprisingly, voluntary surveys of therapists understate the problem. For their part, most patient victims are too ashamed to report the abuse, let alone go public with a lawsuit. In cases not involving sexual misconduct but rather dissatisfaction with the outcome of therapy, many patients would have mixed feelings about suing a therapist with whom they have had a close personal relationship. Former surgery patients probably would be less hesitant to sue a surgeon they saw once or twice for perhaps fifteen minutes.

Patients who want to go to court may have difficulty finding a good lawyer to take a case in which there is no visible, permanent injury and no prospect of a six-figure jury verdict. Others are deterred by the stigma that still attaches to mental illness, a quarter century after Senator Thomas Eagleton was forced off the Democratic ticket after revealing his treatment for depression. These are some of the barriers to meritorious litigation. Unfortunately, there are no effective barriers to frivolous malpractice litigation.

Many psychiatric malpractice cases, particularly suicide cases, have little or no merit. Nevertheless, malpractice trials are a nightmare for psychiatrists—even if they win. They have to sit in court and listen while other psychiatrists with impressive credentials pronounce their work substandard. Their most valuable asset, their reputation, is put at risk before jurors who probably don't understand what they were trying to do.

I included cases that, in medical parlance, had a "bad outcome" for the patient, but in which the psychiatrist was exonerated. Although some psychiatrists may have a negative view of *any* book about malpractice—the less said about it the better—this book is not a polemic against psychiatry. Nor is it a clinical outline or text for psychiatrists or lawyers. While the book is necessarily grounded in psychiatry and law through research and peer review, I wrote it primarily for the general reader interested in, or merely curious about, psychiatrists and the people they treat.

Psychiatric malpractice can occur in a myriad of situations, and I did not attempt to cover the field. Some common cases, for example, prescribing the wrong medication, can have serious consequences but may have little human interest value. Based roughly on three criteria—volume of cases, human interest, and overall significance—I chose four kinds of cases: suicide of a patient, violence by a patient against another person, unusual disputes about the standard of psychiatric care, and sexual misconduct by a psychiatrist.

For each of these four categories of malpractice, I tell the stories of two cases in detail. I then give an overview of the major issues raised by the two stories and place them in a broader context. My criteria for selection mean the cases I chose to treat are not necessarily typical. Some are, but others—like the *Bean-Bayog* case in chapter 10—were chosen for their interesting facts, legal implications, and the public attention they received.

The case chapters are (with one exception) based almost entirely on verbatim transcripts of sworn testimony in court and on hospital records. The court files contained little in the way of therapists' notes of treatment, other than medications. Such notes, where they exist, would be used by one side or the other in malpractice litigation because the plaintiff-patient, by filing suit, waives the privilege of confidentiality that otherwise applies. But therapists aren't legally or ethically required to make notes relating to psychotherapy, and many don't. According to Ralph Slovenko, professor of law and psychiatry at Wayne State University, "most analytically oriented therapists will insist they do not need records to treat patients successfully."

I obtained copies of case records through court clerks or counsel for one of the parties. Most of the records are voluminous; some exceed two thousand pages. The reader should be aware that my relatively short treatments of long and complicated cases had to be highly selective. Many marginal issues and witnesses were omitted altogether. I tried to present straightforward accounts of what happened, letting the record speak for itself. My opinions are given as such, either explicitly or by the context.

Three board-certified, forensic psychiatrists spoke to me at length about general issues as well as about their own experience in the classroom, the clinic, and the court. Certification as a forensic psychiatrist requires both training as a psychiatrist and training in legal standards and procedures. Forensic psychiatrists are recognized as specially qualified to testify as expert witnesses in cases involving diagnosis and treatment of mental illness, including malpractice cases. The three forensic psychiatrists are:

Thomas G. Gutheil, M.D., professor of psychiatry, Harvard Medical School; codirector, Program in Psychiatry and the Law, Massachusetts Mental Health Center; author of numerous articles on clinical and forensic psychiatry.

Seymour L. Halleck, M.D., professor of psychiatry, School of Medicine, adjunct professor of law, School of Law, University of North Carolina; coauthor of *Law in the Practice of Psychiatry* (Plenum, 1980); editor in chief, *Bulletin of the American Academy of Psychiatry and Law*.

Robert L. Sadoff, M.D., clinical professor of psychiatry, University of Pennsylvania Medical School; past president, American Academy of Psychiatry and Law; coauthor of *Psychiatric Malpractice, Cases and Comments for Clinicians* (American Psychiatric Press, 1992).

When former patients sue their psychiatrists for malpractice, they are choosing to open the intimate details of their lives to public scrutiny. Their trials will be open to the public, and court transcripts will remain public records thereafter. In writing this book, I was legally free to use real names and places, and in most cases I did so. Some of the cases don't present strong privacy claims. The standard-of-care cases (chapters 9 and 10) received so much publicity in the past that any attempt at preserving anonymity of the principals would have been futile. Three of the four cases involving suicide and violence (chapters 4, 6, and 7) also received extensive publicity. In chapter 3, however, I changed the names of the family of the teenage boy who committed suicide because several family members may have been victims of sexual abuse and I didn't want to invade their privacy. The patients and psychiatrists in the sexual misconduct cases (chapters 12 and 13) are, presumably, trying to get on with their private and professional lives. I respected their privacy by using fictitious names and places.

The cases I've retold in detail all happen to have involved psychiatrists. The same malpractice rules apply to clinical psychologists and social workers—the other mental health professionals involved in treating patients—and I might have chosen malpractice cases involving them. Psychologists and psychiatrists appear to be about equally implicated in sexual misconduct. On the whole, however, psychologists and social workers are less exposed to malpractice liability, partly because they aren't authorized to prescribe medication. More important, they spend most of their time with the "worried well," a patient population with a lower potential for malpractice claims. Psychiatrists see the sicker patients—

the suicidal and dangerous ones with whom the risk of litigation is much higher.

A note on gender. In parts of the book, and in particular the general discussion of sexual misconduct in chapter 14, the masculine "he" or "him" is used to refer to psychiatrists or other therapists. This is done not merely to avoid the awkward "he or she" construction, but because men greatly outnumber women among psychiatrists and because surveys indicate that sex occurs in therapy much more frequently between male therapists and female patients than vice versa. However, the number of female therapists involved in sex with patients is growing as their numbers grow—and has included such prominent therapists as Dr. Karen Horney, a leading figure in American psychiatry until her death in 1962.

I first became interested in psychiatric malpractice because I was misdiagnosed by psychiatrists in the past. I'm one of an estimated two million Americans who have manic-depressive illness, a disorder marked by extreme fluctuations of mood, between euphoric highs and severe depressions. Most people who have this disorder respond well to medication and can lead normal lives, once they are diagnosed and medicated. Getting a timely diagnosis is critical.

When my symptoms first surfaced in the 1950s, diagnoses of manic depression were rare in this country. According to Dr. Ronald Fieve, a specialist in mood disorders, most cases of elated behavior were being diagnosed as schizophrenia, and treated with tranquilizers or electric shock. Lithium, the current drug of choice for treating manic depression, was proving effective in Europe, but it hadn't yet been authorized for use in the United States. By 1970, however, the symptoms of manic depression were better recognized here, and lithium had been cleared by the Food and Drug Administration for its treatment.

Between 1967 and 1971, during my midthirties, I had three manic episodes, each followed by a long period of depression. I was seeing a psychiatrist who prescribed Thorazine, an antipsychotic, but nothing was said about manic depression or lithium. My last severe depression in 1971 led to a month's stay in one of Washington, D.C.'s leading psychiatric hospitals. Although I was exhibiting the classic symptoms, manic depression still was not diagnosed. Based on what I've learned since, by that time it probably should have been.

Nine years later, after another severe and damaging manic depressive episode—which cost me a job, among other things—a psychiatrist at the National Institute of Mental Health listened to my history, pronounced me a "textbook case" of manic depression, and put me on lithium.

I mention this personal experience as a source of potential bias which ought to be disclosed. I do sympathize with depressed patients in locked hospital wards, having been there myself. My long-standing interest in mental illness is another positive result of an otherwise negative experience. I'm not aware of any conscious bias against psychiatrists or other mental health professionals. I have benefited greatly from their treatment. I respect psychiatrists, particularly those who have the courage to make hard judgment calls about very sick patients who may later kill themselves or someone else.

In the process of writing this book, that respect only grew stronger. But I also came to realize that I do have some unconscious bias against psychiatrists and other mental health professionals, growing out of my long and sometimes negative experience with them. That bias surfaced as judgmental language in drafts of the manuscript. I tried to eliminate bias from the book, but I probably wasn't entirely successful, and the reader should take that into account.

My interest in writing about psychiatrists in court was sparked by a 1989 article in the *Washington Post Magazine*, "A Horrible Place & a Wonderful Place," by Sandra Boodman. Her article focused on two psychiatric malpractice cases brought against Chestnut Lodge, the Rockville, Maryland, hospital that figures prominently in chapter 9 of this book. It described the fascinating controversy between advocates of psychotherapy and those endorsing drug treatment and revealed the tragic human stories behind the legal papers.

The *Post* article linked two strands of my own life: my personal experience with mental illness and my professional life as a lawyer. At the time, I had a solo law practice in Rockville, a few blocks from Chestnut Lodge. I had been a lawyer—mostly with the federal government—for thirty years, including six years as an administrative judge sitting in nuclear power plant licensing cases. In my private practice, I had served as an arbitrator in medical malpractice cases under Maryland's compulsory arbitration statute.

I read everything I could find on psychiatric malpractice in the National Library of Medicine at the National Institutes of Health and the library at Georgetown University Law School. Most of that literature is written in technical language. A psychiatrist friend suggested that I write a book for the general reader, with law and psychiatry in the background.

A book about psychiatric malpractice could be written from the plaintiff-patient's point of view—as a "how to" book about suing your psychiatrist. The basic legal framework of psychiatric malpractice is sketched in chapter 2 and supplemented in the following chapters. I pose some questions and make some suggestions at the end of the book for those who think they may have a claim. But this book isn't a consumer's guide. Those who are considering pursuing a possible claim should consult a lawyer—preferably one specializing in medical malpractice—who would, in turn, refer the case to a psychiatrist for evaluation. As the cases illustrate, a psychiatric malpractice case requires both legal and medical expertise.

Defendant, by Sara Charles, is an example of a book written from the defendant's viewpoint. The author, a psychiatrist, was sued by a former patient who had unsuccessfully attempted suicide. The book describes the psychiatrist's unpleasant experiences as a defendant, in and out of court. Not surprisingly, the book calls for changes in the law to insulate psychiatrists from malpractice liability for suicide.

This is a book about what actually happens when patients take their psychiatrists to court. This is the way we, as a society, deal with people who believe they have been injured by a professional in a position of trust. In drawing that picture, I tried to be neutral between patients and psychiatrists, but I have a point of view on the subject as a lawyer and former judge. In addition to the human element, I'm interested in the issues raised in malpractice litigation: the lawyers' tactics, the judges' rulings, and, ultimately, how the system works or falls short of achieving just results for those affected.

The cases raise fundamental issues about our system for compensating victims of malpractice. The system works slowly; many years may pass before a final judgment. Either side can demand a trial by jury, and plaintiffs almost always do. Some cases suggest that jurors don't understand the psychiatric testimony and decide cases on arbitrary or even whimsical grounds. Some multimillion-dollar verdicts are disproportionate to the plaintiff's injury.

If the cases seem to lack rationality in process and certainty in result, that is attributable as much to the nature of psychiatry as to legal rules and procedures. Medicine is as much art as science, and psychiatry is the most uncertain branch of medicine. The patient comes to a psychiatrist expecting a cure, which even the best of psychiatrists may not be able to deliver. Diagnoses, now standardized in the American Psychiatric Association's *Diagnostic and Statistical Manual of Mental Disorders*, often don't describe real patients. As the late psychiatrist Selwyn Rose observed, "People for some reason refuse to fit into little pigeon holes." Psychiatrists treating potentially suicidal or violent patients can't predict their future conduct and sometimes have to play God—choosing between freedom for the patient or confinement for the safety of others.

In such cases there are no clear rules, and intuition plays a major role. Intuition can be hard to defend in court.

Some of the seeming anomalies in medical malpractice arise from conflicting values represented by psychiatry, law, and the jury system. For example, the psychiatrist views confidentiality of the patient's communications as a paramount value. But if the patient makes a serious threat to injure another person, the law steps in to require the psychiatrist to breach confidentiality in order to protect the other person—"confidentiality must yield," in the words of the California Supreme Court.

Virtually all malpractice cases, if not first settled, are decided by a jury. The jury system is concerned more with citizen participation in the administration of justice than with some objective notion of "truth" or rational process. Which leaves us with the question: do juries usually "get it right" even if they don't understand the testimony of medical experts?

At the end of the book, I suggest a few ways in which some of the problems in the legal system might be fixed or alleviated. But I offer no panaceas or drastic reforms. I conclude that the system works about as well as can be expected.

In writing this book, I should have liked to achieve something approaching the humanity and charm of Oliver Sacks's "clinical tales." But I fell far short of that standard. Quite apart from my limitations as a writer, the sources I used—court transcripts—cannot begin to approximate Sacks's personal experience and rapport with his patients. The formal, ritualized language of testimony in court and the limits imposed by the rules of evidence inevitably flatten personalities and dampen nuances of emotion. It was impossible to interview the scores of people involved. Apart from sheer numbers, some of the principals are unavailable, and others undoubtedly would have preferred to leave an unpleasant chapter of their lives undisturbed, rather than talk to me.

Nevertheless, transcripts of psychiatric malpractice cases can be a rich source of information and insight into people. When a psychiatrist's treatment is challenged in court, the usual rule of confidentiality between therapist and patient is waived, and telling details of the plaintiff's life and the therapist's work go into the record, details which can bring a story to life. The reader will have to judge whether I've been successful.

I hope this book will have some impact on the deep and pervasive stigma that attaches to mental illness in American society. One study of public attitudes found that the mentally ill "are regarded with fear, distrust, and dislike" and that both young and old, educated and uneducated, "tend to regard the mentally ill as relatively dangerous, dirty, unpredictable, and worthless." Another researcher found that the mentally ill came in last in a ranking of twenty-one disability groups, including ex-convicts.

The effects of the stigma are pervasive and cruel. The mentally ill are too often shunned and arbitrarily foreclosed from opportunities open to others. The resulting shame—that most corrosive of emotions—erodes the self-esteem necessary to live a productive life. The stigma reaches beyond the profoundly ill in institutions to the guy next door, or in the next office, who suffers from a debilitating, but often treatable, disorder.

It is inhumane to pile an undeserved stigma on top of an illness that is pain and trouble enough. The patients in these stories are people who, like the rest of us, are trying to make the best of the hands life has dealt them.

CHAPTER 2
▼ ▼ ▼
The Law of Psychiatric Malpractice

Law is a blunt instrument; it can be used to beat down the opposition, but no one should think that the law can chart the path of scientific progress in clinical psychiatry.
—ALAN A. STONE, "Law, Science, and Psychiatric Malpractice," *American Journal of Psychiatry*

Medical malpractice has ancient origins. Under the sixth-century Code of Justinian, a Roman doctor could be sued for damages if he gave incompetent treatment to a slave. The malpractice concept was eventually carried over to English law, and later to the thirteen colonies. Sir William Blackstone, perhaps the most influential commentator in the history of Anglo-American law, cited *Dr. Groenvelt's Case* (1694) for the proposition that "*mala praxis* is a great offense at common law . . . because it breaks the trust which the party had placed in his physician, and tends to the patient's destruction . . . for which there is a remedy in damages."

The historic medical malpractice cases involved invasions of the body. Psychiatric malpractice cases are of more recent vintage. Freud and his colleagues didn't invent psychoanalysis until early in this century, and few people took their psychiatrists to court before World War II.

Most of the early cases involved procedures similar to those performed by traditional physicians—the wrong drug prescription, negligent administration of an electroshock treatment resulting in a broken bone. Such cases focused on physical evidence and didn't require judges and juries to fathom the mysteries of the mind. More recent cases have dealt with the range of mental illnesses and treatments, and with invisible, but sometimes devastating, psychic injuries.

The legal rules governing psychiatric malpractice grew out of, and are much like, those that apply to other medical malpractice cases. However, the law of psychiatric malpractice is less fully developed and less predictable. Lawyers call psychiatric malpractice a "gray area" because the duties of psychiatrists to their patients are often unclear, and the subject matter may be hard for judges and juries to grasp.

There is no federal law of psychiatric malpractice. The legal rules are based on state law—mostly precedents established by judges in particular cases (common law) and relatively few statutes enacted (often piecemeal) by state legislatures. Few states have anything approaching a comprehensive, integrated statute on the subject. As a result, gaps in the law—no statute or relevant precedent—are not uncommon. Judicial attitudes can vary from state to state. In general, California courts have been more hospitable to psychiatric malpractice claims than courts in other states. A winner there can be a loser in New York.

The statutes occasionally reflect different positions on controversial policy issues, such as the ceilings ("caps") in some states of, say, $300,000 on damage awards for pain and suffering. Generally speaking, however, the legal rules are similar from state to state. Many of the rules are, however, subject to exceptions—some narrow, others that threaten to swallow the rule.

Bearing those qualifications in mind, a plaintiff (usually the patient) in the typical psychiatric malpractice case must prove five elements to make a case:

1. The existence of a psychiatrist-patient relationship between the defendant and the plaintiff (as will be seen, there are major exceptions to this requirement).
2. The "standard of care" applicable to the diagnosis and treatment of the patient's illness.
3. A breach of the standard of care by the psychiatrist.
4. A close cause-and-effect relationship (in legal jargon, "proximate cause") between the breach of the standard of care and the plaintiff's injuries.
5. The monetary value of the plaintiff's injuries—medical bills, lost wages, pain and suffering, need for future care, and, in a suicide case, the survivors' loss.

THE PSYCHIATRIST-PATIENT RELATIONSHIP

Proof of this element is not a problem in most cases because it's the patient who is suing the psychiatrist. In some unusual situations, however, a case may fail for lack of a direct relationship between the plaintiff and the defendant-psychiatrist. The *Hinckley* case provides one illustration.

In his abortive attempt to assassinate President Ronald Reagan in 1981, John W. Hinckley, Jr., shot and wounded the president, Press Secretary James Brady, and two members of the president's security detail. Brady sustained grave head injuries and was permanently handicapped. He sued Dr. John Hopper, the psychiatrist who had been treating Hinckley for several months prior to the assassination attempt.

Brady claimed that Hopper had been negligent in diagnosing and treating Hinckley, that the psychiatrist should have controlled Hinckley's behavior, and that if he had, the assassination attempt wouldn't have been made. There was a phalanx of Washington, D.C., legal talent in the Brady camp, but they lost anyway. In dismissing the case without a trial, the judge said, "The legal obstacle to . . . this suit is that there is no relationship between Dr. Hopper and [Brady] which creates any legal obligation from Dr. Hopper to [Brady]." Not only was there "no relationship" between Hopper and Brady, before the assassination attempt they had never even heard of each other.

The *Jackson* case (chapter 13) involved a husband whose wife was seduced by *his* psychiatrist. There, the requisite psychiatrist-patient relationship *does* exist, even though the plaintiff-husband is not the sexual victim. By contrast, there have been several cases where one spouse, not a patient, sues the psychiatrist for seducing the patient-spouse. These cases have been thrown out for lack of a psychiatrist-patient relationship between plaintiff and defendant, even though the moral quality of the psychiatrist's conduct was, if anything, worse—another triumph of legalism over reality.

The most important exception to the psychiatrist-patient relationship requirement comes into play in negligent discharge cases, of which there are many. Patients are confined to mental hospitals because they've been found to be dangerous to others. Before a given patient can be discharged, hospital psychiatrists have a duty to review that individual's history and present condition, and to determine that he is no longer likely to be dangerous. A hoary maxim hovers over every discharge decision: "When in doubt, don't let 'em out."

For example, take the case of the widow of George Laird against the psychiatrist who released Hilton Putney from Delaware State Hospital. While driving down a Delaware highway in a psychotic state, Putney deliberately crashed into George Laird's car and killed him. Putney was tried for manslaughter but found not guilty by reason of insanity. Laird's widow sued Dr. Venkataramana Naidu, a psychiatrist employed by the Delaware State Hospital, from which Putney had been released five months before the fatal collision.

Putney had an extensive history of mental illness dating back twenty years, when he had first been diagnosed as a "severe and chronic paranoid schizophrenic." He had been committed to mental hospitals nineteen times. Only weeks before his release, Putney had been certified as a "mentally ill person dangerous to himself and others." Nevertheless, Dr. Naidu had authorized Putney's release after a superficial review of his history, not including a review of the records from his six prior hospitalizations at the Delaware State Hospital.

Taking a hard line in court, Naidu contended that Putney's prior psychiatric history was irrelevant. That did not sit well with the court. Naidu also advanced a broad policy argument—supported by the National Association of State Mental Health Program Directors (as a "friend of the court")—that he had "no duty to protect the public at large from Putney" because long-term future dangerousness is not predictable. Furthermore, if such a duty were to be imposed, psychiatrists would overstate a patient's propensity for violence, keeping reasonable-risk patients in confinement. The court didn't accept that argument either, and the jury awarded Laird's widow $1.4 million.

THE STANDARD OF CARE

The standard of care is the core concept in psychiatric malpractice. It means the knowledge and skills generally recognized by psychiatrists as necessary to diagnose and treat a particular mental illness. When the standard of care is disputed and the case goes to court, expert witness psychiatrists representing both sides typically testify to different standards—the so-called battle of experts. When that happens, twelve lay jurors have to decide who is right.

Lawyers sometimes dispute whether standards of care are local—where the doctor practices—or national. A century ago, the standard of care was whatever the average doctor, practicing in the same area as the defendant, would have done under the circumstances. It was thought that a rural doctor, isolated from current medical knowledge, couldn't fairly be held to the same standard as doctors in a big city. With the growth of modern communications, the "locality" rule has been largely abandoned. Most courts hold that doctors must adhere to a national standard, whether in obstetrics or psychiatry. The national standard is, in turn, derived from medical texts and journals, and whatever the testifying expert believes.

Standards of care are more clear-cut and widely accepted for physical than for mental illnesses. Orthopedists, for example, are sometimes sued when the artificial knees they implant don't work. Since there is general agreement on acceptable ways to install such a device, the standard of care is easy to prove. Although it is a more recently developed procedure, the same holds true for cardiac bypass surgery.

Proof of the standard of care is not a serious problem in some psychiatric malpractice cases. It's no problem at all in a sexual misconduct case because sex between therapist and patient is categorically forbidden by the canons of ethics of all the major mental health professions and by statutes in a growing list of states. But agreement on standards of care for some mental illnesses—manic depression, for example—has evolved only recently, and large uncharted areas remain.

There are cases where the patient "presents" (as the doctors say) a mixed bag of symptoms, and there is no agreement on diagnosis. The case of Dr. Raphael Osheroff (chapter 9) is one example. Teenagers like Johnny Moore (chapter 3) are committing suicide in growing numbers, and yet psychiatrists don't agree on preventive treatment.

Psychiatrists complain that malpractice litigation puts judges in the position of dictating treatment choice. But this complaint attributes more power to the law than it possesses. To be sure, the standard of care is a legal concept, an invention of judges. But the *content* of the standard of care in any given case is supplied by expert witness psychiatrists, not judges. And standards of care, thus established, often allow for choices among alternative treatments—choices only the psychiatrists can make.

BREACH OF THE STANDARD OF CARE

The plaintiff must prove, again through the testimony of expert witnesses, that the defendant-psychiatrist breached the applicable standard of care. Once the standard is established (usually the higher hurdle), what the psychiatrist actually did is then measured against it. This can be easy in a conventional medical malpractice case—for example, where the results of a botched artificial knee implant are apparent from an X ray or, more graphically, from the plaintiff's inability to walk straight (or at all).

Proving breach is sometimes straightforward in a psychiatric malpractice case. While there might be a spirited dispute over what drug should have been prescribed (the standard of care), there would be no dispute over what drug *was* prescribed. Proving breach can be difficult in a sexual misconduct case, where it is usually the word of the psychiatrist against the patient. Various possible approaches to proof in such cases are discussed in chapter 14.

PROXIMATE CAUSE

In addition to proving breach of the standard of care by the psychiatrist, plaintiffs must prove that the breach was the "proximate cause" of their injuries. There are more definitions of proximate cause than of original sin, most of them complex and legalistic. The Maryland Court of Appeals has said it this way: "Proximate cause exists where there is a complete continuance and unbroken sequence between the act complained of and the act finally resulting in the injury, so that one may be regarded by persons of ordinary judgment as the logical and probable cause of the injury" (*Lashley v. Dawson,* 162 Md. 549 [1932]).

Legalisms aside, the common sense of jurors usually asserts itself. The question for them is whether there was so direct a causal relationship between breach and injury that it's fair to blame the defendant. If, for example, the therapist has sex with the patient, abruptly terminates therapy, and the patient promptly commits suicide, that *is* proximate cause. But if, following sex, the *patient* terminates therapy, experiments with other therapists, and commits suicide a year later, that is *not* proximate cause. Most cases lie somewhere in between.

One might think that sexual misconduct cases would present serious causation problems because the victim's postabuse emotional problems must stem in part from her pretherapy history. But the severe consequences of sex in therapy are well documented, and given persuasive proof of sexual contact, jurors seem to have no difficulty in blaming the plaintiff's deterioration on the therapist. One suspects that however the judge may have instructed them on the technicalities of proximate cause, the jury thought the therapist got what was coming to him.

Suicide cases—the most common kind of case—can raise difficult questions about causation. The families of the former patient may have been led to believe that therapy would help solve the patient's problems. The suicide is then seen as clear evidence that the psychiatrist misled them about his ability to prevent it. In that mind-set, the families are understandably looking for someone to blame—other than the deceased or themselves—and the psychiatrist is the logical candidate.

Dr. Thomas Gutheil, a professor of psychiatry at Harvard Medical School and a veteran expert witness in psychiatric malpractice cases, states that "suicide . . . is the classic example of a bad outcome with bad feelings." Gutheil believes that most suicide cases are filed not because of any demonstrable causal link between the suicide and therapist neglect, but on the assumption that suicidal patients are mere passive objects, subject to their therapists' effective control. By and large, that assumption doesn't reflect reality. If suicidal patients are not out of touch with reality (i.e., not psychotic, in the general sense of that term), despite their depression they are still capable of making a rational decision—to live or not to live.

The case against the psychiatrist is weaker on proximate cause grounds as time passes between the termination of therapy and the injury. We have already looked at *Laird v. Naidu* from the perspective of the doctor-patient relationship. The case also illustrates a stretch of the proximate cause requirement almost to the breaking point. Hilton Putney collided with George Laird five and one-half months after he was released from the Delaware State Hospital. Normally, such an interval would absolve the hospital psychiatrist of responsibility. But Dr. Naidu was at least on notice that Putney might be a continuing danger. Putney stopped taking his medication immediately after his release and didn't appear for a follow-up appointment at another VA hospital. In any event, the court rejected Dr. Naidu's argument that the time interval "was sufficient to dissipate any causal connection between Putney's discharge and the fatal accident."

The case against the psychiatrist becomes even weaker when a long period elapses, and the patient consults other therapists in the interval. In the *Bean-Bayog* case, the subject of chapter 10, patient Paul Lozano killed himself almost a year after Dr. Margaret Bean-Bayog terminated therapy with him, and he had consulted several other therapists in the meantime.

VALUE OF THE INJURIES

People sue psychiatrists for many reasons: for revenge, to purge guilt, to restore self-esteem, and, of course, for money. From their lawyers' narrower perspective, the overriding objective is to make the psychiatrists' insurance companies pay money—a lot of money. When prospective plaintiffs walk into a lawyer's office thinking they have a case (most don't), the lawyer has two questions: what happened, and what's the case worth?

As much as possible, plaintiffs must convert their injuries into dollars, the only thing a jury can award. Actual medical expenses—psychiatrist and hospital bills—can be readily proved with documents, and in some cases they are substantial. A stay in a private psychiatric hospital can cost thousands of dollars per week. Lost earnings may be a factor. The psychic injuries resulting from psychiatric malpractice, however, have no direct dollar equivalent.

The law does not allow compensation for purely "speculative" injuries. Yet an injured plaintiff can be compensated for "pain and suffering." The line between the two is sometimes hard to draw, but it is now pretty well established that psychic injuries may be compensable under the broad rubric of pain and suffering. There have been some quasi-scientific efforts to quantify different kinds of psychic injuries. According to a "Social Readjustment Rating Scale" developed by two psychologists—a "grief" scale suggested for use as evidence in court—the death of a spouse is the most stressful event, rated at 100; divorce is rated at 73 and death of a close family member at 65; Christmas is a 10.

These, then, are the general rules—the five basic elements a plaintiff must prove to make a case: a psychiatrist-patient relationship, the standard of care, breach of that standard, a direct causal relationship between breach and injury, and value of the injury. However, several other legal concepts and rules may come into play in a particular case.

THE "RESPECTABLE MINORITY" DEFENSE

As we have seen, the standard of care is defined as the knowledge and skills recognized by psychiatrists as appropriate to diagnose and treat the patient's illness. In some areas, the mental health professions are virtually unanimous, but there are many areas of controversy. What happens when a competent and conscientious psychiatrist finds himself in the minority?

The respectable minority defense has been recognized by courts to prevent tyranny by the majority in a rapidly evolving medical specialty and to encourage professional innovation and growth. The scope of the defense—how big and "respectable" does the minority have to be—is not entirely clear.

The defense is typically raised where there is a broad (at least majority) professional consensus on the applicable standard of care, but the defendant-therapist deviated from it in the good faith belief that another approach was better or required by unusual circumstances. The *Osheroff* case is an example. The weight of professional opinion was that Dr. Raphael Osheroff should have been given antidepressant drugs during his stay at Chestnut Lodge. The Lodge invoked the respectable minority defense for its exclusive reliance on psychotherapy.

THE "DUTY TO WARN"

Psychiatrists have an ethical duty to keep the confidences of their patients. Prior to an influential 1976 court decision, most psychiatrists believed that their duty of confidentiality extended to situations where a patient threatens the life of another person. In its 1976 landmark *Tarasoff* decision, discussed in chapter 8, the Supreme Court of California held that psychiatrists have a duty to warn the objects of threats by their patients, rejecting arguments by the American Psychiatric Association that psychiatrists could not reliably predict dangerousness. The principle established by the *Tarasoff* decision is now the law in most states.

INFORMED CONSENT

Psychiatrists have a legal duty to inform patients of their diagnosis, the available treatment options, the costs, benefits, and risks of each option, including the option of no treatment—all in language the patient can understand. Patients are supposed to digest this information and give their "informed consent" to the recommended treatment, to another treatment, or to decline treatment altogether.

Few therapists interpret this requirement broadly, and most patients do whatever the therapist recommends. There is an added element of artificiality in the informed consent requirement as it applies to the mentally ill. Unless declared incompetent by a court, a mentally ill person is presumed to be capable of understanding alternative options and of giving informed consent, despite possibly substantial impairments of understanding and judgment.

Informed consent issues arose in the *Paddock* case (chapter 4) and the *Osheroff* case (chapter 9). These cases suggest that psychiatrists sometimes adopt a paternalistic approach to disturbed patients. Linda Kay Paddock, a thirty-seven-year-old woman, was depressed but not psychotic. Nevertheless, her psychiatrist sought consent for hospitalization from her parents, not from her. When Dr. Osheroff, himself a physician, entered Chestnut Lodge, he was severely depressed but capable of understanding treatment options. There was little evidence that those options were presented to him.

Questions of informed consent may also arise in the "managed care" context, where, for example, the patient's insurer may refuse to pay for extended hospitalization. What is the meaning of treatment "alternatives" when the insurance company limits or precludes those otherwise available? These issues are beginning to find their way into the courts as insurers assert more and more authority over treatment decisions, as illustrated by the *Moore* case in chapter 3.

THE STATUTE OF LIMITATIONS

Every state imposes time limits within which lawsuits must be filed. If not filed on time, the suit will be dismissed because the "statute of limitations" was not met. A common statute of limitations for a medical malpractice case, including psychiatric malpractice, is three years from the time the injury occurred. There is, however, an important exception—called the "discovery rule"—under which the time for filing doesn't begin to run until the victim knows or reasonably should have known of the malpractice.

Courts recognize that some people, particularly psychiatric malpractice victims, won't know they've been victimized until long after the event. A Massachusetts decision, *Riley v. Presnell*, illustrates the problem, and the solution. The plaintiff, Robert Riley, was referred in 1975 to the defendant, Dr. Walter Presnell, by the Massachusetts Rehabilitation Commission. According to his complaint, Riley was an epileptic with some emotional problems but no major pathology when he became Presnell's patient. Presnell's "therapy" came to include alcohol, marijuana, liberal prescriptions of Valium, and homosexual sex—all of which exacerbated Riley's psychological condition. Presnell abruptly terminated Riley in 1979 without referring him to another therapist. In 1984, a second psychiatrist referred Riley to another former patient of Presnell's who described similar treatment and problems.

Although the Massachusetts statute of limitations normally would have required Riley to file his suit by 1981, he did not file until 1985, claiming that he could not reasonably have discovered Presnell's malpractice until 1984. The highest court in Massachusetts endorsed the "discovery" rule and gave Riley an opportunity to prove his case.

Broad generalizations about the law of psychiatric malpractice are hazardous because relatively few cases have reached appellate courts for decision in the gray areas. But the basic legal principles are relatively simple and fairly clear. Those principles shape a psychiatric malpractice case, but they don't drive it. Medical science is the dynamic element in that process. Beyond that, one can say that the more concrete the elements of the case, and the clearer the standard of care, the easier it should be for the plaintiff's lawyer. Sympathetic facts are more important to a jury than abstract principles of law, as any experienced trial lawyer knows.

PART I

SUICIDE

CHAPTER 3
▼ ▼ ▼

The Walking Suicide Time Bomb

They told us that he was better. . . . They let us take our kid out of there. . . . Nobody had the common decency to say, "Look, you better watch out."
—JANET MOORE, mother of Johnny Moore

The hospital is a business and when they're looking at a patient who is using resources, but not able to pay, they would like me to find a different alternative for care.
—BRUCE RAU, medical director, Charter Hospital

Johnny Moore, a bright and sensitive sixteen-year-old, was saddened by the suicide of his maternal aunt Vicky in April 1986. She and her family had lived nearby when Johnny was little, and he had always been close to her. Aunt Vicky had shot herself after discovering that her father had molested her eight-year-old daughter. Johnny had taken the call from Aunt Vicky's husband, and he had the terrible task of awakening his mother to tell her that her sister was dead.

Johnny's grandfather's sexual abuses had spanned two generations and had involved every female member of two families. He had abused both his daughters—Vicky and Janet—when they were children. During those years, their father had been a heavy drinker, a violent man who didn't go to church. After she married and bore children, Janet Moore wanted to believe that because her father had been "saved" and become a teetotaling church deacon, he was not a threat to her own daughter, Allison.

Janet Moore later realized that hers was wishful thinking when Johnny, then thirteen, told her that Grandfather had fondled Allison,

Johnny's nine-year-old kid sister. At that point, Janet tried in vain to stop her father on her own. Three years later, after her father had abused her niece and caused her sister, Vicky, to kill herself, she filed a criminal complaint against him. The grandfather was charged with sexual abuse, and a preliminary hearing was scheduled for late July 1986.

Johnny's grandfather's depredations were a major factor in making the Moore family dysfunctional. Other factors contributed. The family had moved frequently, uprooting the children from neighborhoods and schools. When Johnny was seven years old, his mother had attempted suicide. Two years before his Aunt Vicky's suicide, Johnny's father had had an affair, and his parents had separated for nine months. After his parents reconciled, Johnny was overly protective toward his mother and alienated from his father.

The Moores were rarely together as a family. Johnny's father worked two jobs: a shift from 5:30 A.M. to 3:30 P.M. at "Blue Bell," a denim material plant, followed by a 4 to 9 P.M. shift at a Sears Distribution Center. Johnny's mother, a nurse, worked the night shift at a local hospital, leaving for work before her husband got home and returning after he had left for work.

Johnny had always been a good student. A sixth-grade writing project, "Don't You Ever Get Homesick, Marco Polo?" had received special recognition. After his Aunt Vicky's death in April, Johnny finished his sophomore year in high school with a 3.4 grade-point average. But he remained depressed. One night in early June, he came to his mother and said, "Mama, I've got a problem. I've been drinking." Johnny's mother couldn't believe it. "It like to knock my socks off," she recalled. Johnny told his mother that he had started drinking "right after Aunt Vicky died."

The next day, Johnny's mother took him to their family doctor, who referred him to the Guilford County Mental Health Center. A center therapist told Janet Moore that Johnny was suicidal, that he wanted to kill his grandfather, and that he should be hospitalized immediately. Johnny's father came home from work, and both parents took the teenager to Charter Hospital of Winston-Salem, North Carolina, a private psychiatric hospital not far from their home.

Johnny Moore was admitted to Charter Hospital on June 12, 1986. He was discharged on July 14, after the family's insurance coverage ran out. Sixteen days later, he wrote a suicide note and swallowed a lethal overdose of Norpramin—an antidepressant prescribed by his hospital psychiatrist.

Charter Hospital of Winston-Salem and its parent corporation, Charter Medical Corporation, became the defendants in a lawsuit brought by

Johnny Moore's parents charging malpractice in the death of their son. When the case was tried in 1991, Charter Medical, a profit-making organization, owned a chain of ninety-one psychiatric hospitals throughout the country. Daily charges in a Charter Medical facility when Johnny Moore was a patient exceeded $300—about $10,000 per month—over 90 percent of which came from health insurance companies. With outstanding stock valued at $797 million, Charter Medical was, in malpractice parlance, the "deep pocket" in the case. The malpractice case would focus on two issues: whether Johnny's discharge was premature, and whether Charter Hospital had put undue pressure on Johnny's psychiatrist to discharge him when his insurance coverage ran out.

JOHNNY MOORE'S STAY AT CHARTER HOSPITAL

Johnny Moore was placed in the adolescent unit, where all the patients, usually about ten, were being treated by Dr. Larry Jarrett Barnhill, Jr., a psychiatrist, and by Betsy Willard, a social worker. Barnhill wrote in his admission note that Johnny had been "referred following increase in suicidal ideation, with increasing severity of depression," coupled with a "marked increase in alcohol and substance abuse" (Johnny had been smoking marijuana). In his initial session with Barnhill, Johnny denied having hallucinations. Dr. Barnhill's diagnosis: major affective disorder, with the possibility of manic-depressive illness to be ruled out. The initial treatment plan was to assess Johnny for medication and to provide supportive therapy concerning his aunt's death and "the chaos created by the charges against his grandfather." Barnhill estimated Johnny's stay at two weeks.

In an early session with social worker Willard, Johnny spoke of "tremendous stress within the family." He felt he was "no good" and that he would end up "in the gutter." He reported that he had almost drowned at age three and had rheumatoid arthritis at thirteen. Johnny told Willard that he was sexually active and had contracted herpes and syphilis in the past year. (Later in his stay, Johnny began to worry that his girlfriend was pregnant.) Willard observed that Johnny was afraid of suicide, but "in many ways he romanticizes the whole area of death." She quoted him as saying that if he killed himself, "I'll be with my aunt in heaven."

On June 17, Dr. Barnhill called in another child psychiatrist for a consultation about Johnny. The consultant made several recommendations, including: "The patient's bizarre suicidal ideation, including drinking poison from fluorescent lightbulbs, and his homicidal intent toward his maternal grandfather, require that he remain hospitalized until there is clearer certainty that he is stable to the point of having better control and understanding of his ideation."

Dr. Barnhill took a cautious approach in prescribing medication. He thought Johnny's depression might be attributable to withdrawal from alcohol—a type of depression that should pass in a few days—and that antidepressant medication might trigger a manic reaction. After a week of observation, however, Barnhill prescribed a daily dose of 150 milligrams of the antidepressant Norpramin. When a laboratory test showed a subtherapeutic level in Johnny's system, the Norpramin was increased to 200 milligrams daily.

Johnny and his mother had a "family session" with Betsy Willard on June 23. Johnny's unusually close, protective relationship with his mother was the focus of attention. Johnny sat close to his mother and held her hand throughout the session. He spoke of his parents' separation as if he were merged with his mother. Willard's plan for dealing with this "enmeshment" was to "do some work between father and son." She met with them in another family session, which led to a father-son outing on July 4. Nothing more came of the plan, however. After their outing, Johnny felt that his relationship with his father had gotten worse.

Johnny participated in various groups and activities during his hospital stay. His adolescent unit had group therapy four times each week with Betsy Willard. Johnny also talked with other mental health staffers on his unit. There were weekly "leisure experience" and "self-esteem" groups, a class in "anger control," and art therapy.

Nevertheless, Johnny's preoccupations with suicide, violence, and revenge were present throughout his stay. Reporting on a group therapy session of June 30, Willard noted that he "continues to brood on how unhappy his world is, and to focus on revenge [against] his grandfather." The next day, Dr. Barnhill wrote, "Johnny continues his infatuation with death, fatalism, and more nihilistic fantasies." A week later, Barnhill noted Johnny's "obsessive preoccupation with self-destructive behavior."

The term "psychosis" denotes serious mental illness. The term is used in a broad sense to mean that the patient is out of touch with reality. The *Diagnostic and Statistical Manual of Mental Disorders*, psychiatry's diagnostic guide, lists nine separate psychotic disorders that share some common symptoms, notably persistent hallucinations—seeing or hearing things that aren't there. Johnny had been having hallucinations about his Aunt Vicky and his grandfather before he entered the hospital. In early July, those hallucinations returned and became persistent. On July 8, six days before his discharge, Johnny told a mental health staffer he was "tired of hearing voices nearly every day . . . a male voice and a female voice. . . . the female tells him everything is going to work out all right. . . . the male voice tells him that he should . . . just kill himself." Johnny said he was afraid to go on pass the coming weekend because of "what might happen . . . that these voices are now taking control of his body." Also on July 8, Dr. Barnhill noted "questionable auditory hallucinations . . . perhaps related to more significant psychotic symptoms." Barnhill decided to ask Johnny's parents for permission to give him Navane, an antipsychotic drug, in addition to the antidepressant Norpramin Johnny was already taking.

On July 9 Johnny participated in art therapy. He drew a picture he titled "Death," depicting different ways to commit suicide—including a gun, a razor blade, and poison. He told the art therapist that he wasn't ready to leave the hospital the following Tuesday (as it turned out, he left one day earlier) and that he planned to kill himself before that time. The staff on Johnny's ward was notified about his suicidal intentions. That evening, Johnny told the staff he needed to be watched. He was locked out of his room and required to sleep in the dayroom, where the staff could keep him under constant watch.

On Thursday, July 10—four days before Johnny's discharge—Dr. Barnhill noted two "symptomatic changes" in Johnny's chart. First, an increase in auditory hallucinations—the same male and female voices he had heard before. Although these hallucinations were "persistent," Barnhill thought that Johnny seemed "less intensely preoccupied" with them. He prescribed a small dose of Navane to mute the voices.

The second change Barnhill noted was "the recrudescence of self-destructive behavior"—meaning that Johnny was still thinking and talking about killing himself. Barnhill described the staff's approach to Johnny's "suicidal ideation."

> We're handling this matter-of-factly, linking it to his anxieties about discharge and the possible identification with his aunt during this disengagement process. We've reviewed this thoroughly with his family, our concerns about his dramatic symptomology and histrionic style, and both parents seem comfortable with the notion of eventually discharging, in spite of the failure of complete resolution of his suicidal thought.

A laboratory test indicated that the Norpramin Johnny had been taking for three weeks had still not reached a therapeutic level. On July 10, Barnhill ordered an increase in Johnny's daily dose from 200 to 250 milligrams.

On Friday, July 11—three days before discharge—a mental health worker reported a conversation with Johnny. "Johnny made a point about telling me about a dream he had this morning in which he shot himself in the head. . . . Johnny states that he still feels suicidal and cannot believe that Dr. Barnhill is considering sending him home." Johnny had uneventful day passes with his family the Saturday and Sunday preceding his Monday discharge.

Johnny was discharged from Charter Hospital to his family on Monday, July 14. Dr. Barnhill gave Johnny's mother a prescription for 150 fifty-milligram tablets of Norpramin—a month's supply. An unusually large prescription was written at the Moores' request because their insurance paid a larger proportion of a month's supply than of smaller quantities. Barnhill noted that Johnny's mood at discharge seemed "stable," but that his "constant verbal interest" in suicide "may require more close observation." Johnny left behind a letter to a fellow patient saying he was going to kill himself when he got out.

JOHNNY MOORE AS AN OUTPATIENT

Johnny Moore never went back to Charter Hospital. His mood remained depressed after his discharge. Normally a hearty eater, Johnny picked at his food. He stayed close to home, not seeing much of his friends. His mother took him for an appointment at the County Mental Health Center on July 22. The therapist told her that Johnny was "going to be okay." He had lined up a job at a Taco Bell before he was hospitalized. He picked up his uniform in late July but never reported for work.

On July 29, a preliminary hearing was held on the sexual abuse charges against Johnny's grandfather. Johnny went to court with his mother and sister. He didn't testify, but his sister did. The court found probable cause to believe that Johnny's grandfather was guilty and bound him over for trial. Johnny cried at the hearing. Afterward, he stated that his grandfather "got what he deserved."

On the evening of July 30, Johnny hugged his mother as she was leaving for work. "Are you okay?" she asked. "Oh Mama, don't worry about me. I'm fine," Johnny replied. Johnny's father went to bed about midnight and got up about 2 A.M. to go to the bathroom. Passing Johnny's room, he saw him sitting on the edge of his bed. "I asked him did he want to talk about anything. . . . He said 'No. Just go to bed, Daddy, and sleep. I'm fine.'"

Johnny's father got up to go to work about 4 A.M. and found the following note on the kitchen table.

Dear Family,

I am sorry everything came to an end like this. Please forgive me. I love you all so much. . . . I know this will hurt, but what would hurt more—this, or seeing me in a straightjacket in a padded room, staring into space or screaming. That would have destroyed you all, especially Mama. . . . Try to carry on the case in mine and Aunt Vicky's names. She told me to tell you that. . . . Don't let Junior [a nickname for Johnny's grandfather] go to the wake or the funeral. I spent the last few minutes praying and then Aunt Vicky came, heavenbound. Love always,

Johnny Moore

Johnny had swallowed all of the Norpramin remaining of his month's supply—about seventy-five pills. His father tried to force him to vomit, but Johnny gently bit his finger and shook his head. Johnny was taken to the emergency room about 5 A.M. and later transferred to intensive care. He was in a coma and on a ventilator. Shock was applied for an erratic heartbeat. His kidneys failed, making dialysis necessary. He was having seizures.

The evening of his first day in the hospital, Johnny's mother was standing by his bed. As she recalled the visit: "He and I used to play this game. He'd wake me up and say: 'Mama, are you there?' I bent down next to him and I said: 'Johnny, baby, it's Mama. Are you there?' And he turned his head, he opened his eyes and he looked at me. And the nurse that was taking care of him like to fainted. But that's the last time that he ever looked at me."

Johnny remained in a coma for two weeks; his condition deteriorated until tests showed no blood flow to his brain, and the doctors said nothing more could be done. The Moore family was Catholic; a priest was called to say the last rites. On August 16, Johnny's ventilator was disconnected, and he died.

THE MALPRACTICE CASE

Two years after Johnny Moore's death, in August 1988, his parents sued Charter Hospital of Winston-Salem and its parent corporation, Charter Medical Corporation, in the Superior Court of Guilford County, North Carolina, for malpractice. The suit originally included Dr. Barnhill as a defendant, but a settlement was reached with him before the trial. *Moore v. Charter Hospital* was a complex case. The trial began in November 1991 and lasted six weeks, generating a transcript of more than three thousand pages. Twenty-five witnesses testified, including eight experts. Ultimately, the jury returned a $7-million verdict in favor of the Moores.

Was Johnny Moore Discharged from Charter Hospital Prematurely?

THE PLAINTIFFS' CASE. The Moores' lawyers built their case primarily on hospital records and the testimony of former hospital employees, three psychiatrist experts, and Johnny's parents. During his hospital stay, Johnny became close to Fernando Garzon, a mental health worker on the adolescent unit who was majoring in psychology at Wake Forest. Garzon knew Johnny as a "good kid," never a behavior problem. But he saw no improvement while Johnny was in the hospital. Johnny was suicidal when he arrived and again as his discharge approached. "Johnny would talk about suicide kind of like you and I might talk about sports," Garzon said.

James Sims, another mental health worker, had a degree in psychology and had come into contact with Johnny daily. Sims had been involved in Johnny's admission and recalled how "he was hallucinating, both visually and auditorily," and had shown "an intense desire to kill himself and an intense anger toward his grandfather." Johnny was again suicidal and hallucinating toward the end of his stay. Sims thought Johnny was "the sickest child we'd seen in a long time."

The plaintiffs' three expert witnesses on the issue of premature release had impressive credentials. Jonas R. Rappeport, a psychiatrist, was chief medical officer for the Circuit Court of Baltimore, Maryland, and held teaching appointments at the University of Maryland and at Johns Hopkins. Harvey L. Resnik, a psychiatrist with extensive experience in private practice and government research, had authored the first textbook on suicide to be used in American medical schools and had edited two other books, *Suicidal Behavior* and *The Prediction of Suicide*. Gerald Cooke, a psychologist, taught and lectured on suicide and held teaching positions at Villanova and the University of Pennsylvania.

There was a consensus among the plaintiffs' experts that Johnny had been prematurely discharged from Charter Hospital. Dr. Resnik identified nine factors that contributed to Johnny's high level of suicide risk:

1. He was a male adolescent. The suicide rate among adolescents, about six thousand each year, is increasing; moreover, male adolescents are three times as likely as females to succeed in killing themselves.
2. He had an alcohol problem.
3. He felt responsible for his parents' separation.
4. He was depressed.
5. His family had a genetic predisposition to suicide, and he had been strongly affected by his aunt's recent suicide.

6. He was physically impaired from rheumatoid arthritis; he couldn't run and play ball like other kids.
7. He was impulsive.
8. He was an indirect victim of incest—through his grandfather's abuses of his sister, mother, cousin, and aunt.
9. He was experiencing command hallucinations—a hallmark of psychosis. Voices will tell a psychotic patient to jump out a window and fly, or to "walk in the street because you're a human tank and you'll knock the cars over." Unable to appreciate the risk, the patient is driven to obey the voice.

Dr. Resnik told the jury: "I've been in practice over thirty years. I treat adolescents. . . . I can tell you I have never seen a heavier load of suicidal predisposition in my practice or in the literature. This boy right here, before he walks into [Charter Hospital], is a walking suicide time bomb."

The plaintiffs' experts believed that Johnny had not gotten any better, and may have gotten worse, by the time he was discharged. He hadn't reported hallucinations during most of his stay. A few days before discharge, however, he was psychotic, suicidal, and homicidal—hearing Aunt Vicky's voice, dreaming of shooting himself in the head, and drawing instruments of suicide in his art therapy class. According to Dr. Cooke, it takes weeks, not days, to recover from a serious psychotic episode. Dr. Resnik agreed, saying Dr. Barnhill should have had Johnny committed if his parents had not agreed to his transfer to a state hospital.

In a case like Johnny's where antidepressant and antipsychotic drugs are prescribed, the patient should be kept in the hospital until tests show he is stabilized—the doses have reached a therapeutic level, and the patient isn't suffering from serious side effects. Dr. Barnhill had been increasing Johnny's dose of Norpramin gradually, but at the time of his discharge it hadn't been determined that this dosage had reached therapeutic level. Barnhill's discharge note had concluded, somewhat ambiguously, "hopefully, we can stabilize him over the 72 hours after discharge."

Dr. Barnhill prescribed the antipsychotic drug Navane in a four-milligram dose four days before discharge, when Johnny was reporting hallucinations. According to Dr. Resnik: "That is not an antipsychotic dose. It's a tranquilizing dose." At discharge, Barnhill reduced Johnny's Navane dose to two milligrams, which Resnik compared to "water off a duck's back."

Dr. Barnhill and social worker Willard had not taken Johnny's preoccupation with suicide seriously enough. A Barnhill note that referred to

Johnny's hallucinations a few days before discharge as "teenage fantasies" evoked a sardonic comment from Dr. Resnik. "Come on. . . . This is a patient that's got the heaviest premorbid, suicidogenic . . . time-bomb walking set of circumstances I have ever seen." Willard thought that Johnny "romanticized" death. According to Dr. Cooke: "Many people talk about suicide in a romantic fashion. They have a delusion that after they kill themselves, they'll be able to look back—look down, as it were—and see how everybody responds [to] their death. . . . That, unfortunately, does not reduce, but rather increases, the likelihood of suicide."

The plaintiffs' experts agreed that transferring Johnny to a state hospital for longer-term care would have been an acceptable, if not desirable, option. But continued hospitalization was essential. Discharge to the custody of Johnny's parents, with outpatient visits to a clinic, was wholly inadequate.

Dr. Barnhill's chart note of July 10 concluded with this cryptic sentence: "We have informed him that possible transfer to a State hospital would be an option, should these behaviors [hallucinations and suicidal ideation] recur." Dr. Rappeport read this sentence as a thinly veiled threat against Johnny: stop having hallucinations and talking about suicide, or we'll put you in the state hospital. Johnny's mother denied that anything had been said to them about the option of a state hospital—an option she thought "might have saved his life."

The testimony of Johnny's parents focused on what Barnhill and Willard had told them about Johnny's condition at discharge and what they should do with Johnny's drug medications. According to Johnny's mother, "They told us that he was better, and that he was having teenage fantasies about death and suicide, and that he was doing these things to get attention." Dr. Barnhill did not explain why Johnny's medications could be dangerous. As Johnny's mother recalled, Barnhill told her: "Take the medicine and keep it away from him, you put it up from seven to ten days. And after that, you let him have free access to it and dose himself."

Johnny's mother claimed that she had followed Barnhill's instructions "to the letter." The first ten days Johnny was home she had held on to his medications, taking them with her to work and putting them under the mattress when she went to bed. After ten days, she put them on the kitchen table.

CHARTER HOSPITAL'S CASE. The hospital's lawyers were content to rely on Dr. Barnhill's testimony that Johnny's medical condition had justified discharge, without calling any outside experts. Perhaps sensing that they would lose on that question, they concentrated on insulating their client, the hospital, from a questionable discharge decision. Since the hospital's lawyers weren't representing Dr. Barnhill, they were free to leave him twisting in the wind.

Dr. Larry Jarrett Barnhill graduated from medical school in 1975, completed a psychiatric residency in 1979, and was thereafter board certified in child and adolescent psychiatry. He was a professor at Eastern Carolina University until 1983, when he joined a psychiatric practice group in Winston-Salem and became a part-time staff member at Charter Hospital. Barnhill served until 1987 as director of the adolescent program at Charter. At the time of the trial, Barnhill was a professor of psychiatry at the University of North Carolina and director of its children's outpatient services.

Dr. Barnhill disagreed in most respects with the opinions of the plaintiffs' experts: Resnick, Rappeport, and Cooke. He did agree that Johnny had been suicidal at admission, and that he had been the sickest patient on the adolescent unit. Beyond that, however, Barnhill thought he had a good therapeutic relationship with Johnny, that he had begun to improve rapidly in the hospital—with increased sleep, weight gains, and successful day passes—and that, at discharge, he was "better." Barnhill stated that the Charter program for adolescents became redundant, or even counterproductive, after a three- or four-week stay.

Dr. Barnhill believed he had handled Johnny's drug tests and dosages appropriately. He at first testified that he had received a laboratory test result on Johnny's last Norpramin increase before he was discharged and that the level was therapeutic. He later conceded that he had been mistaken, that he had received the result the day after Johnny's discharge, and that it merely confirmed what he had thought—that a therapeutic level had been reached.

Dr. Barnhill had been aware that Johnny told a nurse at his admission about hallucinations—seeing something "floating down the hall" and hearing a "female voice calling his name." Barnhill thought at the time that those hallucinations probably were the result of alcohol abuse, and that they would pass with hospital abstinence. Barnhill believed that Johnny's hallucinations toward the end of his stay were a "discharge regression" brought on by fear of leaving the protective hospital environment; they would, Barnhill felt, dissipate as Johnny adjusted to life on the outside. Barnhill believed that Johnny's dream, three days before discharge, of shooting himself in the head was also a discharge regression, not a worsening of symptoms.

Dr. Barnhill recalled hour-long meetings with Johnny shortly before and again on his discharge day. Barnhill's main concerns were with

Johnny's suicidal thoughts and hallucinations. "At that time, his suicidal risk had diminished drastically. That would not say that two weeks from now, he might not be suicidal again. We also looked at his auditory hallucinations. By his claim, they had diminished. He wasn't particularly troubled with them."

Dr. Barnhill equated "suicidal," in the medical sense, with a serious, present intention to kill yourself. He hadn't seen that intention in Johnny Moore at his discharge. For one thing, Johnny lacked the strongest single indicator of suicide—a prior attempt. Barnhill also testified that because Johnny didn't believe his hallucinations were real, Johnny wasn't psychotic at discharge. For the same reasons, the psychiatrist didn't believe Johnny had been subject to involuntary commitment. As he understood the law, commitment required a "strong suspicion" that the patient is otherwise going to be dead within forty-eight hours.

Dr. Barnhill's testimony about his conversations with Johnny's parents contradicted them in virtually every respect. For example, Janet Moore recalled asking Barnhill whether Johnny should attend his grandfather's court hearing (scheduled for two weeks after discharge), that Barnhill said Johnny *should* go to court, and that "if Johnny could see somebody doing something . . . about his sister being molested, it would make him feel a lot better." Dr. Barnhill testified that he had advised Johnny's parents *not* to let Johnny go to court because the "degree of distress" it would bring up would be "very detrimental." According to Barnhill, he had suggested getting the hearing delayed or even withdrawing the complaint. Such a stark conflict in testimony is unlikely to result from faulty recollection. In any case, the hearing was held on schedule, Johnny went to court, and he committed suicide the next day.

Dr. Barnhill denied that he had threatened Johnny with commitment to a state hospital. Furthermore, he had discussed the option of a state hospital with Johnny's parents; they had rejected that option, leaving Barnhill with the impression that they thought of the state hospital as a "snake pit."

Dr. Barnhill "never" told Johnny's parents to give him free access to medications. In treating hundreds of adolescents for depression, he "never made that recommendation" because the drugs are "very lethal." He had told the Moores that Johnny's Norpramin prescription was "probably enough to kill three or four of us" and to keep it "absolutely out of his reach." Further, that after Johnny was settled at home, they could allow him access to three or four days' doses, at most.

Was Johnny Moore Discharged Because His Insurance Coverage Had Expired?

Johnny's father subscribed to family health insurance through his employer. The policy set a thirty-day limit on psychiatric hospital stays. When Johnny was admitted, Charter Hospital confirmed his coverage with the insurer and thereafter kept Dr. Barnhill informed of the remaining days of coverage. Shortly before Johnny's coverage expired, Dr. Barnhill applied to the Charter administrator for a two-day extension of Johnny's stay, based on his parents' agreement to pay for the additional days on an installment plan. A two-day extension was granted, and Johnny was discharged on July 14, 1986, thirty-two days after his admission.

The plaintiffs contended that Charter Hospital had a policy of discharging patients when their health insurance expired, without adequate regard to the patient's medical condition, and that the policy, as it had been applied to their son, violated the standard of care for hospitals. Charter Hospital denied having any such policy. It claimed that it gave free care—also known as "Charter Care"—to many patients whose medical condition required them to stay after their insurance expired.

THE PLAINTIFFS' CASE. There was no written hospital policy that patients had to be discharged when their insurance ran out. On the contrary, Charter Hospital was committed, in a "Rights of Patients" form signed by each patient, to provide "adequate and humane services, regardless of sources of financial support." The plaintiffs set out to prove that that commitment hadn't been kept.

What patients and their parents are led to believe about a hospital's discharge policy is one indication of what that policy really is. Tracy Cheek, a former patient, had been a friend of Johnny's in the adolescent unit. Johnny had told her he was being discharged "because his insurance ran out." The mother of a former patient testified that when she took her son to Charter Hospital, she had been told that she had twenty-one days of coverage and that her son would be in the hospital for twenty-one days. Another mother recalled that as coverage for her son was expiring, Dr. Barnhill "would count down how many weeks or days we had left."

According to Fernando Garzon and James Sims, former mental health employees on Johnny's unit, it was commonly assumed that patients would be discharged when their insurance ran out. Sims thought that insurance was the "overwhelmingly predominant factor" in deciding length of stay at Charter, and that Johnny's discharge had been for insurance reasons. Sims thought Dr. Barnhill had been trying to keep Johnny in the hospital, that the Business Office had turned him down, and that

"Dr. Barnhill's frustration was quite evident." In Sims's experience, which included the intake department, patients were not told that free care was an option.

The plaintiffs had retained Dr. Umit Akinc, a professor in the business school at Wake Forest University, to perform a statistical analysis of admissions and discharges at Charter Hospital in the year preceding Johnny Moore's discharge, focusing on two variables: duration of stay and duration of insurance coverage. The study involved more than one thousand patients. Akinc found that patients with thirty or fewer days of coverage stayed an average of 19.7 days, whereas those with thirty or more days of coverage stayed an average of 25.8 days—a difference of 6.1 days that bore no relationship to patients' medical conditions. Akinc cautioned that his study didn't show insurance to be the only factor in discharge decisions; many patients get well before their insurance expires. But he concluded there is a significant relationship between the duration of a patient's coverage and length of hospital stay.

The three experts who testified on the issue of premature discharge—Rappeport, Cooke, and Resnik—also expressed the view that expiration of Johnny Moore's insurance had unduly influenced his discharge. In Dr. Cooke's phrase, insurance had "impacted and compromised the clinical decision." Building on the Akinc study, Dr. Rappeport pointed out that "People don't get well by the amount of insurance they have. People get well by virtue of the disease they have, the care and treatment they get."

The plaintiffs called Professor Charles P. Hall, Jr., chairman of a graduate program in health administration and a professor in the Department of Risk Management at Temple University. Hall's areas of concentration included health insurance and risk management. He testified that the standard of care for a hospital, including a psychiatric hospital like Charter, should be "independent of the existence of insurance, or the duration of insurance . . . as it pertains to release of a patient." Patients should be discharged only when their conditions are either "cured, stabilized or under control, or when the patient is being transferred, if further treatment is necessary, to appropriate alternative facilities."

Professor Hall thought that in Johnny Moore's case there were strong indications "the primary motivator in discharge was the expiration of insurance." The strongest was that Dr. Barnhill had been required to get approval from the Charter administrator to keep Johnny in the hospital after his insurance expired. Barnhill's "request for extension" gave as reasons "continued treatment and regulation of medication," which should have been "a red flag" to the administrator that the patient wasn't ready for discharge. "You don't really have to be a rocket scientist," Hall contended, "to figure out that this guy is in trouble."

In such a case, the standard of care required the administrator (or someone acting for him) to "verify that those conditions which were the cause of the extension had been rectified." In Johnny Moore's case, Barnhill's discharge note of July 14—saying that Johnny was not yet "stabilized"—indicated the contrary. Hall testified that failure to stabilize a patient before discharge falls under the heading of "patient dumping."

None of the plaintiffs' experts argued that hospitals and doctors were prohibited from giving any consideration to insurance in planning a patient's treatment. On the contrary, Hall stated that any hospital today, psychiatric or medical, "would try and not keep the patient longer" than authorized by insurance. Therefore, the treating doctor needs to be kept informed of the patient's insurance. In Johnny Moore's case, his limited coverage should have been taken into account from the beginning to facilitate transfer to a state hospital when it became apparent that long-term treatment might be necessary.

But there is a line between prudent treatment planning, based partly on coverage, and discharging patients willy-nilly when their coverage runs out. Professor Hall cited the "well known fact" that some hospital administrators have "brought pressure to bear" for discharges, and that some doctors have yielded to pressure "to retain their privileges . . . with that hospital." During 1986, Dr. Barnhill spent most of his professional time at Charter Hospital, making him potentially vulnerable to pressure. A hospital crosses the line into malpractice when "any kind of pressure or duress is brought to bear on the therapist to sign a discharge order primarily because of the expiration of the insurance, and not based on the medical condition of the patient." Hall concluded that, in Johnny's case, "insurance was the driving force in the discharge" and a cause of his death.

CHARTER HOSPITAL'S CASE. Charter called two former administrators— one had been the manager of its Business Office and the other the medical director—to deny a policy of pressuring doctors to discharge patients when their insurance ran out. They testified that, on the contrary, Charter gave free care to patients who asked for it and who needed further hospitalization after their coverage ran out.

Billie Pierce, a former administrator of Charter Hospital of Winston-Salem and a vice president of its parent corporation at the time of trial, stated that she "in no way put pressure on the physician to discharge the patient," and that she had never turned down a doctor's request to extend a stay after the patient's insurance expired. Her office had monitored insurance closely to protect patients from being "strapped" with bills they couldn't pay, but not to pressure doctors for discharges. Pierce claimed that Charter had accepted some patients knowing they couldn't pay their bills. She estimated that during her four-year tenure as an administrator, free care probably exceeded $1 million.

Dr. Bruce Rau had been medical director when Johnny Moore was at Charter and was a member of the Charter medical staff when he testified. He agreed with Pierce that there had been no policy of automatically discharging patients because their insurance expired, and that extension requests of a few days were routinely allowed. However, Rau acknowledged, "I didn't make free care a major topic of discussion because I didn't want all the other patients on my team to get the idea they could stay a long time for free."

In that regard, Dr. Bernard Carroll, a professor of psychiatry at Duke University Medical Center and, ironically, a witness for Charter Hospital, testified, "If a doctor consistently has patients who end up being financial burdens to the hospital, he can find it difficult to have his admitting privileges renewed."

Whether Charter Hospital had actually given more than token (or any) free care emerged as a critical issue. Without convincing proof of it as a routine practice, the jury would likely find that Charter had a "pay up or get out" policy, as the plaintiffs claimed. Charter had hired a certified public accountant to review its records for the amount of free care it provided between 1986 and 1990. There were no record entries labeled "free care" or "Charter Care." The accountant was told by the hospital controller, however, that a category called "administrative adjustment" represented free care. That category totaled $1.5 million for the five-year period, with $108,000 attributable to 1986, the year Johnny Moore was in the hospital.

The hospital's gross revenues in 1986 were about $8 million, so that free care represented about 1 percent of revenues for that year. By comparison, Dr. Carroll, Charter's witness from Duke University Medical Center, testified that his nonprofit center writes off at least 10 percent of its charges as free care every year and that the standard of care in that regard was the same for a proprietary hospital like Charter. (For the second time, Charter's lawyers had shot themselves in the foot with Dr. Carroll's testimony.)

Charter's free-care figure for 1986 sagged under cross-examination of its accountant witness. He had not done a complete audit of charges to the "administrative adjustment" account; he had only "walked through their [Charter's] procedures and talked to their accounting personnel." He had "no idea," for example, whether charges to that account included refunds to patients. The plaintiffs subsequently called to the witness stand a different accountant who had reviewed the individual records in a random sample of hospital accounts. None of those accounts reflected free care.

Most of the hospital's evidence bore on whether it had an across-the-board premature discharge policy. In the specific case of Johnny Moore, Dr. Barnhill took the stand and denied that anyone in Charter administration had put pressure on him or done anything to affect his clinical judgment.

The Jury's Verdict

After the evidence was presented, the jury heard lengthy, sometimes impassioned closing arguments from the lawyers. Charter's lawyer opened by begging the major question: "Thank God insurance doesn't affect the quality of care we're entitled to." As the Moore family lawyer saw it, his clients had been caught in a system that milked the insurance of working people, and "when that economic clock had ticked down, they were put out on the street and the door slammed shut." Charter's lawyer quoted John Donne, and the family's lawyer invoked the spirit of Sacco and Vanzetti. The judge observed that the trial "has been the most difficult over which I have presided." He instructed the jury on the law and sent them to deliberate.

After hearing testimony for six weeks, the jury reached a unanimous verdict in one day. They found that Charter Hospital of Winston-Salem had violated the standard of care by having a policy requiring doctors to discharge their patients when their insurance coverage expired, and by allowing that policy to interfere with Dr. Barnhill's medical judgment in discharging Johnny Moore. As a predicate for awarding punitive damages, the jury found that Charter's conduct had been "wanton." The jury also found that Charter Hospital of Winston-Salem was an "instrumentality" of its parent corporation, Charter Medical Corporation, making the parent liable for the conduct of its subsidiary.

The jury awarded damages of $1.1 million for medical and funeral expenses and for the monetary loss to Johnny's parents sustained because Johnny had not reached his normal life expectancy. Janet Moore received an additional $40,000 for emotional distress. Finally, the jury awarded punitive damages of $2 million against Charter Hospital of

Winston-Salem and an eye-popping $4 million against Charter Medical Corporation. The verdict totaled $7.1 million, one of the largest malpractice awards in North Carolina history.

The jury foreman said, "We felt that insurance played a major role in the decision to discharge this boy. . . . We are sending a message." Dr. Paul Fink, a past president of the American Psychiatric Association, stated that "the system was what was on trial. It raises very clear ethical and moral questions."

In January 1992, Charter and Charter Medical appealed the decision to the North Carolina Court of Appeals. In January 1995, more than eight years after Johnny Moore committed suicide, the Court of Appeals handed down its decision. The trial court's decision was upheld in all but one respect. The Court of Appeals ruled that the trial court had erred in submitting separate instructions to the jury on punitive damages for Charter Hospital of Winston-Salem and for its parent, Charter Medical Corporation—a technicality if ever there was one. The Supreme Court of North Carolina affirmed the Court of Appeals decision without writing an opinion, leaving the punitive damage question to be settled by the parties or thrashed out in the trial court.

While the malpractice case was working its way forward, the sexual abuse charges against Johnny's grandfather were dropped by the Guilford County attorney.

CHAPTER 4
▼ ▼ ▼

Bum Rap in Orlando

Mrs. Paddock was psychotic. She believed that she was in
mortal danger from a conspiracy.
    —DONALD F. KLEIN, M.D., witness for Linda Paddock

She was mentally competent. She started to cut her wrist
with a penknife. She didn't use a ballpoint pen. She didn't
use a feather. She used a utensil which is designed to cut.
    —ROBERT L. SADOFF, M.D., witness for Dr. Chacko

On June 26, 1983, Linda Kay Paddock, a slender, attractive, thirty-seven-year-old beautician, walked out of her parents' home in Winter Park, Florida, to a nearby wooded area, where she took a butane cigarette lighter from her purse and set her cotton blouse on fire. Paddock's self-immolation caused second- and third-degree burns over two-thirds of her body, but she survived to bring a malpractice case against her psychiatrist, Dr. Chowallur D. Chacko, claiming that he should have had her hospitalized before she burned herself. Unfortunately for Paddock, she lost her case.

Paddock v. Chacko, as it was ultimately decided by an appellate court in Florida in 1988, turned out to be a landmark case on the obligations of psychiatrists when their patients give some indication they may commit suicide. Under the court's decision, if the patient refuses to enter a mental hospital voluntarily, the psychiatrist is not required to resort to involuntary hospitalization in order to avoid a later allegation of malpractice. Such situations are judgment calls, and, according to the *Paddock* decision, the courts are not to second-guess psychiatrists in making them. Apart from its value as legal precedent, the case is a fascinating study in the role of expert witnesses in psychiatric malpractice cases, and in the potential importance of seemingly irrelevant matters—such as Linda Paddock's marriage.

THE PADDOCKS

When Linda Paddock set herself on fire, she and her husband, Bill, had been married for seventeen years; they had a daughter, Stacey, fifteen. Early in their marriage, Bill did a tour of duty in Vietnam as a helicopter pilot, flying 140 search-and-destroy missions. Meanwhile, back home, Linda had an affair.

In civilian life Bill worked for Amway and then, not very successfully, as a sporting goods salesman. Linda had graduated from high school and a college of cosmetology. The Paddocks were usually in financial difficulties, never owning a home of their own. Several times they moved in with relatives.

Linda continued to have affairs after Bill returned from Vietnam. She claimed she eventually told him everything—about affairs in Florida and North Carolina, and one in Georgia with an Atlanta Falcons football player. Bill had slapped Linda around occasionally but not, he claimed, because of her affairs. During their marriage, the Paddocks had separated twice.

In the fall of 1982, Linda and Bill were living with his parents in Clinton, North Carolina, a small town near Fayetteville. Linda went to work at a beauty salon, "The Finishing Touch," removing hair with electronic tweezers. She began joining her coworkers for a "girls' night out" to go bowling in Fayetteville—a soldiers' town serving nearby Fort Bragg. After one of the women developed back trouble and could no longer bowl, some of them started going to the "Heart of Fayetteville" motel bar. Rumors of drug use and prostitution followed them. At the trial, Linda claimed she "never went to any motels," but other evidence cast doubt on that claim.

In the spring of 1983, Linda took up with a wealthy farmer whom she had met on a girls' night out. She had hopes of marrying the farmer, even though he was already married and, as she put it, she had been "with him that way" only once. The affair fizzled when Linda discovered that another woman had the inside track.

Linda's disheartening discovery coincided with the beginnings of her paranoid disorder. She came to believe that the other woman was following her around and would tell Bill about the farmer if she didn't tell him first. Bill later testified that Linda did tell him on June 5, 1983, but that he had not been upset about it—"not a bit." Nonetheless, Bill insisted that Linda quit her job at "The Finishing Touch" that very day. Before dawn the next morning, Linda Paddock slipped out of bed and went to the laundry room, where she drank a large quantity of Jack Daniels and other liquors, followed by protocaine (an anesthetic used by beauticians) and formaldehyde.

When Bill got up that morning, he found Linda unconscious on the laundry room floor and took her to the hospital emergency room. Linda's stomach was pumped, and she survived. Her doctor, not a psychiatrist, prescribed a small daily dose of Navane, an antipsychotic drug. A few days after her discharge, however, Linda stopped taking her Navane. The doctor recommended that she enter, or be committed to, a mental institution for further observation. That advice wasn't followed either. As an alternative, the doctor recommended that Linda be seen by a psychiatrist as an outpatient.

LINDA PADDOCK AND DR. CHACKO

Linda Paddock was discharged from the Clinton hospital on June 9. Her parents, Mr. and Mrs. Burkhardt, picked her up and drove her to their home in Winter Park, Florida. The plan was that Linda would stay with them temporarily. On June 15, Linda called the office of Dr. Chacko, a psychiatrist recommended to her father by his doctor at the Veterans Administration Center in Orlando. She made an appointment for herself on June 22, a week later.

Chowallur D. Chacko is a native of India, as is his wife, Anna. The Chackos live in Orlando with their three children. After leaving India, Dr. Chacko had worked for a time at a hospital in Trinidad and Tobago, followed by a residency in psychiatry in a mental hospital in Connecticut, and thereafter as chief psychiatric resident and staff psychiatrist at other hospitals. Chacko had extensive experience with paranoid and suicidal patients. He went into private practice for the first time in Orlando, about ten months before Linda Paddock walked into his office.

There was to be no real dispute about what happened at Paddock's first, and only, appointment with Dr. Chacko on Wednesday, June 22, although the experts were to differ over her state of mind at that time. Paddock went to Chacko's office accompanied by both parents. Chacko talked to her alone for the first half hour, and to Paddock and her father for the rest of the hour session. She told Chacko about her affair with the rich farmer, about her suicide attempt, and about her fears that an "impact" was going to wipe out her family—either a train, a bus, or possibly the Mafia. Paddock denied hearing voices but reported that she was receiving "messages"; for example, "I saw this Dempster Dumpster and I got a message from the Dumpster: 'Don't tell your trash to Dr. Chacko.'"

Dr. Chacko gave Paddock a mental status examination. She was aware of the time, date, and place, and she demonstrated her ability to explain "a stitch in time" and "people who live in glass houses." Paddock somewhat understated the extent of her fears because she wanted to return to North Carolina as soon as possible and she was afraid Dr. Chacko might want to put her in the hospital.

Dr. Chacko noted in his chart that Paddock was suffering from an "acute paranoid state in partial remission," but that she had "no active suicidal ideation." Knowing that Paddock intended to leave soon for North Carolina, Chacko told her to seek further psychiatric care there, but that if she remained near Orlando longer, to call him for another appointment. Chacko gave Paddock a prescription for a slightly increased dose of Navane. With that, Paddock's father wrote Chacko a check for $75, she and her parents left, and Chacko marked his file "case closed."

Many psychiatric malpractice cases involve a course of treatment over an extended period of time; the psychiatrist gets to know the patient very well. This case was different. Dr. Chacko saw Linda Paddock in person only once, during the June 22 appointment in his office. As events unfolded, a single afternoon, on Friday, June 24, 1983, proved to be the critical time. Dr. Chacko did not see Linda Paddock in person on the twenty-fourth. Whether he committed psychiatric malpractice hinged on two telephone calls, the first between Chacko and Paddock, the second between Chacko and her father, Mr. Burkhardt. Exactly what was said in those phone calls was in sharp dispute at the trial.

The First Phone Call

Linda Paddock testified about the content of her call to the psychiatrist: "I told Dr. Chacko that I was confused and I was upset . . . and I felt there was something I was supposed to do but I didn't know what. . . . I think I need some help. I have never been so afraid in my life before." To which Chacko had replied, "Well, what do you want me to do, Mrs. Paddock? I have plans to go out of town for the weekend."

According to Paddock, she told Chacko that she was experiencing fears and getting "messages," and that she had not been candid with him before about these messages. Chacko didn't ask her about the messages, but he did ask if she "would be willing to come to the hospital," and Paddock said she would do "whatever he thought best." Chacko indicated that he would make arrangements for a hospital bed.

Dr. Chacko's recollection of the same phone call was quite different.

Paddock called and said she was getting "more confused." But she denied hearing voices or having thoughts of hurting herself. He suggested that it "might be a good idea for her to go into the hospital," but she refused to be hospitalized. Chacko asked to speak to Paddock's father, Mr. Burkhardt; he was not at home then, so Chacko spoke to Mrs. Burkhardt and suggested hospitalization for Paddock, not out of concern about suicide but "for a few days to adjust her medication." Mrs. Burkhardt didn't respond, saying that her husband "takes care of the business."

The Second Phone Call

According to Mr. Burkhardt, he and Dr. Chacko discussed Paddock's condition and the possibility of hospitalization later that afternoon. Burkhardt told Chacko that Linda was upset, that she wanted a stronger prescription for her "fears," and that she seemed "a little worse" than she had been at the office appointment. Chacko said that Paddock would have to go into a hospital before he could give her stronger medicine. Three hospitals were discussed as possibilities. Burkhardt told Chacko that Paddock didn't have medical insurance. Chacko replied that she could be admitted into the Orange County Mental Health Crisis Center without insurance. Despite that discussion, Burkhardt testified that "there was no indication that we would admit her [to a hospital] at that time."

As Burkhardt recalled, the discussion of hospitals was "sidetracked" in favor of increasing the Navane "to see if that would do any good." He and Chacko agreed that hospitalization would be reconsidered on Monday if the increased medication didn't help. Chacko said that if Paddock got worse over the weekend, the Burkhardts should call his answering service. He was going to be out of town, but the service would get in touch with a reputable psychiatrist if necessary.

Dr. Chacko's recollection of this conversation differed markedly from Burkhardt's. According to Chacko, Burkhardt refused to agree to Linda's hospitalization. "[Burkhardt] did not feel that the patient needed to be hospitalized at the time. He indicated that the patient was merely upset because her husband had not yet come down to pick her up." Burkhardt had given his daughter an alcohol rub and said to Chacko, "Look here, Doc, she's sitting right in front of me, calm, relaxed. I see nothing wrong with her." Chacko asked Burkhardt if he and his wife could keep a close watch on Paddock over the weekend, and he said they could. Chacko told him they should take Paddock to the Orange County Crisis Center for screening for possible hospitalization if she got worse over the weekend. He also told him they would reevaluate Paddock's condition on

Monday. Chacko had not planned to be out of town for the weekend and said nothing to that effect.

THE SUICIDE ATTEMPT

On Saturday, June 25, Paddock seemed better, as her father recalled. She got "all fixed up," making sure "every hair was in place," and she and her mother went shopping at a nearby mall. (Paddock disputed this testimony, saying that she had felt worse on the twenty-fifth and had stayed home.) On Sunday morning, June 26, Burkhardt got up early for his weekly round of golf. He checked on Paddock before leaving and thought she seemed all right. Paddock got up later and joined her mother to watch a Baptist service on television.

About eleven o'clock that morning, Paddock became restless and bolted out the door. Her mother called out to her to stay and use the exercise bicycle, but Paddock kept going, soon breaking into a run. She entered the wooded area, knelt under a tree, and took a Swiss army knife from her purse. She later testified, "I had this feeling that I was looking up to God." When the knife didn't serve her purpose, she grabbed the butane lighter she carried for her Eve cigarettes and held it to her blouse; her upper torso was rapidly engulfed in flames.

When the flames subsided, Paddock somehow managed to climb to a platform in the tree beneath which she had knelt. She began calling for help and was found about two hours later by a rescue worker called by a neighbor. She was sitting in a state of shock on the tree platform, with second- and third-degree burns over most of her upper body. The third-degree burns had penetrated to deep tissue, destroying nerve fibers. In the burned areas her skin was gone, or shedding off, and her neck, face, and shoulders were black. The rescue worker gave her morphine through a vein in her hand because severe swelling made the veins in her arms inaccessible. Paddock was taken by ambulance to the burn unit of Orlando Regional Medical Center.

Dr. Chacko learned about Paddock's immolation late Sunday afternoon when his beeper activated as he was driving in Orlando. He pulled off the highway and called the hospital. Chacko saw Paddock in the burn unit the next day and continued as her psychiatrist until she fired him three weeks later.

Linda Paddock stayed in the burn unit for ten weeks. Her burns caused her to retain fluids, and her weight ballooned from 120 to 165 pounds. She was in constant pain. She underwent four skin graft surgeries. Paddock testified that the surgeons had sliced her legs for skin grafts "like a cheese slicer." Her neck remained contracted, making her feel like "I'm trying to get myself out of a paper bag every day." Both ears had been disfigured; the outer rim of her right ear had to be cut away.

The psychic impacts of Paddock's burns were equally severe. According to a psychiatrist who treated Paddock after her discharge from the burn unit, she continued to suffer from a major depressive disorder. She became suicidal in December 1983 and was hospitalized for two months, with daily psychotherapy. The former beautician could scarcely bear to look in the mirror. She cried a lot. The plastic surgeons were not offering much hope. She would probably need psychiatric care for the rest of her life.

The Paddocks discovered that Linda's parents maintained a homeowners' liability policy with State Farm Insurance Company. Linda filed a claim with State Farm, maintaining that her parents had been negligent in failing to prevent her burns. State Farm settled with the Paddocks for $101,000. Linda's father thought the State Farm claim was a "low blow" and rarely spoke to his daughter after it was filed.

THE MALPRACTICE LAWSUIT

Linda Paddock filed a malpractice suit against Dr. Chacko in early 1984 in the Circuit Court for Orange County, Florida, in Orlando. Paddock was represented by Miami lawyer J. B. Spence, the colorful dean of medical malpractice lawyers in Florida. Orphaned at sixteen, Spence grew up in poverty in an area so isolated that, as one story went, "for entertainment friends and relatives would rush to the front porch to watch a car pass." But thirty-five years of flamboyant courtroom combat had brought in thirty multimillion-dollar verdicts against doctors and made Spence a wealthy man. He relished his work. "I am out to save the little guy from the American Money Association—that's what I call the AMA. . . . I enjoy suing the bastards. They're more immoral than drug dealers. In all of these years, I have known of only one doctor who stood up there and told the truth."

Dr. Chacko was represented by Harry K. Anderson of Orlando, a seasoned trial lawyer who specialized in defending personal injury and medical malpractice cases for insurance companies. Anderson's style, at least compared with Spence's, was low-key, but he was a hardworking, tenacious, and effective advocate. Anderson had been retained not by Chacko but by the St. Paul Fire and Marine Insurance Company, which insured Chacko against malpractice, but only to a $1 million limit.

The case was assigned for trial to Judge Joseph P. Baker of Orlando, affectionately known to local lawyers as "Crazy Joe." Unconventional behavior is not uncommon among veteran judges who become bored with their jobs, and this may have explained Judge Baker's deportment in his courtroom. Baker declined to wear robes, sported a bushy mustache that made him look like Mark Twain, and was given to wandering his courtroom during testimony, rattling ice in a Styrofoam cup. In the course of the Paddock trial, among other unusual things, Baker took pictures of the jury from the bench. Despite his eccentricities, Baker kept the trial moving with prompt rulings and displayed a keen intelligence in a posttrial opinion that effectively disposed of the case.

After Paddock's suit was filed, the lawyers took depositions of the psychiatrists designated as expert witnesses and of some twenty other prospective witnesses. The trial began in February 1986, about two years after it was initially filed—an average interval in a complex malpractice case like this one.

Like all experienced trial lawyers in medical malpractice cases, Spence and Anderson each built his case around a dominant theme. According to Spence, Paddock was desperately ill, suicidal, and calling for help on June 24; instead of getting her into a hospital, Chacko only talked to her on the phone and left her to the inadequate supervision of her parents; Paddock's attempt to kill herself was predictable—and Chacko's fault.

According to Anderson, Paddock was not suicidal on the twenty-fourth, and it was not necessary for Chacko to see her personally. Paddock's immolation was an impulsive and unpredictable act, caused more by despondency over her marital problems than by her illness; Paddock and her husband were lying to bolster their case.

The Battle of the Experts: Backgrounds

As a general rule, lawyers are entitled to call as many witnesses as they wish in a trial. Malpractice lawyers sometimes try to overwhelm the opposition and the jury with a parade of expert witnesses. Judges can blunt that strategy, and keep the trial within a reasonable time frame, by limiting the number of experts each side may call. In the *Paddock* case, Judge Baker allowed each side four expert witnesses—still a generous quota.

Spence chose Donald F. Klein, M.D., professor of psychiatry at Columbia University in New York City, as Paddock's lead witness. It took twenty pages of trial transcript just to describe Klein's credentials. Highlights included:

- director of research, New York State Psychiatric Institute
- president, National Foundation for Depressive Illness
- fellow, American College of Neuropsychopharmacology
- fellow, American Psychiatric Association (APA)
- chairman, APA Task Force for the Protection of Human Subjects in Psychiatric Research
- member, editorial board of six psychiatric publications
- author of four books and more than two hundred articles on psychiatry
- thirty years' experience in diagnosis and treatment of depressed patients, including suicidal patients.

Anderson chose Robert L. Sadoff, M.D., clinical professor of psychiatry at the University of Pennsylvania Medical School, as Chacko's lead witness. Sadoff's credentials were equally impressive. Highlights included:

- clinical director, State Maximum Security Forensic Diagnostic Hospital
- lecturer at various law and medical schools, and the Wharton School of Business
- founder, past president, American Board of Psychiatry
- director, American Board of Law and Medicine
- past president, American Academy of Psychiatry and Law
- member, editorial board of several psychiatric publications
- fellow, American Psychiatric Association, American College of Psychiatrists, and several other psychiatric organizations
- author of two books and over seventy articles on psychiatry.

Experts in medical malpractice cases—whether psychiatrists, orthopedists, or obstetricians—are expensive. As an expert witness in the 1986 *Paddock* trial, Dr. Klein charged $300 per hour, a rate that might have been considered high at that time—even for someone with Klein's credentials. By the mid-1990s, however, hourly rates of $300 or more for an expert witness in a malpractice case had become common. Some experts charge somewhat less for out-of-court review of documents but $500 or more per hour for testifying in court.

Theoretically, the client is responsible for the experts' fees, but many malpractice lawyers are willing to "front" (advance) their own money if they believe in the case and are willing to gamble on a big verdict. The Paddocks were in no position to pay experts' fees, but Spence was, and he did—$15,000 or more to each of his four experts. The defense called more reasonably priced experts; their fees averaged about $8,000 each.

The Experts' Testimony

The four experts for Linda Paddock agreed with one another on key points, with minor exceptions; the same was true of Dr. Chacko's four experts. Since lawyers hire multiple experts to testify for their side only if their opinions are consistent, it would be surprising if the experts they hired were not at least on the same page. Lawyers see themselves not as seekers of truth but as advocates for their clients. The two objectives are not necessarily consistent.

In addition to the dynamics of advocacy, Dr. Leigh Roberts, one of the experts for Dr. Chacko, suggested a reason for greater areas of disagreement among psychiatrists than among, to use his example, surgeons. "A surgeon looks at something, can see it, can cut it out, can treat it with medicine. There is more science and less art to surgery. There is more art . . . in psychiatry. . . . It means that there is more likely to be a difference between two psychiatrists than there is a difference between two surgeons."

Of course, the two teams of experts disagreed on most key points. Otherwise, there would have been no trial; the case would have been settled or dropped.

June 6: The First Suicide Attempt

THE PADDOCK POSITION. When Linda Paddock tried to kill herself on June 6 by drinking liquor, protocaine, and formaldehyde, she was mentally ill, psychotic, and depressed. This was not a mere suicidal gesture but a serious attempt to end her own life. She was receiving "messages" and believed that unknown people were conspiring against her. She was not competent in the sense of being able to care for herself.

THE CHACKO POSITION. It is unclear whether Paddock was consciously trying to kill herself on June 6. Her action was impulsive, rather than calculated, and later she stated repeatedly that she had never had a thought of suicide. Rather than intending to kill herself, she may have been attempting to quell those distortions of reality—the "messages"—she was experiencing. Other stresses in her life, including her breakup with the farmer, the loss of her job, and trouble with her husband, would have contributed to her action.

June 22: Linda Paddock's Only Appointment with Dr. Chacko

THE PADDOCK POSITION. The Paddock experts didn't seriously dispute Dr. Chacko's diagnosis of June 22: paranoia, in partial remission. They also agreed that the appointment had not been on an emergency basis, that Paddock was coherent and responsive, and that she did not appear to be suicidal. Nor did Paddock's experts take serious issue with what Chacko did in that first, and only, appointment—with one exception. They contended that Chacko's prescribed daily doses of the antipsychotic drug Navane had been inadequate; in the language of medical malpractice, they did not "meet the standard of care."

Dr. Chacko prescribed six milligrams of Navane daily on June 22—up two milligrams from the North Carolina hospital prescription. Dr. Klein, a nationally recognized expert in drug treatments for mental illnesses, took the strong position that "six milligrams of Navane is a tiny, minuscule dose . . . utterly out of keeping with the magnitude of the problem that Linda Paddock presented with. . . . Most people who get Navane for a psychotic state are probably going to get somewhere between 10 and 40 milligrams. Forty milligrams is not a lot. Many patients will get as much as 80 to 100 milligrams." Klein also believed that the increased dose Chacko ordered for Paddock—from six to eight milligrams—when her condition worsened two days later had been inadequate.

Dr. Michael Gilbert, another expert for Paddock, agreed, calling the doses Chacko prescribed "very, very minimal. . . . I liken it to beating somebody over the head with a feather." And when Chacko later increased the dose only slightly, Gilbert likened that to using "two feathers. So you either use an adequate dose or you don't bother."

However, Paddock's experts didn't present a totally united front on the Navane issue. Dr. Gilbert referred to the maximum dose as "about 20 to 30 milligrams"—less than half the dosage Dr. Klein said many patients get. More surprisingly, Dr. Steven Targum, another Paddock expert, thought that Chacko's six-milligram dose of June 22 was "probably appropriate."

THE CHACKO POSITION. Dr. Chacko's experts endorsed his diagnosis of Paddock's condition on June 22 and the actions Chacko took during the June 22 appointment—including his prescribed doses of Navane. Overall, as Dr. John Greist, another Chacko expert, put it, Chacko had done more than the minimum required. He had met "quite a high standard of care."

Regarding Navane, Dr. Sadoff testified that "there is a major difference between the use of Navane for a nonpsychotic person and one who is flagrantly psychotic." Someone who is not psychotic should be started on small doses of six to eight milligrams, while an obviously psychotic person may need "somewhere between 15 and 30 or 40 milligrams." By those standards, Dr. Chacko's prescriptions of small Navane doses for Linda Paddock were appropriate. When he saw Paddock on June 22, she was not psychotic. Giving her a higher dose of Navane could have created a risk that she would not take her medicine—Paddock had stopped taking it before, against doctor's orders. Furthermore, Chacko thought she was going to return soon to North Carolina, and that he would never see her again. Under those circumstances, he didn't know whether she would have follow-up care, and if so, how soon.

June 24: Dr. Chacko's Telephone Evaluations of Linda Paddock

The differing versions of the participants in the telephone calls between Dr. Chacko (from his office) and Linda Paddock and her parents (from their home) on the afternoon of June 24 helped to shape the factual assumptions the experts made in forming their opinions about what Dr. Chacko did that day. As one might expect, the Paddock experts chose to believe what Paddock and her father remembered about the calls (her mother did not testify). Similarly, the Chacko experts accepted Dr. Chacko's recollection of the calls.

THE PADDOCK POSITION. Linda Paddock was psychotic when she phoned Dr. Chacko in the early afternoon of June 24. She was also at risk for suicide in the immediate future, as Dr. Chacko should have realized. Among the indicators of suicide were her recent attempt with liquor, protocaine, and formaldehyde. She felt guilty—she saw herself as a "terrible person" who "deserved punishment." She was reaching out for help when she admitted she had understated her problems at his office to avoid hospitalization.

Dr. Gilbert testified that when a patient has a track record like Linda Paddock's, the psychiatrist is "sitting on a powder keg." While psychiatrists cannot predict when or whether a particular person will attempt suicide, they can determine whether a person is a substantial risk for suicide, as Paddock was on June 24.

What should Dr. Chacko have done when Linda phoned him on June 24? Dr. Klein thought that "the only thing that makes any sense at all is to have a face-to-face, in person examination of the patient to find out if there really is something cooking here that could be deadly. Dr. Chacko didn't do that. . . . his not doing so is a very serious deviation from the standards of good medical care." The other Paddock experts agreed. A face-to-face examination would have enabled Chacko to establish better rapport with Paddock and to observe directly such indicators of mental state as appearance, body language, and demeanor—"affect" in psychiatric parlance. Dr. Harold Morgan saw a phone call versus personal contact as the "difference between reading about something that happened in the newspaper and being there and seeing it for yourself."

According to Paddock's experts, Chacko had several viable options, none of which he chose. He could have had Paddock come to his office; he could have met her at a hospital emergency room; he could have had the police pick her up; or he could have made a house call. If he had done any of those things, instead of evaluating her over the phone, his evaluation would have been more complete, and it should have led to a decision to hospitalize Paddock—involuntarily if necessary. Chacko's failure to hospitalize Paddock on the twenty-fourth, in their opinion, effectively caused her to set herself on fire on the twenty-sixth.

There was a separate issue—part legal and part medical—whether Dr. Chacko would have been able to hospitalize Paddock against her will on June 24 if he had concluded that hospitalization was necessary. Florida and other states have commitment laws governing the conditions under which mentally ill persons can be hospitalized against their will. In the past, the typical commitment law made scant provision for the individual's rights; as a result, some mentally ill but harmless people (and some people who were only eccentric) were railroaded into mental hospitals. Commitment laws, including Florida's, have been revised in recent years to provide a panoply of procedural rights—for example, the right to a hearing, to a formal determination of dangerousness, to a time limit on commitment—before a person can be involuntarily committed.

Paddock's experts testified that Linda was suicidal and that she met the other legal requirements for commitment under Florida law. Their testimony implied that any person who met those requirements was at least a strong candidate for involuntary hospitalization and that it might be the psychiatrist's duty to seek hospitalization of anyone who met those requirements.

The legal question whether a psychiatrist is automatically *required* to try to hospitalize a patient who meets those requirements or whether, in that situation, he has discretion was not addressed by either side or by the trial court. It remained for the Florida appellate court to resolve that question.

THE CHACKO POSITION. Although Chacko might have learned more had he seen Paddock in his office on June 24, based on what he already knew and on what he learned from her and her parents on the telephone, it was not necessary to see her in person that day. Paddock was not suicidal. Nor, as Dr. Sadoff put it, was she "blatantly psychotic," citing the fact that "she didn't call the plumber, she called the psychiatrist." Granted that she needed supervision, her parents appeared to be responsible and to offer her a good support system.

The actions Chacko did take at that time—recommending hospitalization for observation, reserving a hospital bed for her if she chose to accept his recommendation, increasing her medication, instructing the parents to keep a close watch on her, and advising them to call if she changed for the worse—were appropriate under the circumstances.

According to Chacko's experts, telephone evaluations of patients are a practical necessity for psychiatrists. Dr. Greist, in describing his own practice as a university professor and part-time practicing psychiatrist, said, "We very frequently treat people that we don't see. . . . I see about two patients a day in the office and I perhaps speak with another half dozen by telephone every day, and I think we give very good care."

The Chacko experts questioned the practicality of two options suggested by the Paddock experts. It would have been difficult to get Paddock hospitalized by simply signing a form and calling an ambulance to pick her up. Dr. Walter Muller, a private practitioner from nearby Winter Park, gave a realistic view of that procedure in Florida. "Usually the ambulance comes with the police car. And unless I'm there it's very hard to get ambulance drivers and policemen to take patients. They have to observe these people in a bizarre situation, just as the law spells out." As for a house call, psychiatrists rarely do business that way, any more than obstetricians. Dr. Klein, the lead Paddock expert, conceded on cross-examination that he made about one house call per year. Dr. Targum, another Paddock expert, stated that he had never made a house call in three years of Florida practice.

Dr. Chacko's experts took a strong position against the linchpin of Linda Paddock's case—that her condition met all the legal requirements for involuntary commitment and that she should have been committed if she declined to enter a hospital voluntarily. To be sure, Paddock met the threshold commitment requirement; she was mentally ill, at least to some extent. But according to Chacko's experts, she was not a danger to herself. She was in touch with reality; she was not refusing to care for herself; and she had able and willing family members to care for her. And although she had made a recent suicide attempt, several other factors came into play, including levels of depression, lack of suicidal plans, and whether her particular mental illness increased suicidal risk. Paranoid people like Paddock are more likely to injure others they think are conspiring against them than to injure themselves. These factors supported a clinical judgment that Paddock's torching herself on June 26 was an impulsive act—that it was not foreseeable on the twenty-fourth.

One of the Chacko experts, Dr. John Greist, approached the suicide prediction problem armed with a computer program. Greist, a psychiatrist at the University of Wisconsin, is a "suicidologist"—one of perhaps twenty people in the country engaged in intensive study of the causes and prediction of suicide. Greist and his colleagues had developed a computer program incorporating all known variables in predicting suicide. When the relevant data—sex, age, race, type of illness, etc.—concerning a person suspected to be at risk are fed into it, the program has been shown to be more accurate in predicting suicide than a clinician making a judgment call. Greist testified:

> I did try my best to portray Mrs. Paddock to the computer as I thought she might have presented herself on the 24th. . . . The [computer] prediction was that Mrs. Paddock would continue to have no thoughts of suicide over the next six months, and that there was no risk of a serious attempt. . . . Based on everything I can learn about this case, I don't think any clinician would have . . . meaningfully predicted Mrs. Paddock's burning herself on Sunday the 26th.

The Chacko experts also made their case in social policy terms. Statistics show that very few of those at *some* risk of suicide—only about 5 percent—will actually kill themselves within one year. Thus, if hospitalization automatically followed upon a determination of risk, the overwhelming majority would be hospitalized unnecessarily. As Dr. Greist explained, "In order to prevent suicide . . . by hospitalizing people, one would have to have 95 percent of the people at risk in the hospital when they didn't need it in order to catch the 5 out of 100 who might benefit from being in the hospital."

An Alternative Strategy: Making the Opposition Look Bad

The 793 pages of psychiatric testimony in the *Paddock* case were—or, in a more rational system of justice, should have been—the heart of the case. The ultimate issue, whether Dr. Chacko had committed malpractice, is a medical question to which only qualified psychiatrists could testify. But lay jurors have a difficult time making a reasoned choice between conflicting psychiatric testimony, particularly where the two teams of experts are about equally well qualified.

Some malpractice lawyers believe that the opposing experts cancel each other out, that the jury effectively disregards their testimony—which it doesn't understand very well, anyway—and decides the case on some other basis. Harry Anderson, Dr. Chacko's lawyer, was operating on that theory. Having matched the opposition, expert for expert, Anderson stressed the morality theme: Linda Paddock was an unfaithful wife, and both Paddocks were liars.

Anderson hammered away at this theme at every opportunity, On cross-examination, Paddock admitted that she had "engaged in various relationships with different men" over the course of her marriage, only to later deny having had any "affairs." Paddock's recent affair with the rich farmer was relevant to her depressed state of mind. Spence might have objected, however, that an affair dating back to the Vietnam War—while Bill was serving his country—was irrelevant and would only serve to prejudice the jury against his client.

But Paddock had made the mistake of lying about her history. During a pretrial deposition she had testified that the rich farmer had been her only extramarital sexual partner since her marriage to Bill Paddock. She had also lied to one of her doctors about extramarital sex. This gave Anderson an opening; he could go into Paddock's sexual history to test her credibility as a witness. Two incidents say as much about Bill Paddock as about his wife.

Dr. John Nash was an gynecologist practicing in Columbia, South Carolina. The Paddocks had moved to Columbia following Linda's release from the hospital in Orlando. Linda had seen Dr. Nash in December 1983. Anderson called Dr. Nash as a witness. Dr. Nash's records of that first appointment reflected Paddock's statement that "she had had multiple sexual exposures outside her marriage and was concerned regarding this in terms of venereal diseases." Paddock had not indicated when the exposures had occurred, but Nash had assumed they were recent. Nash took a culture which tested negative for gonorrhea.

In November 1984, Anderson requested a copy of Nash's records and, as required, gave notice of the request to Spence. Thereafter, Linda and Bill Paddock went to Nash's office. Bill claimed that Linda's story about sexual exposures in her last visit had not been correct. He wanted the records changed. As Nash recalled the incident: "He told me a story that was different from what Linda had told me the first time. I was told that the sexual exposure that she had gotten was in 1977, and that she was worried about an asymptomatic venereal disease from 1977 until 1983." Dr. Nash thought it was "very unusual" for a person to ask to be checked for venereal disease six years after the event. Nash told Bill that "there was no way I was going to change anything," but that he would enter what Bill had told him in his record as well.

Anderson questioned Linda Paddock about her appointments with Dr. Nash. She flatly denied any attempt to get Nash to change his records. Bill Paddock's recollection differed from Dr. Nash's. "We explained that our attorney had asked us to speak to him to clarify a sentence that was in his records that was confusing. And we explained to him the details and he said that he would make an amendment to his chart, clarify it." There was no reason for Dr. Nash to misrepresent what happened. The Paddocks, of course, had a strong motive to lie: a multimillion-dollar damage award.

When Linda Paddock was discharged from the hospital in Clinton, North Carolina, after her first suicide attempt, her attending doctor, Dr. A. L. Fajardo, had written in her discharge summary, "The patient was discharged on June 8, 1983, after she was seen by the Mental Health Clinic and was advised to commit the patient to a mental institution, but the family refused."

Wishing to portray himself to the jury as Linda's protector, Bill didn't want to appear to be failing to follow medical advice. He denied that he had been advised to commit Linda to a mental institution. He also denied telling Dr. Fajardo that he and his attorney didn't like what was in his discharge summary, and threatening him if he refused to change it. Dr. Fajardo stated in a deposition that Bill had threatened him.

Bill Paddock wasn't the only one accused of trying to distort records. He, in turn, accused Dr. Chacko of writing his treatment record of Linda (except for the initial appointment of June 22) only after Paddock's lawyer asked for copies of Linda's record. If true, Chacko would have had an opportunity to slant the critical record entry for June 24 in his favor. Chacko denied having done that. For their part, Bill Paddock and his brother testified that when they had gone to Chacko's office with an attorney to get the records, they were first shown a record that stopped at June 22 and later that day were given a copy that included other entries. This conflict is not easy to resolve since all those who testified had a motive to falsify. It can be said in Dr. Chacko's favor that if he had been trying to slant the record in his favor, he could easily have done a better job of it.

The Jury's Verdict

As the *Paddock* case went to the six-person jury—four women and two men—the evidence appeared to weigh in Dr. Chacko's favor. Although the lay jury might have found the expert testimony about equally persuasive on both sides, on balance, Chacko's experts had given better-reasoned explanations of their positions. Since Linda Paddock, as the plaintiff, had the burden of proof, the jury should have found in favor of Dr. Chacko.

But they didn't. On the contrary, after deliberating for thirteen hours, the jury found that Dr. Chacko had been negligent, and that his negligence had caused Paddock's injuries. The jury further found that Paddock had not been guilty of contributory negligence. They awarded Paddock $2.15 million, twice the largest malpractice award in the history of Orange County, Florida.

The jury returned the customary bottom-line verdict. They didn't make findings on disputed factual issues, such as whether Dr. Chacko had recommended hospitalization, or whether Linda Paddock had refused it. After the trial, one of the jurors said, "We were so confused we didn't know what to do." The jury's collective rationale (if there was one) behind its cryptic verdict remained obscure. However, some individual jurors offered explanations to reporters.

According to newspaper reports, some jurors thought Dr. Chacko "should have done more to prevent Paddock from hurting herself." Juror Wilson Love said that "Dr. Chacko didn't care. There's got to be a certain amount of caring." Specifically, Love faulted Chacko for not seeing Paddock at once after she was hospitalized for burning herself. Other jurors were influenced by their belief that Dr. Chacko had altered his record to show that Linda Paddock had rejected his hospitalization recommendation. Although the jurors didn't say so publicly, they may have assumed, correctly, that Dr. Chacko had a malpractice liability policy, and that he was in a better position than the Paddocks to pay for her injuries. Their award, however, was more than double Chacko's insurance coverage.

Bill and Linda Paddock raised their arms in triumph on the Orange County Courthouse steps after the jury returned its verdict. Linda said, "I'm usually a conservative person, but he deserves it." Anderson and Chacko were "totally flabbergasted" by the verdict. As Anderson saw it, "The jury is asking the doctor to be a fortune teller and predict what his patients will do. What in the world are these doctors supposed to do?" But Anderson wasn't through yet. He filed a series of motions in the trial court to set aside the jury's verdict.

Nullification of the Jury's Decision

Two months later, Judge Baker granted Anderson's motions, threw out the jury's verdict, and entered a judgment in favor of Dr. Chacko, including a judgment for $58,257.92 in costs—mostly for witness fees, but excluding the largest cost, for attorneys' fees. Judge Baker rejected the contention that Paddock's injuries were Dr. Chacko's legal responsibility, that "he should have anticipated Linda's self-immolation and was legally obligated to take control of her life away and protect her from her self-destructive tendencies." Recognizing that psychiatrists are not able to predict whether a person at risk will actually attempt suicide, he ruled that a psychiatrist is not legally obligated to "provide a cure, either by restraints or by eliminating the cause." Under the circumstances, Dr. Chacko was justified in leaving Linda "where she and her family felt it was best for her to be"—at home.

As additional protection against reversal on appeal, Judge Baker also rejected the jury's verdict because the evidence didn't support the jury's conclusion that Paddock had not been negligent, and because the $2.15 million verdict was "excessive."

The Motion to Disqualify Judge Baker, and Other Acrimonies

J. B. Spence was understandably upset to see his $2-million verdict go down the drain. Spence told the press, "I've been practicing law for 35 years and I think I got shafted here." Although he had emerged the winner, Anderson took no satisfaction in the process either, calling it "without doubt the most abusive and nastiest lawsuit I've ever been involved in."

Illustrating his last point, Anderson had charged Spence with stonewalling, intimidating witnesses, and having his secretary call Anderson a liar. "It takes an extremely small man to hide behind his secretary's skirt," Anderson charged. Spence retorted that he looked upon the case as "amateur hour," that Anderson had "wanted to win that case so bad and knock off Spence, Miami hotshot, that he practically wet his pants to whip me."

Spence, the self-styled Miami hotshot, now had nothing to lose by alienating an upstate judge, so he filed a motion to disqualify Judge Baker, hoping that a new judge would reinstate the jury's verdict. The motion to disqualify charged twenty-four instances of improper conduct—among them, that Judge Baker put his feet on the bench and acted like a clown, and that he had made passes at an attractive female juror. All of this prompted the *Miami Herald* to headline: "Weird Antics Enliven Burn Trial."

Judges have discretion to refer disqualification motions to another judge for a ruling, but the judge charged with misconduct can, as Judge Baker did here, rule on such a motion initially, subject to review by an appellate court. Spence argued his motion orally, charging that Baker's courtroom was like the "Twilight Zone," that Baker ran it "like a kindergarten," and that he had "just rolled over and played dead" for the defense. Baker denied Spence's motion without comment. Spence's remaining hope was to have Judge Baker's ruling reversed on appeal.

The Appellate Court Decision

The final chapter in *Paddock v. Chacko* was written by Florida's Fifth District Court of Appeal in February 1988. The court resolved the key factual disputes in Dr. Chacko's favor. Observing that psychiatry offers "an innumerable variety of remedial therapies to the troubled and ailing souls of modern society," the court approved what Dr. Chacko had done for Linda Paddock. The court upheld Judge Baker's ruling on the commitment issue: there is no legal duty to commit a patient to a hospital involuntarily, at least not in Florida. The court pointed out that the language of the Florida civil commitment statute is permissive, suggesting "no basis for imposing an affirmative obligation on psychiatrists." Such an obligation, the court thought, would "create an intolerable burden on psychiatrists and the practice of psychiatry."

Dr. Chacko said that the appellate court decision "makes me feel that justice is done. . . . that not only am I vindicated but also all good psychiatrists."

Bill Paddock called the decision "probably the biggest tragedy that ever happened to a single family."

CHAPTER 5

Suicide: The Therapist as Scapegoat

I used to practice better twenty years ago in dealing with suicidal patients. I'm doing it by the book now, and thinking about what's going to get me sued.
—SEYMOUR L. HALLECK, M.D.

Suicide is a rare event in the general population. The rate in the United States is about 12 suicides per 100,000 population per year—representing about 1 percent of all deaths—compared with 42 percent for cardiovascular diseases, 24 percent for cancer, and 1.5 percent for AIDS, based on 1992 data. Suicide rates in some selected populations are dramatically higher. Studies of Veterans Administration hospitals have found a suicide rate of 150 per 100,000 patients, about twelve times higher than in the general population. Studies of psychiatric hospital patients have found suicide rates more than double those of Veterans Administration patients—about 370 per 100,000 patients. And the rate among younger hospital patients is nearly double that of all psychiatric patients—about fifty times greater than in the general population.

Suicide is the number one cause of malpractice suits against mental health professionals—about 20 percent of the total. That statistic has little to do with the merits of most suicide cases, however, which are based on the survivors' often mistaken belief that the therapist should have predicted, and intervened to prevent, the death of a loved one.

PREDICTING SUICIDE

The mental health professions have long disclaimed the ability to predict whether particular people will take their own lives. These disclaimers are based largely on sad clinical experience, but systematic efforts to identify future suicides have also fallen short. A study of 954 depressed people conducted by the National Institute of Mental Health suggests some of the difficulties in prediction. Upon admission to the NIMH study, the participants (80 percent of whom were inpatients) were rated by a trained observer for "suicidal ideation"—thinking about suicide. Within six months after admission to the study, eight of the participants did commit suicide. Yet five of those eight had been rated at admission as having "mild or no suicidal ideation."

Dr. John Greist, the "suicidologist" and a defense witness in the *Paddock* case, acknowledged that his computer program—while more accurate, overall, than clinical judgment in predicting suicide—is often wrong in particular cases. Other psychiatrists have expressed skepticism about the computer as a diagnostician. Thus, Dr. Robert Sadoff: "We don't make diagnoses by machine. We do it on a one-to-one basis with a person, over a period of time." Dr. Thomas Gutheil stressed the importance of subjective elements: "In some people you can really see it coming. A lot depends on the state of the relationship, the feeling that you get in the room with the person which usually doesn't make it to the chart."

Despite difficulties in prediction, mental health professionals believe they can assign degrees of suicidal risk to individual patients with reasonable degrees of accuracy, based on the presence or absence of various indicators of suicide potential. Recall that Dr. Harvey Resnik, a plaintiffs' expert in the *Moore* case, listed nine indicators that Johnny Moore was at extreme risk for suicide—in his phrase, a "walking suicide time bomb."

Merely thinking about suicide doesn't equate with suicidal risk. Dr. Seymour Halleck pointed out that "probably everybody at some time in their life has thought about suicide. A lot of people sometimes wish they were dead. But there aren't that many people who are really about to kill themselves." A prior attempt is, by consensus, the most reliable indicator. Serious depression is usually present, along with feelings of helplessness and worthlessness. Traumatic events—the death of a spouse or getting fired, for example—are also common indicators, as are hallucinations of violence. Men are more likely to kill themselves than women are, partly because they make fewer failed attempts.

Lists of indicators can be extended to include sexual victimization, living alone, and depressing circumstances affecting the particular patient. There is no officially sanctioned list, and new indicators are discovered from time to time. For example, the presence of panic disorder has recently been shown to be associated with suicide risk.

As the sheer number of indicators suggests, there is no simple test of whether a patient is seriously at risk for suicide. Beyond that, most of the indicators are not objective checklist items; they require judgment, often a highly subjective judgment. To be sure, most patients who evoke concern about suicide are depressed; the question is: how depressed? Even a seemingly objective indicator like a prior attempt can raise questions requiring judgment: was it a serious attempt or primarily a way of getting attention?

After the therapist works through the list of indicators, making judgments on items as necessary, and taking into account his sense of where the patient is, he must rate the patient on a scale ranging from low, to medium, to high risk of suicide. Few patients will exhibit all of the items on standard lists of indicators, and the intensities of the indicators the patient presents may vary widely. Once again, judgments have to be made, usually on the basis of incomplete information. Linda Paddock saw Dr. Chacko just once before setting herself on fire. On the basis of that brief encounter, he had to decide whether her temporary living arrangement with her parents was safe enough under a complex set of circumstances.

This rather elaborate and highly subjective screening process is considerably better than flipping coins, but it doesn't produce a high correlation between determinations of suicide risk and its actual commission. On the contrary, studies have indicated that only about one in twenty of those patients determined to be at risk will actually commit suicide within one year. Of course, in many cases a correct risk determination and appropriate treatment will prevent suicide, accounting for part of that statistic. But no treatment, not even hospitalization, can guarantee that suicide will not occur. In studies of suicide committed by psychiatric hospital patients and recently discharged patients, 36 percent killed themselves while still in the hospital, usually by hanging themselves with their own clothing. If hospital patients really want to kill themselves, they will find a way.

In recognition of these factors, no suicide expert seriously argues that therapists can predict whether, let alone when, a particular patient will commit suicide. When suicide cases go to court, the argument shifts to whether the therapist assessed the level of suicidal risk correctly and took appropriate action to minimize that risk.

HOSPITALIZATION

When a distraught patient phones at 3 A.M., should the therapist call the police, send an ambulance, or say something reassuring and go back to bed? Although hospitalization for mental illness is commonly associated with an imminent danger of suicide or violence against others—cases where commitment may be necessary—there are other situations where it may be advisable. Dr. Gutheil generalized the issue: "The whole point of hospitalization is to take the heat off patients, and not leave them feeling burdened by external stuff on top of what they've already got internally."

Hospitalization may appear to be the conservative approach, but it can prolong or deepen a depression. A psychiatrist's recommendation of hospitalization can itself be depressing. Many psychiatrists believe that hospitalization fosters dependency, that patients are better off outside if they can somehow continue to function. Some patients have a history of severe regression when hospitalized. As Gutheil put it, such patients "may need to work for their self-esteem, even if they're working poorly."

William Styron's ordeal with depression, chronicled in his book *Darkness Visible: A Memoir of Madness*, illustrates these tensions. After struggling vainly with depression for months, Styron finally consulted a psychiatrist whom he called "Dr. Gold." Twice-weekly sessions with Gold, plus drug therapy, failed to stem Styron's growing despair. Dr. Gold nevertheless advised him to "try to avoid the hospital at all costs, owing to the stigma [he] might suffer."

Dr. Gold asked Styron if he was suicidal; Styron "reluctantly told him yes." In the book, Styron goes on to describe objects in his home that had become, in his mind, "potential devices for my own destruction": attic rafters, the bathtub, kitchen knives. But Styron didn't disclose these thoughts to Dr. Gold—"since there seemed no need to." After contemplating suicide for months, Styron thought one night that he was on the verge of killing himself. He was admitted to a psychiatric hospital the next day, where he stayed for seven weeks. Styron came to view psychiatric hospitalization as benign, convinced that he "should have been in the hospital weeks before," that "the hospital was my salvation."

In his book, Styron asserts that Dr. Gold's failure to hospitalize him earlier was "wrong." That certainly sounds like an allegation of malpractice. Malpractice it may have been, if Styron had reached a point where suicide was a serious danger and Dr. Gold either knew it or should have known it.

Dr. Gutheil stated an operative principle in treating suicidal patients: "If you don't level with me, I can't help you." Styron's admission that he hadn't disclosed the details of his suicidal thinking suggests that Dr. Gold may have been insensitive but not incompetent. On the other hand, once Styron admitted his suicidal thinking, perhaps Gold should have pressed

Styron for more details. Styron's description alone is an insufficient basis for any conclusion about malpractice.

There are other factors that may weigh against hospitalization. Public hospitals are usually crowded and accept only the sickest patients. Some public hospitals are so unpleasant they would make anyone feel awful, so it is not surprising if they deepen the depressions of their patients. Private psychiatric hospitals in the 1990s are charging patients about $500 per day, about $15,000 per month. Costs on that order exclude the unrich and uninsured from private hospitals altogether. Even if a patient has some insurance coverage, the typical policy (as in the *Moore* case) limits psychiatric hospitalization to thirty days or less. And even if the patient is covered, an insurance company with a strict utilization policy may make it hard for the patient's doctor to get advance approval of hospitalization.

Nevertheless, the therapist treating a suicidal patient should consider hospitalization as an option. Dr. Sadoff took the position that "it's better for us to bury our mistakes in the hospital than in the cemetery," and that, in a close case, "if you're going to make a mistake, make it on the side of life." If the patient is at the high end of the suicide risk scale, the therapist may well have an obligation to commit the patient who refuses voluntary hospitalization. In other cases, however, the therapist will perform a cost-benefit analysis, leading to a judgment on the need for hospitalization. If he can show that such an analysis was made in good faith, on the basis of available information, the therapist shouldn't be second-guessed in court if his judgment turns out to be wrong. Unfortunately, this does not deter some survivors from trying.

THE MYTH OF THE THERAPIST'S CONTROL

Judges and jurors sometimes perceive patients as powerless and therapists as omnipotent. During the 1980s, Dr. Gutheil complained that "without actually coming out and saying so, the courts . . . appear to view mental patients as children, as incompetent individuals for whom others must take parental charge." Dr. Halleck protested a de facto assumption in the legal system that anyone who commits suicide does so involuntarily. Such an assumption might rest on reasoning that: (1) no one in his right mind would kill himself of his own free will; (2) X killed himself; (3) therefore, X could not have been in his right mind; and (4) people who are not in their right minds can't truly act of their own free will.

Such reasoning is simplistic. A suicidal patient's ability to make intelligent decisions may be impaired by depression but not to the point of helplessness. Therapists use various techniques to encourage their suicidal patients to assume responsibility. For example, in a typical "suicide prevention contract" the patient signs a form in which she agrees to call the therapist or go to the emergency room if she begins to think she may hurt herself. According to Dr. Halleck, suicide prevention contracts have become so widespread as to approach standard-of-care status.

But a suicide prevention contract does not, of itself, represent effective control of the suicidal patient, especially the outpatient. Dr. Halleck believes that contracts probably do more to alleviate the therapist's anxiety than to safeguard the patient. Once an outpatient leaves the therapy session, the therapist has no real control over her; if she really wants to kill herself, a paper contract won't stop her. Halleck doesn't ask for contracts from his suicidal patients. Instead, he finds it more effective to give them a strong assurance that they will recover from depression in time.

Suicide and the question of control raise a philosophical question. Although rarely prosecuted for lack of a surviving defendant, the law makes suicide a crime. Jack Kevorkian, the Michigan doctor who advocates and practices assisted suicide for the terminally ill, has fueled an ongoing debate whether people should have a "right to die" if that's what they want to do. With suicidal patients, the question is whether they can exercise such a right intelligently in spite of their depression. Most psychiatrists think not. Dr. Sadoff attributed to Harvard professor Alan Stone a "thank you" theory under which the psychiatrist takes the patient by the shoulders and says: "I'm not going to let you die. I'm going to treat you and in a few weeks you'll feel better. Then you'll thank me."

In suicide cases where the patient was hospitalized, plaintiffs have fared better in court because there is much greater control in a hospital environment than in an outpatient setting. Hospitalized patients are under close supervision by the staff. A patient who seems close to the brink can be put under one-on-one observation. While hospitals can't be expected to prevent all suicides, they are held to a higher level of responsibility, commensurate with their ability to oversee, control, and protect their patients.

Malpractice liability in hospital cases is, more often than not, based on the negligence of nurses, orderlies, or other staff who fail to follow standard procedures or to implement the psychiatrist's instructions. A Connecticut case provides a good example. A woman patient was locked alone in a seclusion room with a steel bed after reporting that voices were telling her to kill herself. No one entered the room for several hours to check on her condition. She was found with her head wedged between the side rail and the mattress of the bed—unconscious, with no pulse, blood pressure, or respiratory function. The woman's injuries reduced her to a permanent vegetative state, requiring constant nursing care for every bodily function. The jury awarded a verdict of $3.6 million against the hospital but ruled in favor of her treating psychiatrist.

CHANGING JUDICIAL ATTITUDES TOWARD SUICIDE

In the past, judges and jurors in suicide cases have sometimes engaged in what Dr. Gutheil has called "magical thinking"—characterized by simplistic, hindsight reasoning with undue emphasis on the particular means of suicide. For example, if the patient commits suicide with a medication overdose, the therapist who prescribed it is seen as the "cause" of death, but not if the patient used his own shotgun. In the real world, people usually commit suicide by the most convenient means—whether that's a drug, a gun, or a rope.

More recently, judges (if not jurors) have become increasingly respectful of the uncertainties inherent in the assessment of suicide risk. If a malpractice case goes to trial (most are settled before trial), each step in the therapist's assessment process will be scrutinized. The court will instruct the jury that the therapist is not the guarantor of the patient's safety, that he has only to meet the standard of care, as described by the expert witnesses.

Of course, there is nothing to prevent the jury from resorting to magical thinking in deciding the case. Despite expert testimony to the contrary, they may still believe that the deceased was helpless and the therapist all-powerful—a notion that the plaintiff's lawyer will do everything to encourage. Or the jury may be swayed by irrelevant factors. One of the *Paddock* case jurors explained their verdict by saying that Dr. Chacko hadn't been sufficiently caring. The ability of the jury to disregard the evidence and the court's instructions, within wide limits, is a risk therapists run if they decline to settle and go to trial.

LIMITED LIABILITY IN SUICIDE CASES?

Dr. Halleck has suggested that the detriments of authorizing malpractice litigation for suicide may outweigh any social benefit, that the law should limit the liability of psychiatrists for suicide. "We practice badly in suicide cases because we worry about being sued. We sometimes hospitalize too much, we sometimes control too much. We get so preoccupied with the prospect of litigation, we forget about the person." Speaking as a teacher at a medical school, Halleck noted: "I usually work with residents and I don't want them to get sued. So we do a lot of things which I don't think are in the best interest of the patient."

A malpractice suit can have serious consequences, regardless of its outcome. If a resident is sued, that information goes into the National Practitioner Data Bank and is reported to Boards of Medical Examiners, who may make an issue of it when the resident seeks certification. A history of malpractice litigation may prevent a doctor from being listed as a "preferred provider" (the Blue Cross term) by managed care insurers, who routinely inquire whether an applicant for listing has been sued.

Dr. Halleck didn't call for complete immunity from malpractice liability, recognizing that there are times when doctors are "grossly negligent" with suicidal patients. A change in the law requiring proof of "gross" instead of ordinary negligence might give therapists some additional protection from suit. But if that change were made, plaintiffs' lawyers would routinely charge gross negligence in suicide cases. In the conflicting testimony of experts, there is no bright line between ordinary and gross negligence.

The critical decision in almost all outpatient suicide cases is whether to hospitalize the patient involuntarily. The Florida court's decision in the *Paddock* case takes a big step toward shielding therapists from malpractice liability in such cases. The court deferred to Dr. Chacko's judgment, acknowledging in broad terms that the threat of a malpractice suit for failing to commit a patient would impose an "intolerable burden" on the profession. The decision can be read to mean that Florida therapists will never be held liable for failing to hospitalize suicidal patients, regardless of the circumstances, but such a reading would extend well beyond the facts of the *Paddock* case. Staying closer to those facts, if a therapist recommends hospitalization, reserves a bed, and otherwise acts in a professional manner, he has no further legal obligation to have his patient committed involuntarily.

PART II

VIOLENCE AGAINST OTHERS

CHAPTER 6
▼ ▼ ▼

Man with a Mission

There are lots of people who have delusional beliefs [about] doing harm to other people, and these people are living in the community, and the vast majority of them never act on their delusional beliefs.

—STEVEN M. MIRIN, M.D.

Dennis Gould was suffering from paranoid schizophrenia, all the psychiatrists agreed on that. He experienced delusions of grandeur and violence, and, as events would prove, he sometimes had the will to act on them.

Gould, a Jew, thought of himself as the Messiah whose mission was to save the Jewish people. He believed that his former girlfriend, Shelley Rotman, was impure and that God had ordered him to kill her as a sacrifice. Gould expected that, in the end, he would go to Israel to be crucified.

Gould's readiness to take drastic action in response to his delusions was first demonstrated in April 1975. Boston is one of the few American cities still operating trolley cars. Ambivalent about his divine mission to kill Shelley Rotman and afraid he might actually do it, Gould lay down next to a Commonwealth Avenue trolley track and let the oncoming trolley's iron wheel cut off his right arm. But God's will—through his chosen instrument, Dennis Gould—was not to be thwarted. Three years later, Gould killed Shelley Rotman with his left arm, stabbing her thirty-one times.

The victim's family held Gould's psychiatrist, Dr. Steven Mirin, responsible for Shelley Rotman's death, contending that Mirin should have realized how dangerous Gould was and had him committed to long-term hospitalization. In May 1988, a Boston jury found that Mirin had committed malpractice and awarded the Rotman family $4.5 million in damages.

INNOCENT BEGINNINGS

Dennis Gould came from a working-class family in Nantasket, a town near Boston. His father, operator of a dry cleaning establishment and a snack wagon, was distant, hardworking, and not very giving emotionally. Dennis was closer to his mother, but he also felt that his mother smothered him. Mrs. Gould wanted Dennis to be a doctor, a goal beyond his reach, and he grew up in the shadow of his successful older brother.

Shelley Rotman, the dauther of an electrical contractor, came from a middle-class family in Milton, a Boston suburb. She was a junior in high school when she met Dennis Gould. Shelley was attractive, popular, and a good student. She graduated from high school in 1973 and later earned a degree in social work from Syracuse University.

Dennis Gould was in his early twenties and a student at Suffolk University in Boston when he met Shelley Rotman at a party in 1971. They dated through 1972 and became close, if not intimate. Shelley's father, Alfred Rotman, at first thought Dennis "appeared to be well adjusted, likeable, ambitious, not a bad sort of boy."

That impression didn't last. In late 1972, Shelley was visiting in the Goulds' home when Dennis threatened her with a butter knife. In early 1973, Dennis began telling Shelley that God was talking to him and that he was getting messages from the Bible. Shelley told her father, who began to discourage the relationship, but Shelley (according to her father) had a "motherly concept" and continued to see Dennis.

In early 1973, Dennis Gould experienced a psychotic break; something happened to trigger paranoid schizophrenia. As Dr. Mirin would later testify, people who become schizophrenic—about 1 percent of the population—have an underlying biological vulnerability that "breaks" in response to external stresses. The illness usually surfaces in the late teens or early twenties, manifesting itself in disordered, bizarre thinking. There is no known cure for schizophrenia. Controlling it with medication is the best that can be done, and only for some patients.

IN AND OUT OF THE HOSPITAL, 1973–76

Dennis Gould was first hospitalized for psychiatric problems at Worcester State Hospital in May 1973. According to his intake history, Gould believed he was the servant of God and that God had ordered him to kill his mother and father. Gould was diagnosed as having an "acute schizophrenic episode," from which he appeared to make a rapid recovery. He was discharged after two weeks.

Shelley Rotman thought Gould had suffered a "nervous breakdown" from which, with her help, he would recover. She had visited him in the hospital and invited him to her graduation party. Following his discharge, Gould came to the party, but he was sullen and kept to himself. That night, he slept over at the Rotmans' house. The next morning Gould became agitated and began following Shelley's mother around the house. Mrs. Rotman recounted that bizarre encounter: "He grabbed my arm and he wanted to bring me upstairs, and I got frightened. I yelled at him to sit down at the table and I went to the phone and called his parents." Gould's parents picked Dennis up, explaining that he had forgotten to take his pills.

Shelley Rotman didn't see Dennis Gould again for five years—until she and her parents went to court for an order restraining him from contacting her. After that court appearance, Shelley would see Gould one last time—with a knife in his left hand.

In June 1973, it was apparent that Dennis Gould was much sicker than the psychiatrists had thought when they discharged him from Worcester State Hospital less than a month before. Gould was recommitted to Worcester State, where he stayed for more than ten months. During this second hospitalization, Gould's homicidal delusions about Shelley Rotman came to the surface. Gould told hospital psychiatrists: "In order to be the real Messiah he has to kill his girlfriend, who is like a goddess. He feels he will not be able to kill her. Then he will not be the Messiah. Then he will have to go into show business to be a clown like Jerry Lewis." There were other indications of Gould's potential for violence. He was physically aggressive toward a staff member, he hit another patient, and he threatened his mother.

The Worcester State psychiatrists believed that Gould couldn't be safely released into the community without medication. When Gould was discharged, it was with the understanding that he would return to the hospital periodically for injections. Beginning a pattern of resistance to medications, Gould returned only once.

Six months after his discharge, the Worcester State superintendent telephoned Gould's mother to see how he was doing. She was disappointed that Dennis wasn't making more progress but reported that he was working and that he denied having dangerous thoughts. Mrs. Gould thought a home visit by hospital personnel would be "unwise," so the superintendent abandoned the idea. Six months later, unmedicated and blatantly psychotic, Gould amputated his right arm under a trolley wheel.

A bloody Dennis Gould was taken to Massachusetts General Hospital, where, following surgery, he stayed for about three weeks. He was a difficult patient. Despite large doses of antipsychotic drugs, his delusional thinking worsened, and expressions of "tremendous rage and aggression" increased. One day a hospital psychologist was testing Gould's ability to think abstractly. She asked him the meaning of "strike while the iron is hot." Gould's response was to strike the psychologist. According to Dr. Mirin, Gould thought that "she was inviting him to rape her."

Even with only one arm, Gould was dangerous—a level of dangerousness Massachusetts General Hospital was not designed to cope with. He was transferred temporarily to Worcester State Hospital, where he had spent most of the preceding year. In May 1975, Gould was transferred to McLean Hospital, a private teaching hospital for Harvard Medical School. Gould was a patient at McLean for about five months, until his insurance coverage ran out and he was discharged. While at McLean, he lived in East House, a secure facility to which dangerous patients were usually assigned.

Dr. Steven Mirin became Dennis Gould's therapist at McLean in May 1975, and he continued to treat Gould until he killed Shelley Rotman in July 1978. Mirin had graduated from the State University of New York with an M.D. degree in 1967, followed by a residency in psychiatry at Boston University. After a stint in the air force, Mirin became clinical director of a psychopharmacology research project at McLean. In 1983, Mirin became medical director at Westwood Lodge Hospital, a position he occupied at the time of trial, along with a faculty appointment in psychiatry at Harvard Medical School and a private practice.

After his initial sessions with Gould, Mirin prepared a case report in which he associated various incidents with the onset of Gould's illness. For example, Gould had "reached up and unscrewed the light bulb . . . in the ark in the synagogue"—a light that, in Jewish religious symbolism, was supposed to burn eternally. Religious symbolism pervaded Gould's thinking. He felt "permanently blighted" because he had been circumcised and believed that had been a sign from God. Mirin's diagnosis: paranoid schizophrenia.

Gould's delusions continued through his stay at McLean and throughout the time he was under Dr. Mirin's care. According to Mirin's report, "no combination of psychotropic drugs or psychotherapy has seemed to alter his delusional system." Mirin noted Gould's delusion that "cutting off his right arm gave him the right to kill whomever he liked." Nevertheless, at that point, Mirin believed that "there appears to be some degree of insight and observing ego, making him a viable candidate for long-term support in psychotherapy coupled with the use of psychotropic medicine in a highly structured milieu."

The "highly structured milieu" Mirin had in mind was either a halfway house, where Gould would hold an outside job but have a structured living situation, or a day treatment center, where his time would be spent in supervised programs.

About six weeks after Gould's arrival at McLean, there was a conference of psychiatrists and other mental health professionals to discuss Gould's case. Knowing Gould couldn't afford to stay at McLean for very long—Mirin estimated that McLean would have cost $300–400 per day in 1975—alternative placements were discussed, including a halfway house or a day treatment center. According to Mirin's notes of the conference, "If after three to six weeks of intensive treatment and exploration of treatment alternatives, other than McLean, no progress can be made it would be recommended that the family transfer the patient to a state hospital or any other hospital of their choosing." There was no suggestion, at that juncture, that Gould might simply be released to his parents, without some "structured milieu." Despite intensive psychotherapy and continued heavy doses of drugs, Gould did not improve.

At a July staff conference, the "real possibility [that Gould might] attempt to kill his ex-girlfriend" was discussed. Referring to Gould's "proven tendency to severe psychotic acting out," Dr. Louis McGarry, the head of legal psychiatry at the Massachusetts Department of Mental Health and a consultant to McLean, said that "any overt act in the girlfriend's direction, carrying a weapon, going toward her house . . . might be an adequate basis for a Bridgewater transfer." Bridgewater is the state maximum security hospital to which the most dangerous patients are committed. Dennis Gould eventually ended up in Bridgewater, but only after he killed Shelley Rotman.

In late July, there was a consensus at McLean that Gould was still dangerous, and, as one psychiatrist put it, that "a transfer to Worcester State is our only viable option." Dr. Mirin concurred, later testifying that "he was still obviously psychotic and unable to care for himself, and as a result, was also potentially dangerous to Shelley Rotman." As late as August 20, Dr. Mirin wrote that "at present [Gould] represents a danger to himself and others, and is probably in need of long-term hospitalization." Nevertheless, the McLean psychiatrists decided to get an outside opinion on whether Gould could be discharged.

On August 29, a Dr. Shelton interviewed Gould and concluded—contrary to the unanimous professional opinion at McLean up to that time—that Gould could be discharged "with an outpatient psychotherapy connection and medication for an extended period of time."

Dr. Mirin testified that he had not at first agreed with Dr. Shelton's conclusion. Less than a month later, however, both Mirin and other McLean psychiatrists came around to Shelton's view. No further consideration was given to sending Gould to Worcester State Hospital—viewed two months earlier as the "only viable option"—apparently because Gould didn't like Worcester State, nor did his family.

Gould began getting passes for home visits in late September and was discharged from McLean in October 1975, in Dr. Mirin's care. Had he been willing, Gould might have been placed in a halfway house or enrolled in a day treatment program that provided the kind of structured milieu Dr. Mirin had said earlier was important. But Gould's discharge was not conditioned on his accepting one of those options. He rejected both and went home.

Gould's first nine months as an outpatient passed without serious incident. He saw Dr. Mirin once a week in his office at McLean. In July 1976, however, Mirin observed that Gould was becoming "more paranoid, grandiose and delusional." He was also increasingly agitated but refused an increase in medication. Although Gould hadn't seen Shelley Rotman for over two years, he had found out that she had been studying in Europe and that she was coming home soon.

In mid-August, Mirin learned that Gould had spoken with Shelley on the telephone. Since Gould continued to talk about killing her, Mirin saw the phone call as an ominous sign. He warned Gould that if the contacts with Shelley continued, Mirin would hospitalize him. Mirin sent a letter to McLean's lawyer, outlining the circumstances and requesting his advice. The lawyer wrote back, advising Mirin that Shelley should be warned.

On August 25, 1976, two days before Gould was rehospitalized, Dr. Mirin wrote the following note to Shelley Rotman:

Dear Miss Rotman:

It has come to my attention that you have recently been in contact with Mr. Dennis Gould, a patient of mine. This is to inform you that Mr. Gould still suffers from occasional thoughts of doing you bodily harm, though these are by no means constant. Needless to say, I feel you should eliminate any casual or formal contact with Mr. Gould in the future.

Sincerely,
Steven Mirin, M.D.

When Gould's mother informed Mirin that she had found two knives in the glove compartment of Gould's car, Mirin gave Gould the choice between voluntarily hospitalizing himself and being committed. Gould was admitted on a voluntary basis to Worcester Memorial Hospital, a private institution, on August 27, 1976. Gould's chart reflected that "as in the past, Gould was a problem patient—moderately menacing to several staff members and . . . incorporating into his delusions some confusion between his ex-girlfriend and our occupational therapy student."

The staff at Worcester Memorial believed that "weekly visits to a private doctor's office was an insufficient program." They thought that Gould should be transferred to Worcester State Hospital "in order that he become more integrated into the state supported chronic rehabilitation system." Because Worcester State was the last place Gould wanted to go, Dr. Mirin tried to have him readmitted at McLean. McLean rejected Gould because he had an unpaid bill from his previous admission.

Gould was then transferred from Worcester Memorial to Westwood Lodge Hospital, another private institution, in September 1976. He remained psychotic at Westwood, telling his psychiatrist that he saw "messages from God around him all the time." Gould's "increasing expression of aggressive ideation" toward Shelley Rotman was duly recorded.

Shortly after his admission to Westwood, it was noted in Gould's record that his insurance company would pay only $3,300 more, which, at $300 per day, would cover about eleven more days of hospitalization. Gould was discharged from Westwood Lodge in Dr. Mirin's care after thirteen days. His discharge papers stated that he was "less angry and murderous toward his girlfriend."

From the onset of his illness in May 1973 until September 1976, Dennis Gould was intermittently confined in locked psychiatric wards about half of that time—a total of seven hospitalizations in five different hospitals. From May 1975 until July 1978—more than three years—Gould was under the care of Dr. Mirin. During all but six months of the latter period, Gould was treated on an outpatient basis.

DENNIS GOULD AS AN OUTPATIENT

Gould's ability to function in the community as an outpatient depended on his "treatment alliance" with Dr. Mirin, which Mirin defined broadly as "a sense between a doctor and a patient that the two of them are going to work together to deal with the patient's illness." At a minimum, Gould would have to show up for his appointments and take his medications. In addition, he would be expected to do other things Mirin believed would be helpful. In the absence of a working treatment alliance,

Mirin predicted that Gould's condition would deteriorate and he would be rehospitalized.

For the first year or so, Dr. Mirin saw Gould once a week; after that, he saw him every two or three weeks, except when Gould's clinical state called for more frequent appointments. Generally speaking, Gould had a good record in accepting appointments suggested by Mirin and in keeping them, until the end. Gould's last appointment with Mirin was on July 11, 1978. Mirin had asked Gould to return in a week, but Gould refused, saying he would come back in three weeks. Six days later, he killed Shelley Rotman.

Throughout Dr. Mirin's treatment, Gould was on massive doses of various drugs—doses that are measured in their pharmacologic equivalents to Thorazine, the oldest and most widely prescribed of the so-called psychotropic drugs. The average outpatient dose of Thorazine is in the range of four hundred to eight hundred milligrams per day. Patients on larger doses are usually hospitalized. Gould was, in clinical terms, "refractory" to drugs—that is, drugs had a much smaller effect on him, compared with most patients. As a result, Mirin found it necessary to prescribe doses three or four times larger than those normally given to an outpatient, with Thorazine equivalents ranging from two thousand to over three thousand milligrams per day.

Even with those massive doses, Gould's messianic and homicidal delusions didn't go away. In early 1977, for example, Gould became agitated during a speech by newly elected President Jimmy Carter because he thought he was to play some role in the new administration, and that the speech might refer to him. According to Mirin, however, the drugs did have the effect of diminishing Gould's bizarre thinking and, consequently, the likelihood that he would act on his delusions. Gould's record in taking medications was uneven, however, and hard for Mirin to check on. Gould's parents were supposed to monitor his drug intake, but that system did not always work.

In most other respects, the Mirin-Gould treatment alliance was a failure. Dr. Mirin kept trying to persuade Gould to live in a halfway house or to enroll in a day treatment program, but Gould consistently refused. Sometimes his parents vetoed a promising program. His father rejected Gould's participation in "Project Independence," a vocational rehabilitation program in which he might have learned a trade. The father questioned the program's practicality; Dr. Mirin had a different perspective: "I would have preferred it if he tried anything."

Gould was eligible for a day treatment program at Worcester State Hospital, but his parents didn't want him in that public facility. So Gould remained at home with his parents, an arrangement with some decided disadvantages. He had very little social life, a situation that might have been improved in a halfway house or even in Worcester State. His father didn't understand Gould's illness and thought he needed more discipline. This led to confrontations. His mother pulled in the opposite direction. Mirin saw her as the "intrusive savior" who made him dependent on her—"telling him what to wear and generally hassling him." The stresses of the home situation exacerbated Gould's psychosis.

Loneliness and the heavily religious content of his delusions drew Gould repeatedly to the Hebrew school, the yeshiva, near his home. Dr. Mirin believed that going to the yeshiva was bad for Gould because it fed into his delusions, which could make him more psychotic and more dangerous. Mirin repeatedly told Gould to stay away from the yeshiva. Gould would appear to agree and then break his promise. In the months before killing Shelley Rotman, Gould was going to the yeshiva almost daily.

Gould violated the treatment alliance in other ways. He sometimes refused to take a new drug or to accept an increased dosage. On several occasions, Mirin recommended that Gould undergo electroconvulsive therapy (also called shock treatments or ECT). Gould always refused. Gould began smoking marijuana, which Mirin thought could loosen his tenuous grip on reality; Mirin told him to stop, but Gould didn't stop.

Gould wanted to be fitted for a prosthesis for the stump of his right arm. Mirin was concerned that Gould might be able to use the prosthesis as a weapon. Gould's orthopedist assured Mirin that, given the location of the amputation, Gould would not have sufficient force in his right arm to inflict injury. Mirin gave his approval, provided the hook would be ground down so that it wouldn't have a point on it.

Dr. Mirin told Gould repeatedly to stay away from Shelley Rotman— a link in the treatment alliance Gould repeatedly broke, usually without telling Mirin. Gould would telephone the Rotman home, particularly during Jewish holidays or school vacations when he thought she might be there. Shelley spoke with him a few times, and this left him agitated. On New Year's Day 1978, Gould went uninvited to the Rotman home; Shelley wasn't there. Gould became agitated, and as Mr. Rotman recalled: "He was saying that he didn't want to hurt Shelley, but he was getting messages from God. . . . He kept saying he didn't want to hurt her and he waved up the stump of his arm and he said he made a sacrifice and Shelley had to make a sacrifice." Rotman's lawyer recommended filing a criminal complaint for Gould's threats on Shelley's life, advice the Rotmans followed.

When Gould was summoned to court to answer a criminal charge, his lawyer asked Mirin to write a letter to the judge. Mirin's letter read as follows:

Your Honor:

Mr. Dennis Gould will be appearing before your court and has requested that I provide information pertinent to his past psychiatric treatment. Mr. Gould has been a patient of mine since May 1975, when he was admitted to McLean Hospital, Belmont, Massachusetts, for treatment of a chronic emotional disorder. In the treatment of his illness Mr. Gould has received psychotherapy and medication, both of which are increased in times of stress. In the last two and one half years, Mr. Gould has related transient thoughts of a psychotic nature, but despite this has managed to hold a full time job and lead a relatively normal social life. Despite the chronicity of his thought disorder I feel that at the present time he does not represent an imminent danger to himself or others. He has agreed to continue to see me on a regular basis and I feel that we have a strong treatment alliance. I hope this information will be of some assistance to the court.

Steven Mirin, M.D.

This letter would come back to haunt Mirin in the malpractice trial. It failed to say that Gould suffered from paranoid schizophrenia; it stated that Gould had held a "full time job" for the past two and one-half years— without mentioning that Gould's father was the employer, and that Mirin had hospitalized Gould during that period because he thought Gould was dangerous; Gould was not leading a "relatively normal social life"; perhaps most significant, Mirin and Gould did not have a "strong treatment alliance."

The criminal charge was later dropped in a plea bargain, under which Gould agreed to have no contact with Shelley Rotman and to submit to two years of unsupervised probation. Soon after, Gould violated his probation by sending Shelley Rotman a birthday card signed "Me."

Why was Dennis Gould obsessed with the idea of killing Shelley Rotman? The origins of Gould's delusion were not fully explored at the trial, but some light was shed. Gould was afraid of women, that much was clear. Dr. Mirin thought Gould's notion that Shelley was "impure" grew out his inability to tolerate intimacy in their relationship. As Mirin saw it, "The basis for his delusional belief about Shelley Rotman and his need to kill her had to do with his impotence in his sexual relationship with her, and also his own rage at himself and at her as a consequence of what transpired in that relationship." Mirin thought that Gould's deep feelings of sexual inadequacy made him feel terrible, and that he had transferred the blame to Shelley Rotman—an example of "paranoid projection" in which a person trying to cope with intolerable feelings seeks relief by attributing them to someone else. From there, it was a short step to believing that Shelley was impure and should be killed.

Gould's delusions waxed and waned with changing circumstances—getting stronger, for example, during the Jewish holidays. (Gould had amputated his arm on the trolley track during Passover.) At the trial, Mirin speculated that Gould had become agitated when he misinterpreted a chance remark—mistakenly thinking someone had called him a homosexual—and that this perturbation of his feelings of sexual inadequacy had led him to kill the person who was, in his distorted thinking, responsible for those feelings.

THE KILLING

In the spring of 1978, Shelley Rotman was hired as a social worker at a nursing home in Quincy, a Boston suburb. She continued to live at home. One evening, Gould sat in his parked car near the Rotman home for several hours until a neighbor called the police. The police knew of no connection with the Rotmans, and Gould was allowed to go on his way. Three days before he killed her, Gould telephoned the nursing home and, using the assumed name "David Miller," confirmed that a Shelley Rotman was employed there.

Dennis Gould drove to the Quincy Nursing Home on the morning of July 17, 1978, arriving about 8 A.M. He sat in his car, armed with a hunting knife, and read a book in Hebrew as he waited for Shelley Rotman. She arrived about 8:45, parked her car, and walked down a walled ramp toward a back door to the nursing home. Gould followed her down the ramp.

James McPherson, a construction carpenter, was sitting in his truck nearby when he saw Shelley walk down the ramp, followed by Gould. McPherson heard a scream and ran down the ramp to investigate. He found Gould "on top of the woman, and it looked like he was slugging her." He ordered Gould to back off and sit on the ramp wall while he went for help. When McPherson returned moments later, Gould had renewed his assault. As McPherson remembered it: "And when I run down [the ramp] he drove it [the knife] right into her chest, and I slammed him against the wall . . . and he kept saying: 'Messiah, she's impure.'"

Officer Kevin Murphy, a Quincy policemen, responded in his cruiser to an 8:49 A.M. call from the nursing home. He found Gould sitting on the ramp wall. He found Shelley, her shoulder pinned against the doorway, her arm protecting her face. Shelley's mouth appeared to be moving, and he could hear "a rasping sound, or gurgling type sound."

Officer Murphy arrested Gould and took him to the police station, where he confessed to killing Shelley. Gould's demeanor was calm as he told Murphy: "The rabbi told me right from the pulpit. He looked right at me. The whole congregation looked at me and he, the rabbi, said: 'Thou shalt kill her.'" Gould thought that what he had done was "right," but that "they will probably nail me to a cross."

About an hour after the killing, the Rotmans got a phone call from the hospital; they were told that Shelley had been in an accident. When they arrived, they learned that Shelley was dead. Mrs. Rotman wanted to see her daughter but she couldn't "because they were doing an autopsy. Why did she need an autopsy? She was cut up enough."

About 10 A.M. on July 17, Dr. Mirin got a phone call from Gould's sister, who reported that Gould had been unusually agitated over the weekend, a danger sign that his delusions were growing stronger. Gould's parents had also observed his agitation but had failed to call Mirin over the weekend. By the time Mirin received the sister's call, Shelley Rotman was already dead.

Gould was tried twice for killing Shelley Rotman. The jury in the first trial convicted him of first-degree murder, and he was sentenced to life imprisonment. (Massachusetts does not have the death penalty.) That conviction was reversed on appeal. Gould's second trial resulted in his acquittal by reason of insanity. He was then committed to Bridgewater State Hospital for an indefinite period, subject to an annual psychiatric review of his condition to determine whether he is still dangerous. Some psychiatrists may be reluctant to certify that a person is no longer a danger to others when that person, like Dennis Gould, has committed a brutal homicide. In any event, Gould is still in Bridgewater.

THE MALPRACTICE CASE

Alfred Rotman, as administrator of the estate of his daughter, Shelley, filed a malpractice suit against Steven Mirin, M.D., in March 1980. The wheels of justice turned slowly after that. Various procedural obstacles and a large backlog of cases on the civil docket of the Middlesex Superior Court in Cambridge delayed a jury trial for eight years, until April 1988.

There was little disagreement about the facts. The disputes centered on whether, given those facts, Dr. Mirin had been negligent—whether he had failed to meet the applicable standard of psychiatric care, as represented by what the average psychiatrist would have done in similar circumstances. Like most medical malpractice cases, *Rotman v. Mirin* became a battle of the experts. Their combined testimony consumed over nine days of the twelve-day trial, filling more than twelve hundred pages of transcript.

THE CASE AGAINST DR. MIRIN

Mr. Rotman's principal expert witness was Bernard S. Yudowitz, M.D. Yudowitz had earned joint degrees in medicine and law from Cornell University and the University of Glasgow, and had completed a residency in psychiatry at McLean Hospital. He had other qualifications that made him particularly suitable as an expert in this case. Yudowitz had served as director of Bridgewater State Hospital from 1975 to 1978. In that capacity, he was in charge of evaluating violent patients referred there by the courts—patients like Dennis Gould.

Dr. Yudowitz took the position that Dennis Gould was a dangerous paranoid schizophrenic who should have been committed to a hospital long before he killed Shelley Rotman. He pointed to several places in Gould's records, including the results of psychological tests at Massachusetts General Hospital, taken shortly after the trolley car amputation, which stated that "[Gould's] aggression, plus the inability to inhibit the expression of his violent impulses, give him the potential of being a very, very violent and dangerous person." Referring to Gould's subsequent stay at McLean, and stressing the impressive credentials of the McLean psychiatrists, Yudowitz noted that "everyone at McLean felt that this man needed long-term treatment in a hospital setting." In Yudowitz's opinion, Gould's stabbing Shelley thirty-one times exhibited a "maniacal rage" which "only illustrates how psychotic and sick this guy was." Yudowitz predicted that "the likelihood of this patient ever coming out of the hospital is minimal, almost nil."

Dr. Yudowitz testified that although paranoid schizophrenia is a "dangerous category," not all those so diagnosed are as dangerous as Dennis Gould. Dangerousness increases with the presence of other variables:

> You have those with fixed delusions, and then you have those with fixed delusions of harming someone. And then you have someone with fixed delusions of harming someone, who might from time to time get ideas from whatever's mentioned in the movies . . . to go

and do it, and then you have those individuals who are highly resistant to medication, and then you have those individuals in no treatment program, and then you get to the top of the pyramid of those who are most dangerous. . . . That is the picture of Mr. Gould.

Dr. Yudowitz thought there had been "*no* treatment alliance" between Mirin and Gould. Merely showing up for appointments was not, in his view, an alliance, and Gould had rejected most of Mirin's recommendations. The Mirin-Gould alliance had also relied heavily on participation of Gould's parents, since Gould had refused to live in a halfway house. Yudowitz believed that "to appoint parents to be part of a treatment team, in this particular case, is, in my mind, beyond reason."

Dr. Yudowitz thought that Gould's visit to the Rotman home on New Year's Day 1978 demonstrated the need for long-term commitment. "He makes a statement to her father that 'I want you to know that I have to kill your daughter,' as if he's saying 'hello' and passing the time of day." Yudowitz saw this as the culmination of an escalating series of events, beginning with Gould's phone calls to Shelley months before. Mirin's failure to commit Gould at that point was, in Yudowitz's opinion, a "gross deviation" from the standard of care.

Mr. Rotman's second expert was Dr. Robert M. Weiner, a psychiatrist with a medical degree from Columbia University. Weiner holds a teaching appointment in psychiatry at Harvard Medical School and is board certified in forensic psychiatry. Like Yudowitz, Weiner had experience pertinent to the issues in this case. From 1971 to 1983, Weiner had been clinical director for a Massachusetts trial court. In that capacity, he had examined over one hundred people each year for dangerousness.

Weiner agreed with Yudowitz that only a minority of patients diagnosed with paranoid schizophrenia are dangerous. Like Yudowitz, however, Weiner described the mind-set of that dangerous minority in a way that fit Dennis Gould precisely: they share the belief that they have a duty to kill a particular person.

Weiner testified about commitment procedures, drawing on his considerable practical experience. In Massachusetts, a patient can be committed if there is a "likelihood of serious harm." That phrase, in turn, is defined as "a substantial risk of physical harm to other persons as manifested by evidence of homicidal or other violent behavior." Under those standards, Weiner believed that Mirin should not have been discharged from McLean in the fall of 1975, and he could not "conceive of any reasonable psychiatrist having a differing opinion."

Weiner also believed that following the McLean discharge, Gould should have been recommitted when he refused to enter a halfway house or a day treatment program. Weiner's reasoning was simple: "At that point you have a patient who is mentally ill, there's a likelihood of serious harm, and [he is] not in treatment of such a nature to change that likelihood significantly."

According to Weiner, the "likelihood of serious harm" determination includes the present and the foreseeable future. It's a judgmental assessment of the person's *potential* for violence, which may or may not occur. Applying those standards to this case, Weiner thought that Gould had been committable at any time after he began calling Shelley on the telephone in the fall of 1977.

Dr. Weiner testified that Mirin's warning note to Shelley Rotman of August 1976 had been inadequate. Mirin should have told her and her parents that Gould was suffering from a serious mental illness, that his illness involved "the fixed delusion that he must kill Shelley Rotman," and that her life was in danger.

Dr. Mirin's Defense

Dr. Mirin called as his expert witness Dr. Thomas Gutheil, the Harvard professor and forensic psychiatrist whose views on numerous issues are cited elsewhere in this book. Gutheil has written extensively in professional journals, contributing articles about paranoid schizophrenia and determinations of dangerousness. Gutheil also carries on a private practice—including potentially dangerous patients.

Dr. Gutheil agreed that Gould was correctly diagnosed with paranoid schizophrenia and with having persisting delusions whose strength waxed and waned over time. He stressed, however, that it was "extremely rare for individuals with delusions involving harm to actually act on them." For that reason, paranoid schizophrenics are not automatically committable. Moreover, the concept of the "least restrictive alternative," consistent with an equivalent level of safety, underlies modern commitment laws. Therefore, the relatively drastic alternative of commitment is not appropriate unless the person is "responding to those delusions or is in the process of deciding to act" on them.

Gutheil's position means that at the time of commitment there must be proof of actual dangerousness, based on the person's present state of mind—not merely potential dangerousness based on a violent history. If a candidate for commitment was violent shortly before the commitment hearing—for example, by amputating an arm under a trolley wheel—that might suffice to prove dangerousness. But if there was no recent violent conduct and the person's delusions of violence, like Gould's, waxed and waned, commitment might not be justified during a waning period.

Under this view, a psychiatrist considering commitment of a potentially dangerous patient must periodically check the strength or weakness of the patient's delusions. Gould's visit to Shelley Rotman's home on New Year's Day illustrates the issue. Both Mirin and Gutheil testified that they would have committed Gould if they had known, soon after the visit, about Gould's matter-of-factly informing Shelley's parents that he had to kill their daughter. But Mirin did not find out about the New Year's Day visit until January 9. When he examined Gould nine days after the event, Mirin concluded that "he is not more dangerous to Shelley than in the past, and he recognizes that he has to stay away from her or suffer the consequences." Gutheil agreed with Mirin's conclusion.

Dr. Gutheil testified that Dr. Mirin's letter to Shelley Rotman in which he warned her of possible "bodily harm" from Gould complied with the standard of care. Gutheil thought Mirin's letter may even have exceeded that standard because the duty to warn of a patient's possible violence "was only gradually beginning to be taken into account by clinicians in Massachusetts at that time."

Dr. Mirin took the stand in his own defense. Broadly stated, Mirin's position was as follows: "Mr. Gould is clearly, by anyone's imagination, an extremely sick individual who needed continuing care. The issue is whether one can simply lock this person up forever and throw away the key, and that option is not available to me."

Dr. Mirin had no illusions about curing Dennis Gould. As he saw it, when a doctor undertakes treatment of someone like Gould, he must anticipate that "it will be for your lifetime or his." Other psychiatrists had not wanted to take Gould as a patient. Mirin apparently felt obligated to do what he could for a very sick person. However one assesses Mirin's responsibility for the death of Shelley Rotman, the picture of a caring doctor emerges from the trial record.

Dr. Mirin shared Gutheil's view that commitment required actual dangerousness, based on the patient's present state of mind. Mirin agreed that Gould had been dangerous, and therefore committable, through his time at McLean in 1975, and that there had been incidents, such as the amputation by the trolley wheel, when he had not been able to control his violent impulses. Mirin believed, however, that Gould had not been commitable during most of the period 1975 to 1978. Although his delusions had persisted, they had fluctuated with external circumstances. Gould's medications had not made his delusions go away, but they had largely prevented him from acting on them.

Dr. Mirin did not see long-term hospitalization as a "viable alternative"; it was more like a revolving door. "He has been in five or seven hospital stays. All of the hospitals discharged him, and I wasn't in charge of his being discharged." Mirin thought that with the cooperation of Gould's parents, he could effectively monitor Gould through his regular office appointments. He would explore Gould's current mental state, the depth of his psychotic thinking, and whether he was likely to be harmful to others. This would be done by direct questions, such as: do you still think God wants you to kill Shelley Rotman? Mirin would also pick up indirect clues from Gould's behavior—whether he was agitated or disheveled, his tone of voice, his body language.

Dr. Mirin's system for monitoring Gould might have worked well enough if Gould's mental states had remained stable between his appointments. Most of the time, they did. Unfortunately, Gould's delusions could be activated suddenly by unpredictable events. Mirin conceded that Gould's thoughts about killing Shelley Rotman could change "from one day to the next." This meant that if Gould were to become unusually agitated—at the yeshiva, or by misinterpreting a remark to reflect on his sexuality—he might strike before Mirin found out about his altered state. Gould was like a land mine, ready to explode when someone stepped on a sensitive spot. That's what happened on the weekend of July 15, 1978.

Dr. Mirin conceded that Gould had not accepted many of his recommendations. The minimum requirements of a treatment alliance were, as Mirin saw it, keeping appointments, taking medication, and holding a job. Mirin thought there was no way to enforce his other recommendations. As both Mirin and Gutheil pointed out, a patient cannot be "committed" to a halfway house. On the other hand, they did not explain why a psychiatrist could not require a patient like Gould either to enter a halfway house or to be hospitalized, on the theory that the close supervision afforded by the halfway house was necessary as a safety measure.

Dr. Mirin tried to defend his letter to the court, the letter in which he said that Gould had a "relatively normal social life" and that they had a "strong treatment alliance." He pointed out that he had given a detailed clinical history to the court psychiatrist over the phone and that his letter had been prompted by a request from Gould's lawyer. Mirin was apparently trying to keep his patient out of jail and thought a reassuring message from the psychiatrist would be helpful. He might have been better off admitting that his letter had been misleading.

The Jury's Verdict, and a Compromise

The lawyers made lengthy final arguments to the jury. Mr. Rotman's lawyer revisited the record, stressing—as he had throughout—Gould's obsession with killing Shelley Rotman and his history of violence. He made an emotional appeal for damages to compensate for Shelley's conscious suffering before her death: "The last thing in this world Shelley saw was not her her parents, not a friend, not a physician. But Gould. With a knife." He asked the jury to make an additional award for the Rotmans' loss of their only daughter.

When it came to persuading the jury, Dr. Mirin's lawyer had by far the harder job. He couldn't claim that his client had done everything perfectly, that Shelley Rotman's death was inevitable. He told the jury they shouldn't judge Mirin by hindsight. His client had had to made judgments about an unpredictable patient, based on limited information. Mirin had been conscientious, and his actions reasonable.

The judge complimented the lawyers—"two of the most able attorneys who practice law in this State"—instructed the jury, and sent them off to deliberate. The jury was out for one day. They returned with findings that Dr. Mirin had committed malpractice, and that his malpractice had caused Shelley Rotman's death. The jury awarded $2.25 million for Shelley's conscious pain and suffering and an additional $2.25 million for the Rotmans' loss of their daughter—a total award of $4.5 million.

Dr. Mirin's lawyer filed an appeal from the trial court's decision. While the case was pending on appeal, it was settled for an undisclosed, but substantial, amount.

Dr. Mirin testified at the trial that Dennis Gould had telephoned him from Bridgewater State Hospital two years after he killed Shelley Rotman. Gould was still delusional. He believed that Shelley was alive, but that her spirit was in another woman's body. Gould told Mirin that he hadn't told him in advance he was going to kill Shelley because he thought Mirin would have hospitalized him.

CHAPTER 7
▼ ▼ ▼

Search and Destroy

> He perceived himself in a combat situation, which was a
> gross distortion of what was actually going on. He was not
> in Vietnam in a village, he was in an IBM plant. But he
> didn't seem to know that.
>
> —SELWYN ROSE, M.D.

In the afternoon of August 30, 1982, Leonard Avery, a Vietnam veteran
suffering from post-traumatic stress disorder, drove onto the five-thousand-
acre IBM site in the Research Triangle Park near Durham, North Carolina.
Employed on an IBM assembly line until ten days before, Avery had been
fired for chronic absenteeism and for making threats. He was dressed
in camouflage army fatigues and combat boots. His army medals—combat infantryman and master parachutist badges and a bronze star—
were pinned to his "boonie hat." Avery was armed with a .45-caliber, semi-
automatic rifle and several homemade Molotov cocktails.

Avery went first to the Medical Department, where, just before he
was fired, he had had an altercation with a Dr. Connor about his excuses
for missing work. As a parting shot, Avery had told Connor: "I'll be back,
and I'm going to blow this place up. And I'm going to start right here."
When Avery appeared, rifle raised, in the entrance to the Medical Department on August 30, a secretary cried out, "Oh my God, it's him,"
and fled. Another secretary crawled under her desk. Avery fired several
shots, hitting no one. When Dr. Connor heard the shots, he locked his
office door and, in his phrase, "played possum." Avery threw a Molotov
cocktail against Connor's office door; the resulting fire was extinguished
by the sprinkler system. Avery moved on.

Ralph Glenn, a stockman, had been in a men's restroom when he heard shots. Glenn went into the adjoining hall, where he encountered Avery with his rifle. Glenn said to Avery, "Hey buddy, how about let's calm down a little bit and talk this thing over." Avery replied, "I don't want to talk. Just get out of my way." Then Avery shot Glenn in the chest. Glenn walked a few steps and collapsed dead in the hallway. Glenn had not known Leonard Avery.

After the first shots, the IBM security system began to respond to Avery's assault. Word went out over the public address system that employees were to barricade themselves in their offices, but that directive was widely ignored. Charles Davis, a label specialist, recalled the general commotion: "I noticed people running in all different directions and I knowed something was definitely wrong because people do not run at IBM." IBM security personnel weren't armed, so they called for support from the Durham County Sheriff's Department and the North Carolina Highway Patrol. By the time Avery was in custody, Raleigh and Durham City Police had also responded.

As the police began to close in on him, Avery returned to his car and fled the scene, his chrome-plated rifle pointed defiantly out the window. A deputy sheriff fired his shotgun at Avery's retreating car, shattering the rear window and puncturing the gas tank. A high-speed chase ensued, until Avery was stopped by a police roadblock. Having good reason to consider Avery armed and dangerous, the police approached his car cautiously. In the interval, Avery took a .22-caliber "Little Ace" derringer pistol from under the front seat and shot himself in the forehead.

The police took Avery to a hospital, where a neurosurgeon removed metal fragments from his brain, in the process cutting out a major portion of the left frontal lobe. According to the neurosurgeon, the operation should have had no long-term effect on Avery's memory, but the concussion from the bullet's impact could have affected his memory of events around the time of the incident. When Avery took the stand in his trial for the first-degree murder of Ralph Glenn, he didn't remember going to IBM on August 30 or anything that happened there.

In the course of his mission at IBM that afternoon, Avery fired twenty-eight rounds of .45-caliber ammunition. In addition to killing Ralph Glenn, he wounded four other IBM employees, none of whom knew him. He also threw three Molotov cocktails, causing minor fire damage.

NICE KID, MODEL SOLDIER

Leonard Avery was born in rural Wake County near Raleigh, North Carolina, in 1943. During his senior year in high school, when Wake

County schools were still segregated, Avery played baseball and had been starting point guard on the basketball term. His coach recalled him as an "easygoing fellow" who "got along well with others." Avery had been a staff member of the school yearbook, *The Tiger*, and he drove a school bus. He didn't drink and attended the Wake Grove Baptist Church.

Avery graduated from high school in 1961 to discover a world that limited opportunities for a black teenager in North Carolina. He worked in Raleigh as a shoe clerk for six months, as a department store elevator operator for two weeks, then quit to enlist in the army. After basic training, Avery graduated from jump school at Fort Bragg and became, by all accounts, a model soldier. He competed frequently for "Soldier of the Month." Both his conduct and efficiency ratings were "excellent." Avery made sergeant. In 1964, Avery married his first wife, Iris. In 1965, he reenlisted for six years.

Sergeant Avery participated in the U.S. intervention in the Dominican Republic in 1965 as a radio mechanic with the Eighty-second Airborne Division. His unit came under hostile fire, and he was awarded a combat infantryman's badge. When he returned to Fort Bragg after five months in the Dominican Republic, Iris was one month pregnant. The marriage began to founder.

VIETNAM

Sergeant Avery was sent to Vietnam in July 1966, as the war was escalating. Owing to a shortage of replacements, he was assigned as an infantry squad leader—a role for which he hadn't been trained. Avery found a mentor and friend in Sergeant Kelly, his platoon sergeant, who was also black. Kelly showed Avery what he needed to know, and once saved his life.

Avery's platoon was frequently in combat. He killed his first enemy soldier with his M-16 rifle from about fifty yards. Later, he described the effect of that first kill: "From then on, you killed someone, don't bother you no more." Avery started to drink in Vietnam.

An incident that was to haunt him years afterward occurred when Avery's platoon was on a search-and-destroy mission in the Central Highlands—going from village to village, hunting for Vietcong or sympathizers, sometimes burning everything in sight. Friendly villagers would bow or ask for food. But according to one participant, if the villagers "broke and run, ninety percent of the time they were hostile. We would give them one warning, and if they didn't stop, we shot them."

A member of Avery's squad described a standard technique with the village huts: "Some of those hooches . . . have like a hole dug down in it where they would hide. Sometimes you have to go in there and root them out. The best way was to throw a grenade in there."

As his squad swept through a village one day, Sergeant Avery stood outside the door of a hooch, pulled the pin on a grenade, and threw it inside. Then he fell to the ground and threw two more grenades into the hooch. Avery later told his squad that there were people in the hooch, possibly a family.

Fifteen years later, Avery was given sodium amytal (truth serum) and interviewed by a court-appointed psychiatrist in an effort to recover recollections of his assault on IBM. That interview produced nothing about the IBM assault, but the grenade incident did resurface in Avery's consciousness, along with his feelings of guilt that he might have killed an innocent family.

Toward the end of his first tour in Vietnam, Sergeant Avery was transferred to a communications unit. Sergeant Kelly, his friend from his old unit, was killed in a firefight and brought back by helicopter in a body bag. Avery was sent to help unload the casualties and was told that Kelly was among the dead. Another member of his unit described what happened next. "Sgt. Avery opened the bag and saw Sgt. Kelly, and then he just went off . . . he became hysterical. . . . He wanted to get on the chopper to go back out . . . to avenge his death. . . . I had to physically restrain him." Avery himself recalled, "I wanted to go back to the field to get another VC for Kelly."

In July 1967, after a one-year tour in Vietnam, Sergeant Avery was transferred back to Fort Bragg. He spent one day with his wife, Iris, and her infant of unknown paternity, then left her for good. In August he met Jackie, who would become his second wife. A few months later, elements of his unit were being transferred back to Vietnam as replacements. Either he or another sergeant—who had also served a tour in Vietnam— would have to go back. Because the other man was married and had four children, Avery volunteered to go.

In February 1968, Sergeant Avery was back in Vietnam as a forward observer. His job was to get as close as possible to the enemy and radio their positions back to artillery or mortar units. Avery particularly remembered one event from that time: He was ordered to retrieve the body of one of their men who had been killed two days earlier. He found the badly decomposed body, hoisted it over his shoulder, and carried it back to the company area under hostile fire. Avery's second tour in Vietnam was abbreviated to three months when additional replacements arrived.

HOME FROM THE WAR

Leonard Avery's family thought he was changed when he returned from Vietnam the second time. Never one to court trouble before, he bought a souped-up Plymouth with loud mufflers and eventually accumulated enough tickets to have his driver's license suspended. He was quick to anger and was drinking heavily. He told his mother that drinking kept him from smelling dead people. When he saw Oriental actors on television, he would become upset and walk away. Sometimes he refused to eat.

Sergeant Avery got into trouble at Fort Bragg as well. In June 1969, his unit was to fly to West Point. Avery missed the plane and was reduced in rank ("busted") from sergeant to corporal. He was absent without leave (AWOL) for days in August and again in October. In March 1970, Avery left North Carolina, intending to go AWOL indefinitely. After thirty days, the army formally declared him a deserter.

Avery settled in Baltimore, driving a cab and later a Coca-Cola truck. In November 1970, his girlfriend, Jackie, came to Baltimore and they were married. A son was born in 1972. In March 1973, the FBI arrived at Avery's door and arrested him as a deserter. The army didn't prosecute Sergeant Avery for desertion, but the former model soldier was given an undesirable discharge, under "less than honorable conditions."

Avery and his family returned to the Raleigh area, where a daughter was born in 1974. He continued to have a hard time of it. He was drinking heavily again, often mixing boilermakers of Colt 45 malt liquor and gin. He once fired a gun during an argument with a neighbor. In 1977, both his father and his brother (who was also his closest drinking buddy) died of heart attacks. He attended a local college briefly but quit when he ran out of money. His home mortgage was foreclosed. He belonged briefly to Van Masters of Raleigh, a motor club that took trips to various destinations. The club president recalled, "Every time I saw Leonard Avery, he was drinking." Avery had to leave the club when his van was repossessed.

Avery held a series of dead-end jobs: as a stock clerk in a Winn Dixie warehouse, a laborer in a knitting mill, and a maintenance man at the North Carolina State campus in Raleigh. He finally got a good job at Rockwell Nuclear as a drill press operator. But he got into an argument with his boss: Avery thought he was being blamed for rejected parts that should have been the responsibility of another operator. He hit his boss and was fired.

IBM EMPLOYEE / VA HOSPITAL OUTPATIENT

In 1979, Avery wrote a letter to the chairman of IBM objecting to the practice of bringing in people from out of state to fill many of the jobs at IBM's Research Triangle facility and urging that more local people be hired. Avery was hired by IBM in late 1979, according to him, because of the letter he had written. Although he was to be on the IBM payroll for over two and one-half years—until his Rambo-style assault of August 30, 1982—his path there was seldom smooth.

Avery had a succession of medical problems that usually led to sick leave. First it was trench foot, which he related to his experience in Vietnam. Then there were repeated chest pains, but tests indicated no significant cardiac problem. Later, his long and frequent absences would be related in one way or another to mental problems and their treatment at the Veterans Administration (VA) Hospital in Durham. During 1981, Avery was out sick 42 percent of the time. That percentage improved slightly—to 39 percent—during the eight months he was employed by IBM in 1982.

Extended sick leave was a major concern to IBM, not only because of its effects on employee morale but because the company had a policy of paying employees when they were out sick—regardless of how long—if a doctor certified that it was justified. Within months after Avery was hired, IBM management began to discuss his health and attendance and whether he should be let go.

Avery had recurrent nightmares about the Vietcong attacking him. He slept with a pistol under his pillow. One night he woke up attacking the dresser in the bedroom; another night he bit his wife; one morning he woke up to find his hands around his son's neck, imagining he was a Vietcong soldier. Avery also lost control during his waking hours, at various times hitting two of his sisters, a brother-in-law, and friends. Finally acknowledging that he needed help, Avery made an appointment with the VA Hospital in April 1981.

Avery was first diagnosed as suffering from "borderline disorder with paranoid ideation." Subsequent psychological testing and observation led to the diagnosis of post-traumatic stress disorder (PTSD) by Owen D. Buck, M.D., who would be Avery's primary therapist at the VA. Buck was a resident in psychiatry at the nearby Duke University School of Medicine, working part-time at the VA Hospital. He assigned Avery to weekly group therapy sessions with other Vietnam veterans suffering from PTSD.

Post-traumatic stress disorder was first recognized as a distinct mental illness in 1980, in the aftermath of the Vietnam War. PTSD is defined by several symptoms, most of which must be present before the diagnosis can be made. The PTSD patient has had an experience that would evoke severe stress in anyone—such as being in close combat or in a concentration camp. (Divorce or loss of a job doesn't qualify.) Intrusive thoughts and images—killing another person, decomposed corpses—that haunt the patient's mind years later are a common symptom. Others include paranoia, feelings of estrangement from others, hyperalertness or exaggerated "startle responses," loss of impulse control, difficulty sleeping, and guilt about having survived when others didn't.

It's been estimated that about 40 percent of all combat soldiers in the Vietnam War came home with some degree of PTSD. Most of them had mild to moderate cases and, apart from minor adjustment problems, managed to lead relatively normal lives. Many of those with severe cases deteriorated, often with drugs or alcohol, to the point of losing jobs and family and any semblance of a normal life. A few, like Leonard Avery, became violent and ended up being charged with murder.

There were twelve to fourteen members of Avery's therapy group, with attendance typically ranging from three to ten. He attended his first group session in July 1981 and, according to his chart, "participated and expressed feelings well." He attended regularly over the next several months. Violence was a principal preoccupation of the group. Dr. Colvard, who co-led the group with Dr. Buck, recalled how "a number of members talked . . . about wanting to go blow up something, or wanting to kill somebody." Most members of the group, including Avery, owned guns—some more than one.

In September 1981, Avery asked for a separate appointment with Dr. Buck. He reported hearing voices calling his name, seeing faces, and feeling a crawling sensation on his skin. Buck prescribed five milligrams of Haldol, an antipsychotic drug, but Avery was not hospitalized.

In October, Avery sought another appointment with Buck because his first wife had gone to court to demand several thousand dollars in child support arrears. Avery had guns in his car, and he told Buck he would kill anyone who tried to take his guns away from him. Buck noted that Avery had been "functioning at a marginal level for several months," that the child support demand had caused him to deteriorate further, and that he was a "significant homicide risk." Avery accepted Buck's recommendation of voluntary hospitalization. When he checked into the hospital that evening, Avery expressed his feelings about his former wife to a social worker: "I'm not going to pay that tramp. I'll kill her first." But Avery improved dramatically by the next day and was released.

In November 1981, a member of Avery's therapy group who was regarded as a leader committed suicide. Having missed only one session since he began group therapy, Avery missed ten sessions in the next several months, attending only about half the time. Overall, Avery's attendance at group sessions was poor.

In early July 1982, Avery went on sick leave. Weeks later, while still on sick leave, he was involved in an automobile accident that led to a fistfight with the other driver and assault charges against Avery. Avery was still taking Haldol, the antipsychotic drug. On July 29, one month before Avery's assault on IBM, Dr. Buck advised IBM's Medical Department that Avery "would have hurt somebody if he had been to work in recent weeks" and that his "return to work date is questionable at this time." Noting that Avery had attended all group therapy sessions in July, Dr. Buck certified that Avery's absences from work during July were legitimate.

APPROACHING FLASH POINT

Avery remained out of work and also failed to attend the first three group therapy sessions in August. On August 18, Avery was called in to discuss his absences with Dr. Connor of the IBM Medical Department. Connor confronted Avery with his misrepresentations about attending the August therapy sessions. The meeting ended with Avery's threat to blow up the IBM facility, starting with the Medical Department.

Dr. Connor told his superiors at IBM and Dr. Colvard at the VA about Avery's threats. As a psychiatrist who had been working with him, Colvard advised Connor that Avery "did have the potential for acts of violence, that IBM should take his threats seriously" and take precautionary measures, including contacting law enforcement authorities. Dr. Colvard also suggested that IBM consider petitioning for Avery's commitment "on the basis of their observations and immediate contacts with him." (IBM never acted on that suggestion.) Soon thereafter, Dr. Buck phoned Avery, who agreed to enter the hospital voluntarily that evening. But Avery didn't show up as promised.

The next day, August 19, IBM phoned Avery and told him he was fired. On August 20, Avery phoned Dr. Buck, and the following conversation occurred:

AVERY: I've been fired.
DR. BUCK: Yes, I know. Dr. Connor told me.
AVERY: I want to see you. I want you to write a letter saying it was ok to be out of work.
DR. BUCK: I don't see how I can write you a letter. IBM knows that

you haven't been coming for your appointments when you were
saying that you were.

AVERY: I tried to call you.

DR. BUCK: There were no messages left in my box until this last
Wednesday.

AVERY: It's too late for me to start over. There's nothing to be done.
You'll read about it in the papers.

Avery then hung up on Dr. Buck. Buck called IBM right away because
he interpreted Avery's statements as a threat against them. Buck then
talked to his immediate supervisor and the chief of the VA Psychiatry
Service about what to do next. Based on what Avery had said on the
phone, Buck and his supervisors thought Avery might be dangerous, but
Buck also thought that "it didn't seem like he was in the throes of any
mental illness at that time. He was aware of reality, he knew who I was,
who he was, and where he was."

At that point, the VA psychiatrists talked to IBM officials, ultimately
urging them to file charges and to have Avery arrested for making threats.
Commitment had been discussed "at great length" as a "pretty debatable point," Buck recalled, but "all of us at the VA ended up deciding
that would not be the best thing to do." For one thing, they thought that
Avery's dangerousness didn't stem directly from his PTSD, but from his
being fired and from Buck's refusal to cover for him. In addition, however, according to Buck the VA psychiatrists had a more pragmatic reason for opposing commitment. "Mr. Avery was mentally intact enough
so that we were sure he would be released very quickly from the mental
hospital, and perhaps even angrier than before. Our thought was he might
even go ahead and do something he might not have otherwise."

On August 23, Avery went to the Dixie Loan Company, a pawn shop
in Raleigh, and bought a "Commando" Model .45-caliber rifle, two boxes
of Smith and Wesson ammunition, and two thirty-round clips for $318,
plus tax. The "Commando" isn't intended for sport; it's an assault rifle
that, according to a police forensic expert, looks "like the old Thompson
submachine guns." Avery returned on the twenty-sixth to exchange the
rifle for another of the same model because it had jammed.

Also on August 23, as Avery was buying his rifle, his case was discussed at a weekly staff meeting of the VA's Mental Hygiene Clinic by a
group of eight psychiatrists, seven of whom were both board certified
and faculty members at the Duke University School of Medicine. They
concluded, unanimously, that Avery couldn't be committed under North
Carolina law. However, the basis for that conclusion does not appear in

the court record. A week later, on the day of Avery's assault, the same group reached the same conclusion.

Dr. Buck didn't want to close the door entirely on Avery at that point. He called Avery on August 26, and the following conversation ensued:

> DR. BUCK: Mr. Avery, this is Dr. Buck. I called to see how you are doing.
> MR. AVERY: I'm doing all right.
> DR. BUCK: Will you be coming to the group?
> MR. AVERY: I'm not going back to that group. You sons of bitches never did anything to help me. I can find you.
> DR. BUCK: I'm sorry, what did you say? Are you making a threat?
> MR. AVERY: I would like to get all you guys in the same place at the same time. I would blow you asses away.
> DR. BUCK: Mr. Avery, I hope you aren't going to do anything to hurt someone, or get yourself in trouble with the law.
> MR. AVERY: I don't have time to talk with you.
> DR. BUCK: I hope things go better for you. Good-bye.

Buck hung up, "shaking like a leaf." He reported Avery's latest threats to his VA superiors, who tried unsuccessfully to involve the FBI. Buck notified the Durham police, asked them to patrol his house, and left town for the weekend with his family. Avery mounted his assault on IBM the following Monday.

STATE V. AVERY

Leonard Avery was indicted and tried by the State of North Carolina for the murder of IBM employee Ralph Glenn, for wounding four other IBM employees, and on lesser charges flowing from his actions on August 30, 1982. Avery pled not guilty by reason of insanity, in effect, admitting the facts, including the shooting of Glenn. Avery's insanity plea was based on his claim that he had been suffering from PTSD and that, as a result, he met the standard legal tests of the insanity defense: he hadn't known the difference between right and wrong, and had not understood the nature of his actions. Indeed, according to Avery's lawyer, Avery hadn't even known he was at IBM on August 30; he had thought he was in combat in Vietnam.

Some Vietnam War veterans suffering from PTSD experience "dissociative episodes," or "flashbacks," in which a trigger event takes them out of present-day reality and back to the time and place of original stress—back to combat in Vietnam. When that happens, the veteran may go into a combat survival mode; a civilian setting like an IBM plant becomes the jungle, and a passing employee becomes a Vietcong soldier.

In some cases there has been convincing proof of a dissociative episode that led to violence. In others, however, it was apparent that claims of combat trauma leading to PTSD had been fabricated. As an example of the latter, a Vietnam veteran helicopter pilot sued the government, claiming that he had witnessed the death of four fellow crewmen, that his helicopter gunship had over four hundred confirmed kills, and that once, when shot down, he had had to shoot three children at close range. The government produced the pilot's former commanding officer and a crew member as rebuttal witnesses. They testified that the former pilot's helicopter had not been a gunship but was used to ferry people and supplies, that it had no confirmed kills, and that there was no record of the alleged killings of children.

Avery's counsel went to great lengths to prove that his client had actually experienced traumatic events in Vietnam. Army records and testimony showed that Avery's unit had been in combat. A former member of Avery's squad testified that he had seen Avery throw a grenade into a hooch on a search-and-destroy mission. Another witness testified that he had seen Avery open Sergeant Kelly's body bag and then go berserk.

But the jury remained skeptical about the claimed connection between Avery's Vietnam experience and the shootings at IBM. For one thing, some of them must have known other Vietnam combat veterans who hadn't come home with this strange PTSD disease, and who didn't go around in fatigues shooting people. What was different about Leonard Avery that made him do those things? And why did Avery erupt fifteen years after leaving Vietnam?

The court had appointed Dr. Selwyn Rose, a psychiatrist and lawyer, to examine Avery and give his opinion on the PTSD issues. Rose's twenty years' experience in general and forensic psychiatry covered a broad spectrum of cases, from murder defendants to director Roman Polanski's alleged sexual abuse of young girls.

Rose had no doubt that Avery had PTSD: "Avery is a model kid up until the Vietnam war," and he went steadily downhill afterward. Rose supported Avery's insanity defense unequivocally: "He didn't know where he was and what he was doing in a realistic sense at the time of the shooting." But Rose was unable to give the jury much help in understanding why Avery had lost control when other combat veterans don't.

Rose spoke of PTSD as "emerging knowledge." Psychiatrists believe that personality structure determines a person's vulnerability to PTSD, but they don't know which characteristics in personality structure make the difference. As a result, psychiatrists "can't predict whether a particular person is going to have the disease or not."

Furthermore, it can be hard to tell whether a veteran has erupted in violence as a result of PTSD or because of an upsetting event in his present life—such as being fired. Rose believed Avery's assault grew out of his PTSD because he had dressed and acted as if he were in combat, carried an assault rifle, and shot at people when they moved. "He acted as though he were going through an enemy village on a mission." Another psychiatrist witness agreed and also thought it significant that on the evening before his assault, Avery had been listening over and over to "The Message," a song by Grand Master Funk and the Furious Five that refers to being in the jungle and going over the edge.

The prosecution strategy was to portray Avery as an antisocial malcontent who was acting in revenge, and who knew exactly what he was doing. They pointed out that many of the same factors—the fatigues, the assault rifle—were consistent with a revenge attack. In the period 1978 to 1982, Avery had written over forty bad checks at places like Winn Dixie, Penney's, and Radio Shack. He even managed to buy a car with a bad check.

Avery's counsel did their best in a losing cause. Jury selection alone took three weeks, finally producing a jury of seven blacks and five whites. The jury convicted Avery of first-degree murder, as well as the other charges against him, and the court sentenced Avery to life imprisonment. He remains incarcerated today. Even if one agrees with the jury that Leonard Avery was not legally insane on August 30, 1982, it seems likely that his life would have turned out better if he hadn't been sent into combat. In a real sense, Avery is an unmourned casualty of the war in Vietnam.

CURRIE V. UNITED STATES—THE MALPRACTICE CASE IN THE DISTRICT COURT

In May 1985, after Avery had been convicted of murder, a daughter of Ralph Glenn, the father of four, filed a malpractice suit against the federal government in United States District Court in Durham, North Carolina, seeking $4 million in damages. A federal statute makes the government liable for damages caused by the negligent acts of its employees acting within the scope of their employment, including, for example, psychiatrists employed by the VA.

Linda Currie claimed that Avery's VA doctors had committed malpractice in failing to seek his involuntary commitment before he shot and killed her father. Unlike many malpractice cases, the *Currie* case didn't go to a full-scale trial. Instead, the government filed a motion for summary judgment, an expedited procedure that allows a case to be resolved by the judge if there are no real disputes about the facts. The motion was accompanied by affidavits from psychiatrists and other witnesses to key events. There was no dispute that Avery was suffering from PTSD, or about the facts surrounding his treatment at the VA, his threats of violence, or his assault of August 30.

There was also no dispute about the adequacy of the many warnings exchanged between the VA, IBM, and local law enforcement authorities in the days preceding August 30. Although Avery's threats had not been explicitly directed to particular people (except, perhaps, Dr. Buck), they implied violence against the VA doctors, the IBM Medical Department, and possibly other IBM employees. Everyone in those categories had been warned, but Glenn had been killed, and four others wounded, anyway—a clear example of the futility of warnings.

The *Currie* case turned on whether the law should impose a duty on a psychiatrist to seek commitment of a dangerous patient like Leonard Avery, in addition to giving warnings. No statute answered the question, and there were few relevant precedents. The district court found itself in the position of lawmaker, weighing the pros and cons of a "duty to commit" on the basis of policy considerations.

In a detailed and thoughtful opinion, the court recognized an "inherent conflict between protecting society at large by confining the dangerous" and protecting the patient by giving him "the least restrictive environment." The court rejected the government's argument that there should never be a duty to commit, reasoning that "a psychotherapist, perhaps the only one with knowledge of the danger posed by his patient, may have a duty to protect society by taking the only practical action he can." In addition, it is settled law that psychiatrists who negligently release dangerous patients from mental hospitals can be held liable for resulting injuries to others. The therapist's responsibility to protect society from a dangerous patient should be the same, whether the patient is in—or out of—the hospital. Furthermore, if there were no duty to commit, there would be no practical remedy against the therapist who disregards the danger posed by some patients.

The district court considered possible adverse effects of a duty to commit, including whether the mentally ill would be deterred from seeking treatment if they realized their therapists might later feel obliged to commit them to avoid a lawsuit. That prospect seemed speculative. The court also discounted the possibility of an "adverse backlash" leading to overcommitment by therapists seeking to avoid liability. For these reasons, the court concluded that therapists have "some duty not to let known dangerous mental patients whom they treat run around in public."

The next step was to establish the scope of that duty. Under the traditional malpractice standard of simple negligence, a duty to commit might cause therapists to refuse to treat potentially dangerous patients altogether. Seeking to avoid such a result, the court drew an analogy to the so-called business judgment rule, under which, in business litigation, courts defer to the decisions of disinterested corporate directors, in the absence of bad faith or self-interest. The rationale underlying that rule is that judges are not equipped to second-guess businesspeople in their decisions, even if in hindsight those decisions appear to be ill advised, negligent, or even stupid. The court reasoned that, as with business decisions, courts aren't well qualified to review decisions whether to commit seemingly dangerous people.

Under its newly minted "psychotherapist judgment rule": "The court would not allow liability to be imposed on therapists for simple errors in judgment. Instead, the court would examine the good faith, independence and thoroughness of the psychotherapist's decision not to commit a patient." Like many legal rules, the psychotherapist judgment rule wasn't as simple in practice as it sounded. How is the "good faith" of a therapist treating a dangerous patient to be determined? The court listed five factors:

1. The therapist's competence and training.
2. The adequacy, promptness, and independence of the therapist's review of the patient's case.
3. The therapist's efforts to check his judgment against the opinions of other therapists.
4. The therapist's application of proper standards.
5. Other evidence indicating the therapist's good, or bad, faith.

It remained for the court to apply its five factors to the actions of the VA psychiatrists in the *Currie* case. The first three factors were clearly satisfied. Although Dr. Buck was only a resident, Avery's case was considered twice, promptly after his threats to Dr. Buck, by a VA staff of eight other psychiatrists—seven of whom were board certified, and all of whom were on the faculty of the Duke University School of Medicine.

The fourth factor—application of proper standards—cut against the VA psychiatrists' good faith. They had concluded, unanimously, that Avery could not be committed under North Carolina law. Although their reasoning wasn't entirely clear, they apparently believed that a patient had to be psychotic before he could be involuntarily committed.

North Carolina law (and the general rule elsewhere) does not require that a candidate for commitment be psychotic. For example, most people who are committed as potential suicides aren't psychotic. It's enough if the patient has a mental illness that makes him dangerous to himself or others. Avery did not appear to be psychotic at the time. But there was no dispute that he was suffering from PTSD, that he had a record of violence, that he was armed, and that he had threatened to kill his psychiatrist and others. On that basis, as Dr. Rose had testified in the criminal case, Avery could have been committed.

It's hard to understand how eight faculty psychiatrists at Duke University School of Medicine could have been wrong about such a fundamental legal requirement, a requirement which would arise in their work on a regular basis. The court found that their "overly restrictive interpretation cuts against a finding that the therapists acted in good faith." But the court thought that their mistake about commitability was more than outweighed by the realization that Avery threatened not only IBM but also the therapists themselves. Since their decision not to seek commitment "involved serious personal risk to themselves," it must have been made, the court believed, "in the utmost good faith." In light of that conclusion, the court granted the government's motion for summary judgment and dismissed the case.

THE *CURRIE* CASE ON APPEAL

Linda Currie appealed the district court's decision to the United States Court of Appeals for the Fourth Circuit. In a 1987 decision, the three-judge appeals court ruled that there is *no* duty to seek commitment of a patient the therapist believes to be dangerous—at least where the therapist has given adequate warnings to the objects of threats.

The court cited the general rule: one is not liable for the conduct of another person unless one has the right to control that person's conduct. Thus, employers can control employees, parents small children (but not teenagers). The trouble with general rules is that they never fit all of the arguably analogous situations. *Currie* is a case in point. The court recognized that once a dangerous person has been involuntarily committed to an institution, authorities there have the power to control him, and they may be held liable for a negligent release resulting in injuries to others. But as the court saw it, that principle "has little bearing upon a situation in which the one sought to be charged had no right of control, and the complaint is that [he] should have taken affirmative action to acquire the right of control."

The court misstated the realities of the situation. Under a "duty to commit," the therapist is not being asked to "control" an outpatient; he is being asked to seek a court order of commitment—which is entirely within his control. If the court denies the therapist's request (a rare event), he has fully discharged his duty.

The appeals court had little to say about the policy implications of its position. It expressed concern that involuntary commitment at the therapist's initiative would destroy the therapeutic alliance, although it was not in a position to speculate along those lines. It implied that warnings could be effective, despite the contrary indications from the warnings in this case. The court's reasoning implied that even if adequate warnings were not given, there would still be no duty on the part of the therapist to seek commitment of a dangerous patient under any circumstances. If the court had any concern about leaving Linda Currie without a remedy for the loss of her father, it was left unexpressed. The implications of this court's decision are explored further in the next chapter.

CHAPTER 8
▼ ▼ ▼

A Danger to Others

Violence is an American as apple pie.
—KARL MENNINGER, quoted in Stone, *Law, Psychiatry, and Morality* (American Psychiatric Press, 1984)

A few of the many angry people in therapy today will someday kill a lover, a parent, an employer, a rock star, perhaps a total stranger. John Hinckley's attempted assassination of President Reagan was one highly publicized example. Can the therapist be expected to anticipate and take steps to prevent violence—by warning the object of threats, by calling the police, by having the patient committed? In the *Rotman* case, the subject of chapter 6, Dr. Mirin was held responsible for failing to anticipate violence by his patient, Dennis Gould. But the results in these cases are often inconsistent. Consider the *White* case.

Dwayne White had an "explosive personality" and a long history of violence, culminating in the slaying of a policeman. Tried for murder, White was acquitted by reason of insanity and committed to St. Elizabeth's Hospital in the District of Columbia. After ten years of close confinement, and despite continued violent behavior, the hospital granted him grounds privileges but failed to supervise him adequately. White walked off the grounds and stabbed his wife, Genoa, fifty-five times with a pair of scissors. Genoa White somehow survived and sued St. Elizabeth's for damages.

Dwayne White's therapist testified at the trial about a fantasy White had related to her in which he attacked his wife with a gun. But the therapist had not considered the fantasy a serious threat to Genoa White because Dwayne had not been "afraid that he would act on it" and because he "had no history of assaulting women, and had not assaulted anyone in recent months." The court accepted the therapist's explanation. But the question lingers: if violence by the likes of Dwayne White—a convicted murderer with a history of violence—couldn't have been predicted by his treating therapist, can it ever be predicted? Or is the *White* case simply wrong?

PREDICTING VIOLENCE

According to Dr. Seymour Halleck, it's harder to predict violence than it is to predict suicide. Violence involves two or more people, and more variables, than suicide. As with suicide, psychiatrists can look to historically validated indicators of violence—a history of violence is an obvious red flag. But Halleck believes psychiatrists are wrong more often than right when they attempt to predict, for the long term, whether a person will become violent. For these reasons, the American Psychiatric Association has long taken the position that "neither psychiatrists nor anyone else have reliably demonstrated an ability to predict future violence or 'dangerousness.'" But the courts have usually rejected the APA's position, saying, in effect: do the best you can.

In a 1983 death penalty case before the United States Supreme Court, the APA filed a friend-of-the court brief urging that psychiatrists not be permitted to testify as expert witnesses concerning a criminal defendant's long-term future dangerousness. The case involved the testimony of a perennial prosecution witness—known irreverently as "Dr. Death"—who could be relied upon to make firm predictions of future dangerousness by convicted murderers. While conceding that psychiatrists can make reasonable short-term predictions of violent behavior—the necessary predicate for a civil commitment—the APA contended that medical knowledge had not advanced to the point where long-term predictions could be made "with even reasonable accuracy," and that such predictions would be wrong "in at least two out of every three cases." Rejecting the association's position brusquely, the Supreme Court likened it to "asking us to disinvent the wheel." The court seemed to believe that in deciding on the death penalty, psychiatric testimony, with all its shortcomings, was better then nothing.

Death penalty cases aside, it isn't necessary to predict whether a particular person *will* commit a violent act. As in the case of suicide, there is a crucial distinction between a firm prediction of violence, on the one hand, and assessing the level of risk of violence a person appears to present, on the other. Specific predictions of violence—for example, that Dennis Gould will kill Shelley Rotman in the coming month—will turn out to be wrong most of the time. But an assessment of risk—a judgmental process based on recognized indicators of violence—can be a reasonable basis for clinical and legal decisions, even if the patient never harms a fly.

The civil commitment statutes don't distinguish between potential suicide and violence. In either case, mental health professionals assert that they have examined the patient and that, in their opinion, the patient is (in the words of a typical civil commitment statute) an "imminent danger to himself or others." A strong argument can be made that it should be easier to commit a potentially violent person than a suicidal person. After all, those who kill themselves are taking their own lives—which may be pretty miserable—not someone else's. In practice, there may be a double standard in commitment cases, depending upon whether concern about violence or suicide is driving the process. Dr. Halleck reports that when a patient makes an unambiguous, serious threat against another person, commitment is virtually automatic.

Persons suffering from paranoid schizophrenia—like Dennis Gould (chapter 6)—are among the most dangerous of the mentally ill. Schizophrenia is incurable. Nevertheless, many people with this diagnosis *are* able to control their impulses, hold jobs, and live free. Recently developed medications, notably Clozapine, don't "cure" schizophrenia, but they have enabled thousands to leave institutions for near-normal lives outside.

Paranoid schizophrenics with delusions of violence present some of the most difficult judgment calls for treating psychiatrists who must consider the commitment option. It's impossible to predict with assurance whether the patient will act on his delusions. If there is a recent history of violence, like Dennis Gould's self-amputation by trolley wheel, there is some solid evidence that the patient is capable of it. Therapists who fail to seek commitment in such a case—bypassing the opportunity to share the decision with judges who have a more direct responsibility for protecting the public—are playing God and may be risking a malpractice suit.

Whether the law should recognize a "duty to commit" is debatable. The *Currie* case (chapter 7) answered the question for North Carolina in the negative, but it remains open in many States. The decision in *Rotman v. Mirin* (chapter 6) was based on Dr. Mirin's duty, under Massachusetts law, to seek hospitalization of his patient Dennis Gould after he threatened to kill Shelley Rotman. Under the *Currie* "no duty" rule, no matter how clear the indications of a patient's future violence—threats, guns, physical assaults—the therapist has no legal obligation to seek commitment. One could say in defense of that position that therapists are conscientious and that they will seek commitment in cases where it's clearly needed. But the facts of the *Currie* case undercut that argument. Leonard Avery's repeated threats and possession of weapons made him a strong candidate for commitment. The treating psychiatrist didn't recommend commitment—not because he wasn't concerned about violence—but because he anticipated Avery would be released quickly, perhaps more dangerous than before.

The district court in the *Currie* case had a sounder approach: recognize a duty to commit but respect the therapist's good faith decision not to seek commitment. This would give therapists some protection from second-guessing in court, while leaving the door ajar for injured plaintiffs to try to prove rare cases where a psychiatrist exhibits reckless disregard for the dangerousness of his patient.

If the *Currie* "no duty" decision comes to be widely accepted, it would create an anomaly in psychiatric malpractice law. While not entirely clear on the point, the *Paddock* decision (chapter 4) appears to leave room for a limited "duty to commit" in suicide cases. Although the court found that Dr. Chacko's treatment of Linda Paddock had not violated the standard of care, it left open the possibility that a therapist who failed to seek commitment, and who otherwise acted in reckless disregard of a suicidal patient's welfare, might be held liable. The net result under these decisions is some obligation to seek commitment in suicide cases, depending upon the circumstances, and no duty in violence cases, regardless of the circumstances. In terms of social policy, that result is backward because potentially violent people are a greater danger to others than the suicidal. Magnifying that danger is the fact that violent people are less likely to enter a mental hospital voluntarily.

THE *TARASOFF* CASE

On October 27, 1969, Prosenjit Poddar, a citizen of India studying at the University of California, killed Tatiana ("Tanya") Tarasoff. Born into the Harijan (untouchable) caste in Bengal, Poddar had come to Berkeley for graduate study in naval architecture. He attended folk dancing lessons at the International House, where he met Tanya Tarasoff. They dated for several months, and on New Year's Eve Tanya kissed Poddar. He interpreted her kiss as confirmation of a serious relationship. But when Poddar declared his love for her, Tanya said she wasn't interested in a relationship with him.

Following Tanya's rebuff, Poddar became severely depressed. He kept to himself, neglecting his studies, speaking incoherently, and often weeping. Poddar saw Tanya from time to time and tape-recorded some of their conversations, hoping to discover why she didn't love him. Tanya went to Brazil in the summer of 1969. In her absence, Poddar's condition improved, and he went into outpatient psychotherapy at a university clinic. When Tanya returned from Brazil, however, Poddar stopped seeing his therapist.

Shortly after Tanya's return, Poddar went to the Tarasoff home, armed with a pellet gun and a kitchen knife. She refused to speak to him and screamed when he persisted. Poddar then shot Tanya with the pellet gun, and she ran out of the house. Poddar caught up with Tanya and killed her with the knife.

Tanya Tarasoff's parents filed suit against the university, a Dr. Moore (a psychologist and Poddar's primary therapist), three university hospital psychiatrists, and five members of the campus police. An understanding of the case requires some additional background.

When Poddar had been a therapy patient, he had told Dr. Moore that he was going to kill a girl he didn't name (but who was readily identifiable as Tanya Tarasoff) when she returned from Brazil. Moore, in consultation with two psychiatrists, decided that Poddar should be committed for observation, and he requested campus police assistance. Three campus police officers then took Poddar into custody. After questioning him, however, they were satisfied he was rational, and they released him upon his promise to stay away from Tanya. Remarkably, the police overruled the psychiatrists' commitment decision. Perhaps more remarkably, the director of the Department of Psychiatry concurred with the police, even though he had never seen Poddar.

In the midst of all this activity, neither Dr. Moore, nor the psychiatrists, nor the police took steps to warn Tanya of danger from Poddar. Following his encounter with the police, Poddar, undoubtedly feeling betrayed, didn't return for therapy. Shortly thereafter, Poddar carried out his threat.

The trial court threw the Tarasoffs' case out, without a trial, on the theory that they couldn't win even if they proved that a "negligent failure to warn" had caused Tanya's death. The judge reasoned that under the circumstances, the therapists and the police owed no "duty of care" to Tanya.

The Tarasoffs appealed to the Supreme Court of California. Concerned about the judicial creation of a novel "duty to warn" arising from patient threats—a commonplace in therapy sessions—the American Psychiatric Association entered the case as a friend of the court, taking the position that "a psychiatrist cannot predict dangerousness with sufficient reliability to make reasonable a duty to protect others from dangerous conduct." But the California court rejected the APA position: "In this risk-infested society we can hardly tolerate the further exposure to danger that would result from a concealed knowledge of the therapist that his patient was lethal." How knowledge of dangerousness was to be acquired the court did not explain. The court also brushed aside an argument that requiring warnings would unduly compromise confidentiality of the therapist-patient relationship, reasoning that confidentiality "must yield" where "disclosure is essential to avert danger to others."

But the psychiatric community did not come away empty-handed. The court recognized that routine reporting of all patient threats need not be required, and that evaluation of a threat involved "a high order of expertise and judgment." If the therapist turns out to be wrong, he won't be held liable if he used his best judgment. As one psychiatrist put it, "That's our out."

The *Tarasoff* case had multiple denouements. The police had been charged with negligent failure to commit Poddar. The court ruled that the police were immune from civil suit, letting them off the hook altogether. After the appellate court remanded the case for trial, the Tarasoffs settled, reportedly for a modest amount. Poddar was prosecuted for murder, invoked a "diminished capacity" defense, and was convicted of voluntary manslaughter. After serving a short term in prison, Poddar returned to India, where, by his own account, he was happily married.

THE DUTY TO WARN

The *Tarasoff* "duty to warn" doctrine has been adopted, either in court rulings or by statute, in more than half the states. Although the psychiatric community initially resisted its spread, they later bowed to the inevitable and sponsored their own model statute for consideration by State legislatures. Under that model statute and the statutes of several states, the therapist has a choice of warning the intended victim, notifying the police, or hospitalizing the patient—involuntarily, if necessary.

The duty to warn has been expanded to include a threat against property that is likely to lead to serious personal injury or death. John Peck, age twenty-nine and living at home, was an outpatient at a Vermont counseling service. He got into an argument with his father, who called him "sick and mentally ill." Enraged, John packed his suitcase and left home. At his next counseling session, John told his therapist he "wanted to get back" at his father. When the therapist asked how he would do that, John replied, "I don't know, I could burn down his barn." After discussion, John promised not to burn the barn—located 130 feet from his father's house—and the therapist didn't report the threat. John then set fire to the barn, which burned to the ground. The court ruled that the therapist should have warned John's parents, and the counseling service had to pay for the barn.

There is an important limitation on the therapist's responsibility: the patient's threats must be directed toward a specific or readily identifiable person. Generalized threats of violence—for example, against "the police"—wouldn't trigger an obligation to send warnings. We have already seen that James Brady's case against Dr. Hopper, John Hinckley's former psychiatrist, lacked the normally required patient-therapist relationship between plaintiff and defendant. The *Brady* case also illustrates the need for a specific threat of violence against others.

Brady had claimed that Hopper should have warned law enforcement officials of Hinckley's potential for political assassination. But the judge threw the case out because there was no claim that Hinckley had ever threatened the president or, indeed, anyone else. Without a specific threat against "a readily identifiable victim," the court reasoned, the possibility Hinckley might have injured someone else was "a matter of conjecture." There is a further practical complication: absent a specific threat, who would one warn?

The law protected Dr. Hopper from malpractice liability, but his former patient did not fare so well. John Hinckley was prosecuted for attempted murder, acquitted by reason of insanity, and is confined to-day in a hospital for the criminally insane.

Despite the increasing emphasis on warnings generated by the *Tarasoff* decision, many psychiatrists have come to regard warnings as useless, even counterproductive. Dr. Gutheil, for example, noted that "warnings never work, and they can precipitate violence. If I'm warned that you're out to get me, I can say: 'I'd rather sleep comfortably every night in prison knowing that I got you first, rather than worry every day that the ax will fall.'"

Dr. Halleck cited his own experience in questioning whether warnings lead to real protection. "Once warned, what do you do? Years ago, one of my colleagues warned me that a patient was threatening to kill me. I didn't know what to do. I don't carry a gun. I called the police and they said walk home in a different direction." Halleck also pointed out that the breach of confidentiality inherent in a warning can unnecessarily undermine the treatment alliance between therapist and patient. He thought that "some people just need to be told, not told on." If asked, potential victims probably would say they'd prefer to be warned about a threat—forewarned is forearmed—but most aren't likely to make radical changes in their lives as a result. Surely Tanya Tarasoff would have returned from Brazil even if she had known of Poddar's threats.

With these considerations in mind, both Gutheil and Halleck saw civil commitment as the only realistic option when a patient makes a serious threat. An involuntary commitment can damage the treatment alliance between therapist and patient, at least temporarily. According to Dr. Gutheil, however, the damage need not be serious if the need for commitment is explained to the nonpsychotic patient.

FREEDOM AND VIOLENCE

According to the polls, violence has become the prime concern of Americans today. Much of it is, of course, caused by poverty, broken homes, bad schools, and drug trafficking. Violence in the media also gets a share of the blame.

The violence committed by the mentally ill in American society in the 1990s is due in large part to causes that aren't widely recognized. Much of this violence represents negative fallout from a well-intentioned "deinstitutionalization" movement—begun in the 1960s—to empty long-term mental hospitals, liberalize civil commitment laws, and require treatment of the mentally ill in the "least restrictive" manner, usually in community mental health centers. Community centers have failed to meet the treatment needs of the seriously mentally ill, but deinstitutionalization has undoubtedly had some beneficial effects.

The total patient population in public mental hospitals dropped dramatically, from about 500,000 in 1950 to about 130,000 in 1980. Thousands of the mentally ill who can somehow function on the outside are no longer being warehoused, without any real treatment. Revisions of civil commitment laws have made it more difficult to commit the mentally ill. Where once a psychiatrist's certification of illness and a need for treatment may have sufficed, now there must be proof that the patient actually is "a danger to himself or others." Patients have new procedural rights to enable them to contest commitment, with a lawyer. As a result, the danger that a disturbed but not seriously ill person will be railroaded has been reduced.

The dangers to the public from deinstitutionalization of the mentally ill are real, but they shouldn't be overstated. Statistics indicate, for example, that mentally ill people are only slightly more dangerous than the general population and that males between the ages of eighteen and twenty-five are *more* dangerous than the mentally ill. While such comparisons are suggestive, they are far from precise analogies. For example, there is no reason to anticipate violent crimes by infants or the aged (included in the general population statistic), and we have no basis for institutionalizing young men to prevent violence merely on the basis of age. Furthermore, the potentially violent—some of whom can be identified by a history of violence—comprise a relatively small group within the much larger group of the mentally ill.

Still, deinstitutionalization does mean that significantly greater numbers of potentially violent people are no longer being committed or are being released prematurely. Society pays a price for this. Some of these people are going to assault and kill other people. Dr. Halleck posed the philosophical issue through a concrete case.

It's whether you're more patient oriented or more society oriented. If you're really worried about risk to society and you're willing to keep a person locked up forever, that's one way to handle it. But most of us, sooner or later, become worried about the individual. There's a guy at our state hospital who was a drug abuser and went very psychotic and actually believed the four people he killed were demons. There's no question that he was really crazy. He was found not guilty by reason of insanity. In six months his psychosis was gone. The question is: do you ever let this guy out? He's never committed a crime, in theory, but you know he's a bad kid. You know that his psychosis had something to do with his abuse of drugs. I think most civil libertarian types would be trying to get him out.

PART III

STANDARDS OF PSYCHIATRIC CARE

CHAPTER 9
▼ ▼ ▼
Dr. Osheroff's Case

I went into a hospital where I wasted seven months of my life. . . . I was driven crazy, yes, but I wasn't treated for the disease I had.
—RAPHAEL J. OSHEROFF, M.D., former patient at Chestnut Lodge

He felt all this hate which he focused on Chestnut Lodge and me . . . and stopped turning the hate against himself. Now that is a way station in the path of treatment.
—MANUEL ROSS, M.D., Dr. Osheroff's Chestnut Lodge psychiatrist

Dr. Raphael Osheroff paced up and down the hallway of his locked ward, day and night, during the seven months he was a patient in Chestnut Lodge, a private mental hospital in Rockville, Maryland. The orderlies taunted him: "Here comes Ray. How many miles will you pace today?"

Dr. Osheroff, a forty-one-year-old kidney specialist, was severely depressed. He thought his depression might be related to biological factors—an imbalance in his brain chemistry—and he repeatedly asked for antidepressant drugs. His Chestnut Lodge psychiatrist refused his requests, believing that drugs would obscure Osheroff's main problem, which he thought was a narcissistic personality disorder growing out of his early family relationships. Instead of drugs, Osheroff was treated with psychotherapy four times a week.

When Dr. Osheroff signed himself into Chestnut Lodge in January 1979, he was depressed and suicidal, but he was clean shaven and fashionably dressed in a three-piece gray pinstripe suit, and he had at least a tenuous grip on himself. His mood and physical condition deteriorated during his stay. He was confined with hallucinating schizophrenics, many of them in restraints. Osheroff lost forty pounds at Chestnut Lodge; he couldn't sit still long enough to eat. As his depression persisted, his self-esteem eroded, and he stopped getting haircuts, shaving, and bathing.

After seven months at Chestnut Lodge, Osheroff was no longer capable of making informed decisions about his own welfare. His lawyer and stepfather were appointed his guardians. Shocked by his condition and prodded by his mother, Osheroff's guardians had him transferred to Silver Hill, a private mental hospital in New Canaan, Connecticut, in August 1979.

Dr. Osheroff's psychiatrist at Silver Hill diagnosed a "psychotic depressive reaction, agitated type" and prescribed antidepressant drugs—the same drugs Osheroff had been refused at Chestnut Lodge. After only three weeks on medication, Osheroff improved markedly. After three months, he was discharged from Silver Hill to start picking up the pieces.

Dr. Osheroff was convinced he had been the victim of malpractice at Chestnut Lodge, and he was deeply angry about this. In July 1982, Osheroff sued Chestnut Lodge and his psychiatrists there. He also sued his former partner, who had taken advantage of his illness to appropriate his medical practice. Before it was all over, Osheroff would spend $1 million of his own money on litigation growing out of his experience at Chestnut Lodge.

DR. OSHEROFF—BEFORE CHESTNUT LODGE

Raphael Osheroff was the only child of a doting mother and a distant, disapproving father. According to his therapist at Chestnut Lodge, Osheroff's mother had treated her little boy like "a glass doll that would shatter in the slightest breeze." When young Raphael went sledding with the neighborhood kids, his mother would wait protectively at the bottom of the hill.

Raphael Osheroff grew up precocious, talented, and popular. His IQ in junior high was 150. He attended the High School of Music and Art in New York City and earned his undergraduate degree at Columbia. In his senior year, he met and married his first wife, Evelyn. The young couple went to Omaha, where he earned his medical degree at Creighton University, but the marriage ended in divorce.

During an internship in Chicago, Osheroff met and married Carol, a nurse. They later moved to the Washington, D.C., area, where he began his practice, and Carol gave birth to their two children. The marriage began to founder. Despite therapy for both, the Osheroffs separated in 1972 and divorced in 1974. The children lived with Carol, but Osheroff visited them frequently.

Dr. Osheroff met his third wife, Joy, when she was a medical student at Georgetown. They lived together for two years (Osheroff was not yet divorced), married in 1974, and bought an expensive house in the Old Town area of Alexandria. The Osheroffs had a son in 1977, separated in 1978 (just before he signed himself into Chestnut Lodge), and divorced in 1980. In retrospect, both thought they had married before he was over his divorce from Carol. Apart from that, Joy thought that Osherhoff's possessions were his main interest. He was a train buff and also had an impressive collection of musical instruments.

During the early 1970s, Osheroff had been working hard to establish a kidney dialysis practice. One of his psychiatrists spoke admiringly of his "tremendous drive" in "building up a multimillion dollar dialysis empire out of practically nothing." Osheroff's success exceeded his expectations: "I brought a new modality of medical treatment to the area. My services were very much in demand. My practice was thriving. I had a new woman in my life. I had a very busy, active social life. I played music." Life in the fast lane. Osheroff felt so good he quit therapy. But it wasn't to last.

In the fall of 1976, Carol, Osheroff's second wife, announced plans to move to Luxembourg with their two children. Osheroff was devoted to the children, and the overseas move would virtually nullify his visitation rights. He became depressed. His depression deepened when conflicts arose with his partner in his dialysis practice. Osheroff finally decided to let a competitor buy him out—a decision he came to regret, despite the seven-figure purchase price.

Osheroff returned briefly to his former psychiatrist, who advised him to go to court to prevent Carol from taking the children to Luxembourg. Joy opposed his getting involved in a custody fight and convinced him to see another psychiatrist, who took a passive stance on the issue. Osheroff would sit in the psychiatrist's office and weep over the loss of his children and his business. During one session, overwhelmed with anger and frustration, he broke his hand on an upholstered chair. Psychotherapy two or three times weekly for almost two years went nowhere. The children went to Luxembourg.

During 1978, Osheroff's depression grew progressively worse. He had trouble sleeping, even with a sedative. He woke up early, dreading the day ahead; he couldn't concentrate or relate to people. He was getting "no pleasure from living. Food, sex, children, interests, hobbies, everything was black, bleak." Osheroff ruminated on suicide, and he began to pace. He recalled going to a movie when he "had to stand in the back of the theater and pace back and forth." He went to a restaurant and "had to go out in the street and pace."

Increasingly desperate, Osheroff went to New York City to consult Dr. Nathan Klein, a psychiatrist regarded as a maverick by his peers. Dr. Gutheil, a witness for Chestnut Lodge in the malpractice litigation, observed that Klein used endorphins, which, as far as he knew, were used "by no other human on earth." Klein prescribed Sinequan, an antidepressant drug, and lithium, but there were no records showing how much of those drugs Osheroff had actually taken, or for how long. After Klein, Osheroff consulted another psychiatrist—the fourth in two years— who decided that he was not a suitable subject for hypnosis.

Like many victims of agitated depression who spend hours each day reciting their woes to whomever will listen, Osheroff reached out for support wherever he could find it. Before Chestnut Lodge, he would buttonhole his colleagues and employees. For over a year, he had been telephoning his mother every day in New York City—sometimes two or three times a day—with lengthy recitations of his troubles. When her son's calls became too much for her, Mrs. Osheroff's psychiatrist phoned Osheroff's psychiatrist to discuss putting limits on his calls—an expedient later adopted at Chestnut Lodge.

Osheroff's persistent depression and suicide threats were taking their toll on his marriage. His wife, Joy, began pressing him to hospitalize himself. There was a trial separation in the summer of 1978, with Osheroff moving into a hotel for a few weeks. The couple tried again, but Joy moved out for good at Thanksgiving, taking their son with her.

Osheroff developed a severe peptic ulcer, and he had to spend two weeks in the hospital. Discharged during Hanukkah, alone in the house and deeply depressed, he bought one hundred Seconal capsules but stopped short of swallowing them.

Raphael Osheroff had fallen from a pinnacle of success to failure and suicidal depression in only two years. He had lost his children, his wife, and his practice, and he feared he was losing his mind. Four different psychiatrists had failed to pull him out of his tailspin. As Joy Osheroff saw it, her husband finally decided to sign into Chestnut Lodge because "he ran out of people to take care of him."

CHESTNUT LODGE—THE DOMINANT ETHOS

Founded in 1910, Chestnut Lodge developed an international reputation for its work with the seriously mentally ill. During Osheroff's stay there, perhaps half of its patients were psychotic at one time or another. The average duration of patient stays was about fifteen months, much longer than that in other private psychiatric hospitals. Some patients stayed for years. The best-selling novel *I Never Promised You a Rose Garden* was written by a woman who recovered from schizophrenia at Chestnut Lodge.

The central issue in Dr. Osheroff's case was whether Chestnut Lodge committed malpractice in relying exclusively on psychotherapy and refusing him antidepressant drugs. All patients there, including schizophrenic patients in restraints, received four hours of psychotherapy weekly. According to a 1989 article in the *Washington Post Magazine*—the first extensive article about this rather reclusive institution—Chestnut Lodge's commitment to intensive psychotherapy traces to "interpersonalist" therapists, particularly Frieda Fromm-Reichmann and Harry Stack Sullivan, who came to the Lodge in the 1930s.

Unlike the distant Freudians, the interpersonalists maintained that an analyst's job was to forge an intense bond with patients. This method usually involved letting patients regress to the point of trauma in childhood or infancy, and then properly "reparenting" them, thereby curing the illness. Drugs were viewed as coercive agents that would mask a patient's real problem.

When Dr. Osheroff filed suit in 1982, Chestnut Lodge psychiatrists may not have been as averse to prescribing drugs as the *Post* quotation implies. According to Osheroff's therapist at the Lodge, about 70 percent of the patients were on some form of drug treatment by that time. But the Lodge was still widely viewed in the psychiatric community as biased against drugs and overly committed to psychotherapy. Dr. Gerald Klerman, a professor of psychiatry at Harvard Medical School and a nationally known psychopharmacologist, reflected that view. "A number of individual staff people have sort of jokingly said: 'We don't use medication at Chestnut Lodge.' Some of them have said they think it ought to change, but that is the dominant ethos." Of course, a psychopharmacologist like Klerman might be expected to view the Lodge's treatment philosophy with skepticism. But a reluctance to use drugs also emerges from the actions and testimony of the Chestnut Lodge psychiatrists.

THE CHESTNUT LODGE DIAGNOSIS

Dr. Osheroff was admitted to Chestnut Lodge on January 2, 1979, by Dr. C. Wesley Dingman, supervisor of the ward to which Osheroff was assigned. Patients at Chestnut Lodge are assigned two psychiatrists, each having distinct duties. Dingman was Osheroff's "administrative" psychiatrist. He was responsible for conducting an intake interview and making an initial diagnosis. After admission, Dingman was responsible for coordinating Osheroff's care and for prescribing drugs, if any, in consultation with Osheroff's psychotherapist, who had the dominant role in treatment.

Dr. Dingman interviewed Osheroff upon his arrival. His "Admission Note" recited Osheroff's troubles of the preceding two years and his futile efforts to cope with them. Dingman's "Initial Differential Diagnosis" listed three possibilities:

1. Manic-depressive illness, depressed type, *DSM II* 296.2.
2. Depressive neurosis (severe), *DSM II* 300.4 and Personality disorder (unspecified), *DSM II* 301.9.
3. Psychotic depressive reaction, agitated type, *DSM II* 298.1.

("Psychotic" depression in *DSM II* terminology means very severe to disabling depression; it does not necessarily include hallucinations and loss of touch with reality.)

Dingman's *DSM II* numbers refer to mental illnesses recognized in the *Diagnostic and Statistical Manual of Mental Disorders, Revision II*—the revision in use in 1979. The *DSM*, as it is commonly called, is as close as psychiatry comes to a diagnostic bible, but a careful examination of the patient against *DSM* standards doesn't necessarily yield the correct diagnosis. For one thing, many different illnesses have similar symptoms. For another, some patients suffering from a particular illness don't exhibit many of the symptoms listed in the *DSM*. Patients should display at least half of the listed symptoms before they can be diagnosed with that illness.

Dr. Dingman's "Admission Note" concluded with an "Initial Treatment Plan" that included "intensive individual psychoanalytically oriented psychotherapy." The plan contained no reference to drug treatments of any kind. Most psychiatric hospitals hold an initial diagnosis and treatment planning conference shortly after admission. Osheroff's "Initial Conference" was held in March—two and one-half months after his admission. During his seven-month stay at Chestnut Lodge, Osheroff's case would be discussed in only one other group meeting, held shortly before he left for Silver Hill. Osheroff's initial diagnosis was modified at the March conference, but only to omit manic depression. His final diagnosis, upon his discharge to Silver Hill in July, remained unchanged: psychotic depressive reaction, agitated type, and personality disorder (unspecified). The latter diagnosis was "unspecified" because, unlike the *DSM IV* currently in use, the *DSM II* did not separately recognize a "narcissistic" personality disorder. Dingman and Ross made it clear, however, that they thought Osheroff suffered from pathological narcissism.

TREATMENT: PSYCHOTHERAPY WITH DR. ROSS

Dr. Osheroff was assigned to Dr. Manuel Ross for psychotherapy. After medical school, Ross had completed a residency in psychiatry and graduated from the Washington Psychoanalytic Institute. Dr. Ross was treating long-term patients in psychoanalysis or psychoanalytically oriented psychotherapy, seeing perhaps ten patients per year. Almost all of his professional experience had been at Chestnut Lodge.

Osheroff saw Ross for psychotherapy four times each week. In mid-March, after some forty therapy sessions, Ross drafted an "Initial Case Presentation," stating his clinical views on Osheroff's case. Ross believed that Osheroff had a narcissistic personality disorder growing out of his early family history. Osheroff thought he could never please his father. He had felt that when his kidney dialysis business was a success, he could finally prove to his father (long since dead) that "he was really going to amount to something after all."

Osheroff's mother was a different matter altogether. She loved him no matter what he did, and believed that nothing was ever his fault. This meant that Osheroff's wives were never able "to compete with his relationship with his mother." Osheroff and his mother "shared a fantasy that he was destined for greatness." As Ross saw it, "part of Dr. Osheroff's difficulties stem from his wish to reinstate that early oral glow and symbiotic unification with his mother." Deflating his patient's grandiose self-image was one objective of therapy. Osheroff remembered Ross saying to him, "I am going to get you a tin cup . . . and you can go out on Connecticut [Avenue] and beg."

Ross believed that Osheroff's loss of his dialysis business weighed more heavily on his mind than his failed marriages and child custody problems. Although he had realized a large profit in its sale, money was secondary. The business meant "rewards in terms of power and prestige and narcissistic gratification." More than that, "He saw the business as being a giant breast that would provide him with everything that he ever wanted."

Ross thought Osheroff's prognosis was only "fair." He questioned whether Osheroff had the "psychological constitution" to stay in therapy long enough to see results because he was "always looking for the miracle fix." By "miracle fix," Ross apparently meant Osheroff's requests for antidepressant drugs. Osheroff described those requests in a narrative of his Chestnut Lodge experience titled "A Symbolic Death." In his first session with Ross, for example, Osheroff had asked, "What medication will I be on here?" Ross replied, "None. Next question." As Osheroff recalled, Ross later derided medication as "a bottle of pills. Ha! Absurd."

There was a collegial evaluation of Osheroff's case in July, two weeks before he left Chestnut Lodge. Ross and eight other psychiatrists discussed and rejected the "modalities" of antidepressant drugs or electroconvulsive therapy to treat Osheroff's depression. The group believed that "his problems over the long term are best handled with the modalities [i.e., psychotherapy] we are now applying."

Psychotherapy with Ross continued for seven months, until Osheroff left for Silver Hill. After he was sued, Ross saw some progress. "I thought he was beginning to focus some of his hostility on us [instead of himself], and we thought we were on the right track." Ross even saw the lawsuit in positive terms—as an expression of his former patient's negative transference toward him. But Ross's monthly progress reports mostly tell a different story. The last report noted that Osheroff's "extreme narcissistic vulnerability . . . remained in place."

SILVER HILL

Raphael Osheroff arrived at Silver Hill, disheveled and distraught, on August 1, 1979. At intake, Osheroff described himself as "a ne'er do well who had finally made it, and then lost everything." Dr. Joan Narad, Osheroff's psychiatrist at Silver Hill, recalled her first impression: "He was grungy. He needed a bath. . . . He was the most pathetic person I've ever seen."

Dr. Narad was a 1968 graduate of the Medical College of Pennsylvania. Following an internship at Stanford, she returned to Pennsylvania for adult and child psychiatry residencies and was trained in adult and child psychoanalysis at the Philadelphia Psychoanalytic Institute. Narad's initial diagnosis of Dr. Osheroff was: (1) psychotic depressive reaction, agitated; and (2) manic-depressive illness, depressed. Narad's diagnosis was virtually identical to Dingman's at Chestnut Lodge, except that she did not find significant evidence of a personality disorder.

Dr. Narad prescribed Elavil, an antidepressant, for Osheroff's depression and Thorazine, an antipsychotic, for his severe agitation. He was still pacing; Narad had to follow him around the parking lot for one of their early therapy sessions. The medical director bought Osheroff a pair of tennis shoes for his blistered feet.

Osheroff was suicidal when he arrived. Dr. Narad placed him on suicide precautions, with extra personnel, hired at Osheroff's expense, to monitor his movements. Osheroff continued to neglect personal hygiene; he had to be forced to take a bath.

Dr. Narad saw Osheroff three times each week in psychotherapy, but she never considered treating him with psychotherapy alone. Although she is a psychoanalyst and a self-described "conservative" about drugs, Narad thought that Osheroff "was so agitated and in such a state that the words were not enough."

Asked if a time had come when she had seen a marked improvement in Osheroff, Dr. Narad replied, "You bet . . . August 17th"—less than three weeks after he entered Silver Hill. According to Dr. Narad's "Progress Note" of that date: "His mood has improved and there is little of the pacing . . . . He has become more interactive with staff and patients. . . . Last weekend a woman friend visited him and he discussed the possibility of living together with her after leaving Silver Hill." Osheroff's suicide precautions were lifted at that time. Narad thought the Elavil, not psychotherapy, was the main cause of Osheroff's recovery. Indeed, in her opinion, Osheroff couldn't have been reached in therapy without that drug.

Osheroff's improvement continued after that. He participated in group therapy. As Narad recalled, "At times he could be rather charming in telling stories or playing the piano." He became interested in the literature of depression and told Narad he planned to express his anger by writing a book about his experiences. He telephoned and wrote to his children in Luxembourg and was hurt when Carol wouldn't permit him to speak to his son. Dr. Narad wrote a letter recommending that Osheroff's guardianship be terminated. During October, he went on passes to New York City and Washington, D.C.

While Dr. Narad was taking care of Osheroff, his mother was trying to get her son a different psychiatrist. Narad recalled: "His mother didn't have very much use for me. She tried to get me transferred from his case. She called the medical director and felt that I was probably an incompetent woman and that someone of his magnitude should be treated by someone more competent. So I didn't have much use for her, either."

Osheroff was discharged from Silver Hill after three months. Narad concluded that he no longer needed inpatient psychiatric treatment, provided he resumed outpatient therapy and continued his drug treatments.

OSHEROFF V. CHESTNUT LODGE

Most patient-plaintiffs in medical malpractice cases leave matters to their lawyers. Not Dr. Osheroff. He was the driving force and principal architect of his own case. He read widely on the medical issues, interviewed numerous candidates to serve as expert witnesses, sat in on depositions, and put his own stamp on the formal complaint against Chestnut Lodge.

In Maryland, medical malpractice claims must first be taken through arbitration, with the possibility of a later jury trial if either side is dissatisfied. A hearing is held before an arbitration panel—composed of a lawyer-chair, a health care professional from the defendant's discipline (here, a psychiatrist), and a "public" member.

Maryland's arbitration scheme tends to favor the doctors; one of their own is an arbitrator, and they (in practice, their insurance companies) are not under heavy financial pressure to settle; they can afford to drag the dispute through arbitration and then a jury trial. Although this scheme theoretically gives the injured party two bites at the apple, the high costs of litigation can make it hard to take the second bite.

Osheroff went into the arbitration hearing loaded for bear. His expert witnesses were nationally known psychiatrists, specialists in psychopharmacology with extensive experience in treating depression. According to Harvard's Professor Alan Stone, himself a former president of the American Psychiatric Association, Osheroff's experts "rival in eminence any group that was ever assembled to testify on the patient's side of a malpractice case in psychiatry." Chestnut Lodge also assembled a team of well-qualified experts to backstop Drs. Dingman and Ross. In some respects, however, the Lodge's experts didn't entirely agree with Dingman and Ross.

The arbitration hearing focused on a series of related issues: What was the correct diagnosis of Osheroff's illness? Should his depression have been treated with drugs in addition to psychotherapy? If Osheroff was suffering from both depression and a personality disorder, which illness should have had priority in treatment? If Chestnut Lodge committed malpractice, how had Osheroff been injured?

The Diagnosis of Osheroff's Illness

THE CHESTNUT LODGE DIAGNOSIS. Dr. Dingman observed that people with elusive and intractable mental problems gravitate toward Chestnut Lodge. "These folks come to us because they do not fit cleanly and neatly into one of the diagnosis categories." That was true of Osheroff, whose "initial differential diagnosis" had been tentative. Osheroff's depression had been obvious at intake, but Dingman had wondered whether he had experienced episodes of hypomania (distorted and elated thinking), which would have pointed toward manic depression. Complicating diagnosis further, Osheroff's three failed marriages by age forty-one, and his unusually close attachment to his mother, suggested a personality disorder. Dingman had eventually concluded that Osheroff's "main Achilles heel" was a personality disorder.

From the beginning, Dr. Ross, Osheroff's psychotherapist at Chestnut Lodge, thought that his patient's basic problem was a narcissistic personality disorder. Ross pointed to Osheroff's grandiosity and sense of entitlement—both symptoms of narcissism. Osheroff "kept presenting himself as a figure who had been struck down by fate"—like a hero in a Greek tragedy. Dr. Ross had ruled out a psychotic depressive reaction, agitated type because he thought Osheroff's depression was not disabling. He cited the facts that Osheroff had gone to work until he entered Chestnut Lodge and that he seemed capable of enjoying himself; he played the trumpet and the piano two days after signing into the Lodge. Ross thought that Osheroff's depressed mood and threats of suicide were evidence of "pathological grieving" over the loss of his business—an outgrowth of his narcissism. Ross also discounted Osheroff's other indications of depression, saying that his weight loss had resulted from a diet and that his pacing was not compulsive.

Dr. Keith Johansen of Timberlawn Psychiatric Hospital, a private hospital in Dallas, basically endorsed the Chestnut Lodge diagnosis: personality disorder, primarily narcissistic. He listed typical symptoms: fantasies of unlimited success, easily damaged self-esteem, feelings of entitlement, and occasional depressed moods. Osheroff's miles of pacing also fit into that picture. Depressed people, Johansen testified, "don't have the kind of energy" Osheroff had displayed; they take "small little steps" and "don't get very far." Johansen based his diagnosis on his review of records. He had never met Dr. Osheroff.

Chestnut Lodge called Dr. Gutheil, a professor of psychiatry at Harvard Medical School, as an expert witness. Like Johansen, Gutheil had never seen Osheroff. Since he was basing his opinions on medical records and depositions, he felt he could not offer a specific diagnosis. He believed, however, that the Lodge's diagnosis of personality disorder was more consistent with the evidence than a diagnosis of psychotic depression. Gutheil thought that Osheroff had experienced a "narcissistic recovery" at Silver Hill, not because of drugs but because his ego had been temporarily boosted by the comparatively genteel atmosphere and the new woman friend he had found there. Gutheil agreed with Ross that Osheroff's depression was "reactive"—that it had been caused by business and family losses, not his biological makeup.

Other than Dingman and Ross, the only psychiatrist witness on either side to examine Dr. Osheroff personally was Dr. Michael Spodak, a forensic psychiatrist from Baltimore. In addition to the records reviewed by the other experts, Spokak conducted a six-hour interview with Dr. Osheroff for several purposes: to assess his current level of functioning, to determine whether he had been harmed by his stay at Chestnut Lodge, and to make a psychiatric diagnosis. Spodak concluded that Osheroff was functioning at a high level and that he had not been harmed by his stay at Chestnut Lodge, except perhaps by delaying the cure of his depression.

In Spodak's opinion, Osheroff did not have a personality disorder, though he did have certain traits commonly associated with such disorders. For example, he was histrionic, aggrandizing, ebullient, and narcissistic—but those traits were not disabling in him and therefore did not qualify as a mental disorder. On the contrary, Osheroff had shown himself capable of purposeful action in various ways, such as taking Chestnut Lodge to court, not to mention playing trumpet in a Salvation Army Band.

THE OSHEROFF EXPERTS' DIAGNOSIS. Osheroff's experts didn't disagree with Dingman's initial diagnosis. Dr. Gerald Klerman, a professor of psychiatry at Harvard Medical School, thought the three alternatives Dingman had identified, "given the information available to him, were very appropriate and reasonable."

As time went on, however, Osheroff's experts thought the Lodge's continued emphasis on its personality disorder diagnosis had been a major error, partly because severe depression can easily be mistaken for a personality disorder. Patients can be clinging, dependent, and demanding, leading to marked interpersonal difficulties—all signs that may indicate a personality disorder. But those same signs are associated with depression.

A true narcissist can't handle success, and that's one way to distinguish depression from narcissism. As Dr. Donald Klein, a professor of psychiatry at Columbia University put it: "If the narcissistic person is receiving adulation, they say it's really true, I am God. They become more and more impossible, rather than functional." A soundly based diagnosis of a narcissistic personality disorder in a depressed patient would require evidence that the person was having marked interpersonal difficulties when he was *not* depressed. Chestnut Lodge had not attempted to find such evidence. Osheroff's exceptional professional success before the onset of his depression indicated the contrary—that he was quite capable of functioning effectively with others.

According to the Osheroff experts, the passage of time and greater opportunities for observation should have reinforced the psychotic depressive reaction diagnosis. Osheroff continued to have feelings of worthlessness, despair, and guilt; he was agitated, paced continually, and had difficulty sleeping; he lost weight; his suicidal thoughts had receded after admission, but they had resurfaced from time to time. Klerman testified that Osheroff's symptoms of depression were "all classic, almost out of a textbook." His case was "bread and butter psychiatry," a diagnosis that can be made "usually by a first year resident."

To sum up, Osheroff's experts took the position that he *may* have had a personality disorder, but that no such disorder had been established. On the other hand, Osheroff clearly *did* have a psychotic depressive reaction, agitated type. As we will see, in their opinion Osheroff's depression required drug treatment or ECT, and those treatments should have taken precedence over treatment of any personality disorder he may have had.

The Standard of Care for Depression: Psychotherapy versus Drugs

THE CASE FOR PSYCHOTHERAPY. Dr. Dingman maintained that psychotherapy was the appropriate treatment for a psychotic depression, particularly where—as Dingman claimed had occurred in Osheroff's case—drug treatments had already been tried without success. Dingman was referring to the Sinequan and lithium Dr. Nathan Klein had prescribed for a few months in 1978. However, Dr. Gutheil, one of the Lodge's experts, acknowledged that Dingman had not had enough information to assess the effectiveness of that medication.

Dingman testified that at no time "had we gotten discouraged with our treatment plan to the point where we were going to try something else." He thought Osheroff would have eventually gotten better at Chestnut Lodge. He conceded, however, that Osheroff hadn't made any progress during his seven-month stay there.

Dr. Ross rated Osheroff's narcissistic personality disorder severe enough to require hospitalization, partly to protect him from suicide. Ross proposed to cure Osheroff's disorder by changing his personality structure—a process that could take five to ten years of psychotherapy. Ross thought psychotherapy was starting to work when Osheroff left because he was "beginning to focus some of his hostility on us"—a positive sign of a therapeutic negative transference.

Dr. Ross didn't think that antidepressant drugs would have alleviated Osheroff's depression more quickly than therapy, noting that Sinequan had brought "symptomatic improvement" but hadn't changed the "clinical picture"—the underlying personality disorder. But Ross knew no more about Osheroff's drug history than Dingman did. Ross also thought that drugs might have inhibited treatment of Osheroff's personality disorder because they could mask his symptoms by giving false indications of improvement.

Dr. Ross recalled discussions of drug treatments with Osheroff. He told Osheroff that drugs wouldn't help him in the long run but that "he was free to get a consultant . . . or go to another hospital if he wanted to." Ross thought that Osheroff would have been capable of shopping around for another hospital at the time; he didn't "see any gross breaches in his reality system."

Dr. Johansen asserted that psychotherapy is the only treatment for a personality disorder and the depression that sometimes accompanies it. However, he didn't know of any studies demonstrating the efficacy of psychotherapy for such disorders. His opinion rested on his own clinical experience.

Assuming that Osheroff had both a personality disorder and a psychotic depression, Johansen was asked whether drugs would be appropriate to treat the depression while psychotherapy continued for the personality disorder. Johansen saw "considerable risk" in that approach. Osheroff was "forever looking for magical solutions to his problems." If he were to alleviate his depression with drugs, he might believe he was well, terminate psychotherapy, and stop looking at his underlying problems.

Dr. Gutheil largely agreed with Johansen on the appropriateness of psychotherapy in Osheroff's case. It was a judgment call. While a prudent therapist might have given Osheroff drugs, the decision to refrain from drugs was "defensible" because they might have diverted attention from his fundamental problem. However, Gutheil didn't know of any studies showing that medication would undercut psychotherapy in that way.

THE CASE FOR DRUGS. The crux of the Osheroff experts' disagreement with the Chestnut Lodge psychiatrists was their failure to try other treatment options, particularly drug treatment, after it became apparent that psychotherapy alone was not alleviating Osheroff's severe depression. As Dr. Klerman saw it, Chestnut Lodge "failed to pursue the differential diagnosis and . . . they allowed the [depression] to go on unnecessarily long, failed to consider the available known effective treatments, such as medication or [electro]convulsive therapy, and by so doing continued the suicidal danger." The result, Klerman thought, was that "the standard of care was severely violated." According to Osheroff, he asked for antidepressants repeatedly. In any event, the obligation to suggest alternative treatments arises, whether or not the patient asks about them.

Osheroff's experts contended that when his severe depression continued despite psychotherapy, the standard of care required that drugs be used within thirty to ninety days. (Dr. Gutheil, a witness for the Lodge, agreed that drugs should get serious consideration as a treatment option within ninety days.) Withholding drugs from Osheroff for seven months was, in Klerman's opinion, "almost criminal . . . cruel and negligent." Dr. Klein agreed: "It's the sole reliance on exploratory psychotherapy that is really the killer here. . . . I don't think you are going to find any, even a tiny minority of the medical schools in the United States that would tell you intensive inpatient psychotherapy is the appropriate form of treatment for such a case."

The effectiveness of drug treatments against depression has been demonstrated by controlled studies, using methods approved by the Food and Drug Administration. Klerman cited studies showing that certain drugs were 60–70 percent effective against depression within six to twelve weeks. Only a small minority of depression patients, perhaps 10 percent, don't respond to drugs at all. In light of that evidence, Klerman was "appalled" that drug treatments were not even referred to in Dingman's treatment plan.

According to Dr. Klerman, there was "no evidence, positive or negative," only "speculation" that psychotherapy—the only treatment Chestnut Lodge ever gave Osheroff—is effective against severe depression. Building on that theme, Klerman asserted that one is expected to surrender a "philosophical belief" in psychotherapy when the evidence supporting it changes, and that "Chestnut Lodge had held its beliefs way beyond the time when the evidence was available."

Assuming Osheroff had a personality disorder along with severe depression, his experts agreed that the depression should have been given treatment priority, and with drugs. Severe depression is a painful and life-threatening illness. Pathological narcissism, on the other hand, usually is not life threatening and, of itself, usually doesn't require hospitalization.

Even in the unusual case where depression is a secondary concern compared with a severe personality disorder, Osheroff's experts argued that the depression should be treated with an appropriate drug, concurrent with treatment of the personality disorder. Dr. Klein acknowledged the common belief among psychiatrists, before the development of modern antidepressants, that "medication got in the way of therapy." An extensive study of that issue has demonstrated that drugs don't interfere with therapy and, in many cases, may promote its efficacy. In apparent recognition of that principle, Silver Hill's Dr. Narad, a psychoanalyst, gave Osheroff Elavil and Thorazine to facilitate his response to psychotherapy.

Dr. Osheroff's Desire for Drugs: Who Chooses the Treatment?

For the most part, the experts for Dr. Osheroff and Chestnut Lodge presented reasoned bases for their differing conclusions. On balance, the Osheroff experts presented a more convincing case. But the Lodge's position might have qualified, in legal parlance, as a "respectable minority" view, which would normally insulate it from malpractice liability. Except for one thing.

The legal doctrine of informed consent requires that if alternative treatments exist, the patient has a right to be told about their advantages and disadvantages and to make the treatment choice himself. Until he was legally declared incompetent shortly before he left Chestnut Lodge, Osheroff had a right to choose his treatment or to decline a treatment even if his judgment may have been distorted by his illness. Osheroff wanted out of Chestnut Lodge as quickly as possible. To that end, he wanted quick-acting drugs—not years of psychotherapy.

Dr. Gutheil, a witness for the Lodge, acknowledged that treatment goals and methods should be discussed with the patient. Yet there was nothing in Osheroff's Lodge records indicating that he had been told about drug options, so that he could make an informed choice. According to Osheroff, his exchanges with Ross involved Osheroff requesting drugs and Ross deprecating them. The only "option" Ross had suggested was that Osheroff, in his pathetic state, try another hospital if he wanted drugs.

Damages

Dr. Osheroff's expenses for his seven months at Chestnut Lodge were $42,465. In addition to a refund of expenses, the main items of damage were disruptions of his family, loss of business opportunities, continuation of suicidal danger, and pain and suffering. Dr. Frank Ayd, an Osheroff expert who had treated thousands of depressed people, tried to describe how depressed people feel: "It is an anguish almost beyond description . . . from the moment they awaken until they go back to sleep."

Ayd spoke of a Catholic priest he had treated for recurrent depressions over twenty-five years. When the priest was diagnosed with a fatal cancer, his response was, "Thank God, my suffering is coming to an end."

Dr. Spodak, speaking for Chestnut Lodge, questioned most of Osheroff's damage claims. Spodak thought Osheroff's family and business troubles had their origins long before Chestnut Lodge and would have occurred anyway. Although he didn't believe that Osheroff had gotten any better at the Lodge, he also didn't believe he had gotten any worse, nor that his stay at the Lodge had added to his psychological difficulties.

The Arbitration Award

The arbitration panel initially split three ways on the *Osheroff* case. The doctor voted to award actual medical expenses of $42,465; the public member voted to award $442,465—medical expenses, plus $400,000 for pain and suffering; and the lawyer-chairman, apparently concluding that the standard of care had not been breached, voted to award nothing. No opinion was written. The panel later compromised and voted unanimously to award $250,000. Both sides appealed to the Circuit Court for Montgomery County, Maryland, but the case was settled before trial for an undisclosed amount.

The *Osheroff* case began with a flourish and ended with a muffled compromise. Dr. Osheroff resumed practicing as a kidney specialist. Long after the case was settled, its implications were being debated among psychiatrists and malpractice lawyers. Those implications are explored in chapter 11.

CHAPTER 10
▼ ▼ ▼

Dr. Bean-Bayog:
The Therapist as Mom

I'm your mom and I love you and you love me very, very much. Say that ten times.
—card written by Margaret Bean-Bayog, M.D., for her patient Paul Lozano

In July 1986, Margaret Bean-Bayog, M.D., a Harvard-trained psychiatrist, began treating Paul Lozano, a Harvard Medical School student, in weekly psychotherapy sessions. The therapy later intensified to four or five sessions a week and continued for four years. In June 1990, Bean-Bayog terminated Lozano's therapy after he refused to submit to special supervision in connection with his clinical duties at Harvard Medical School. Lozano had a serious drug problem—including cocaine, hallucinogens, and alcohol—which Bean-Bayog feared would pose a danger to patients unless he were supervised.

Lozano's condition deteriorated in the months following termination of treatment. He left Cambridge in early 1991 and went to live with his parents in El Paso, Texas, where, with Harvard's permission, he continued his senior rotations at a local hospital. On April 2, 1991, Lozano took a shower, sprayed himself with Calvin Klein cologne, and injected himself seventy-five times with cocaine. Lozano was found dead at his desk. According to his sister Pilar Williams, Lozano had been hearing Bean-Bayog's voice "telling him to kill himself." The El Paso medical examiner determined, however, that Lozano had died of accidental cocaine intoxication.

In September 1991, the Lozano family sued Bean-Bayog for malpractice, setting in motion the most highly publicized psychiatric malpractice case in American history. The suit charged that Bean-Bayog had deviated from accepted standards of psychiatric care—by having a sexual relationship with Lozano, among other things—and that she had caused him to commit suicide. The Lozanos' lawyer called it "a very bizarre case of a fellow who was troubled by his disorientation and feelings of inadequacy when he got to medical school, who sought help and was abused by a woman who was, in an abnormal and deviant way, sexually attracted to him. She regressed him to a 3-year-old and caused him to believe she was his mother."

Bean-Bayog denied having any sexual contact or doing anything unethical or inappropriate with Lozano. She maintained that Lozano had been suicidal when he began treatment with her. She had provided him with "life sustaining care for almost four years." Bean-Bayog claimed that Lozano had been "completely out of control"—a sociopathic liar who abused drugs and alcohol, entertained delusions of sexual conquest, and, in retrospect, "may have been an untreatable patient." Bean-Bayog's background lent credibility to her statements.

Dr. Margaret Bean-Bayog had a distinguished career and, before the Lozanos' charges were filed, an unblemished reputation. The daughter and granddaughter of doctors, she grew up in Iowa City, Iowa, where her father was Sir William Osler Professor of Medicine at the University of Iowa. She graduated from Radcliffe and Harvard Medical School, earning a Harvard master's degree in public health along the way. In 1984, she married Rogelio Bayog, a Philippine-born psychiatrist. Corazon Aquino, a friend of the groom, attended the wedding.

In addition to a clinical practice, Bean-Bayog had a long record of academic appointments at Harvard Medical School and other prestigious institutions. Until placed on administrative leave of absence (without any finding of fault) in the wake of the Lozanos' charges, Bean-Bayog taught several hours a week at Harvard, where, according to a colleague, she was "revered by her students." She is a fellow of the American Psychiatric Association and has served as president of the American Society of Addiction Medicine. In some twenty years of clinical practice, no other complaints had been lodged against Bean-Bayog. Significantly, no complaints were lodged against her *after* the avalanche of publicity the Lozanos' complaint generated—the time when, in some similar cases, numerous additional complaints have surfaced for the first time.

1986 TO 1991: AN OVERVIEW OF EVENTS

The basic chronology and many of the facts about Lozano's course of treatment with Bean-Bayog are not in dispute. Lozano began weekly therapy sessions in July 1986 after hearing Bean-Bayog lecture at Harvard Medical School. Bean-Bayog kept detailed notes of their sessions—987 pages over the course of treatment. According to her notes, Lozano was depressed and suicidal from the first day of treatment, when he spoke of being hit by a car because he was "inattentive."

Bean-Bayog diagnosed Lozano's primary problem as a "borderline personality disorder," a mental illness characterized by impulsive, manipulative, and suicidal behavior. In the course of hospitalizations in four Boston-area hospitals during his treatment with Bean-Bayog, several other psychiatrists diagnosed Lozano as borderline. Experts say that borderline patients use suicide threats as a way to get attention or to manipulate their therapists. Research indicates that borderlines are more likely than other patients to falsely accuse their therapists of sexual abuse. All these characteristics fit Lozano's behavior, if one believes Bean-Bayog's side of the story.

The Lozano's lawyer charged that Bean-Bayog had "regressed" Lozano to a three-year-old. However, Lozano was already regressed when he came under Bean-Bayog's care. In the early sessions, he confessed to a "bad habit"—that he liked stuffed animals and owned "a cute little dog." He had fantasized a childlike relationship with his stuffed dog, "Pound Puppy," whom he brought to some of his therapy sessions. The notes of one session, for example, quote Lozano as saying, "I looked at Pound Puppy and said there's going to be a scolding."

While not involved in its creation, Bean-Bayog did respect Lozano's Pound Puppy fantasy, writing in a vacation note, "Give the Pound Puppy my regards." Lozano once photographed her cuddling the stuffed dog during a therapy session. According to Bean-Bayog, she had embraced the dog because Lozano had tricked her into believing there was no film in his camera. The photograph later appeared in a *Newsweek* article, "Dr. Bean and Her Little Boy."

In September 1986, after three months of therapy, Lozano told Bean-Bayog that he had gone to the top floor of the Harvard School of Public Health and calculated his "free fall time" were he to jump. Bean-Bayog had Lozano admitted to McLean, a private hospital affiliated with Harvard, where he stayed for two months.

After his discharge from McLean, Lozano saw Bean-Bayog only monthly until the following April. During that time, Bean-Bayog tried conventional therapy techniques, such as drug therapy and a cognitive-behavioral technique that included giving Lozano written reminders not to drink, to take his medications, and so on, but those techniques proved ineffective. Lozano became deeply depressed, and Bean-Bayog began seeing him almost daily. On May 3, 1987, Lozano returned to the top floor of the School of Public Health. He phoned Bean-Bayog, saying he had spent fifteen minutes "dangling his legs out and thinking of jumping."

Bean-Bayog persuaded Lozano to come to her office and later drove him to McLean. Lozano stayed there until his insurance ran out, when he was transferred to Faulkner Hospital in Boston. He was released from Faulkner in September 1987 and took a two-and-one-half-year leave of absence from medical school.

Lozano managed to stay out of psychiatric hospitals during his leave of absence. For part of that period, Bean-Bayog saw him several times a week and kept in close touch through phone calls, cards with supportive messages, and audiotaped readings of children's stories. Bean-Bayog considered these unconventional techniques necessary to save a very sick patient. This chapter will focus on whether Bean-Bayog's approach—the therapist as "nonabusive mom," to use her phrase—was appropriate in Lozano's case.

Lozano returned to medical school in January 1990. Shortly thereafter, Bean-Bayog told him she was planning to adopt a baby and would be taking maternity leave. Lozano became upset at the prospect of being displaced in her affections. He was also angered by her insistence that he pay more of her bills (she had been treating him almost on a pro bono basis). In March, Lozano had a psychotic episode. He came to her home where her two stepchildren were home alone, shouted for her, and pounded on the doors and windows. Bean-Bayog called the police and had him readmitted to Faulkner. Lozano had admitted to Bean-Bayog that he had seen patients while under the influence of drugs. In June 1990, while Lozano was still in Faulkner, Bean-Bayog terminated him as her patient, primarily because of his refusal to submit to supervision for his drug problem when he began clinical rounds as a medical student. The staff at Faulkner developed an aftercare plan for Lozano, and he began seeing another therapist before Bean-Bayog finished terminating with him.

Lozano was discharged from Faulkner in time to return for his senior year of medical school, but his condition deteriorated. He continued to threaten suicide and was hospitalized three more times. About six months after his termination with Bean-Bayog, Lozano was to undergo a series of electroshock treatments for severe depression. His sister Pilar, a nurse in El Paso, came to Boston to be with him. Lozano told her about his therapy with Bean-Bayog, which he said included sex, and asked her to go to his apartment and look at the things Bean-Bayog had given him.

Williams was startled by what she found:

- Children's books (*The Velveteen Rabbit, Goodnight Moon*) inscribed "Love, Dr. B."
- A Valentine's Day card, including an elephant holding a "with love SON" balloon, and the following verse:
    The elephant brings lots of love
        Because it's plain to see
    That you are loved as much
        As any son could ever be!
    Have a Happy Valentine's Day!
                Dr. B.
- Audiotapes of Bean-Bayog reading children's stories.
- Cards labeled "Handy multipurpose emergency and reference flashcard deck." One card read: "I'm your mom and I love you and you love me very, very much. Say that ten times. You're my mom and I love you very, very much."

Williams also found graphic accounts of sadomasochistic sexual fantasies, from a woman's viewpoint, in Bean-Bayog's handwriting.

Williams dumped what she had found into a bag and carried it to Dr. William B. Gault, a psychiatrist who had taken over Lozano's care after Bean-Bayog terminated with him. Gault examined the contents of the bag and advised Williams to call a lawyer from his office. Thereafter, Gault wrote to the Lozanos' lawyer that Paul's story

> would be scarcely believable were it not for the large quantity of apparent written documentation which his sister showed me. . . . He initially consulted feeling homesick, frightened, depressed and daunted by the prospect of shouldering increasing adult responsibilities. It would appear . . . that Dr. Bean-Bayog responded by encouraging him to indulge in an infantile fantasy of her loving him and caring for him as a mother while simultaneously provoking him with intense sexual stimulation, including vivid sadomasochistic sexual imagery and sexual activity.

Gault also wrote to the Massachusetts Board of Registration in Medicine in the fall of 1990, citing a "morbid emotional bond" between Bean-Bayog and Lozano, and lodging a formal complaint against Bean-Bayog. The board initiated an investigation, but the Gault complaint did not receive priority handling.

Lozano left Boston in early 1991 and returned to El Paso. His parents were managing a motel, and Lozano moved into one of the units. On April 2, 1991, after talking with Dr. Gault long-distance from Boston, Lozano sat down at his desk and injected himself with cocaine.

LITIGATION ON TWO FRONTS

The Lozano family's malpractice suit was filed five months after Paul Lozano's death. In March 1992, the Board of Registration in Medicine commenced a disciplinary proceeding against Bean-Bayog, separate from the malpractice suit. The board held an emergency, closed-door session and thereafter issued a statement alleging its "reason to believe" that Dr. Bean-Bayog had "used an unconventional method to treat [Lozano] in a manner which *did not conform to the standards of accepted medical practice at that time*" (emphasis added). The board did not cite any specific "standards of accepted medical practice" to which Bean-Bayog had allegedly failed to conform. She was specifically faulted:

- for contributing to Lozano's belief that she was his "mom" and he was her "boy," and for using flash cards to deliver that message;
- for giving Lozano children's books inscribed "to the boy" or "for the baby";
- for giving Lozano audiotapes of her reading children's stories; and
- [referring to her explicit sexual fantasies about Lozano] for failing to terminate or "otherwise address" those fantasies.

The board decided that Bean-Bayog's continued practice pending a full hearing on the charges against her, but under the supervision of another psychiatrist, would not constitute "an immediate and serious threat to public health."

The next day, Bean-Bayog's lawyer filed a brief answer to the board's allegations, essentially denying any impropriety. He stated that Bean-Bayog had tried conventional therapy methods with Lozano "for almost a year without success." Lozano had remained recurrently suicidal. At that point, Bean-Bayog began using "supportive therapy techniques . . . to calm him down when he was feeling or acting out of control." As the lawyer explained:

Mr. Lozano told her that he found comforting the idea of a "nonabusive mom"—i.e., a benevolent mother who would not abuse him. Thereafter, Dr. Bean-Bayog and Mr. Lozano, on occasion, used this concept to help calm him down when he was out of control. Dr. Bean-Bayog made it perfectly clear during therapy, and Mr. Lozano understood, that she was not his real mother, that he was not her real child, and that the therapeutic process was aimed at allowing him to relive and come to grips with his childhood memories of abuse.

The children's stories and flash cards were described as part of Bean-Bayog's "nonabusive mom" technique.

Bean-Bayog conceded that her treatment of Lozano had been "unique and somewhat unconventional," but that it had been justifiable under the unusual circumstances of Lozano's case. She stated that Lozano was the only patient with whom she had used such unconventional techniques.

In September 1992, rather than defend herself in a public hearing, Bean-Bayog chose to surrender her medical license, calling the board of Registration's proceeding a "media circus." The lure of a female Harvard professor, a younger male patient, and intimations of kinky sex had proved irresistible to the media, even before the hearing.

The *Boston Globe* gave the story frequent front-page coverage in the weeks after it broke, including titillating excerpts from Bean-Bayog's graphic descriptions of her sexual fantasies and the flash cards. The tabloid *Boston Herald* had been even less restrained, featuring such headlines as "DOC: I NEVER HAD SEX WITH PATIENT." Boston television and radio stations had taken up the hue and cry. Extensive stories also appeared in the *Washington Post* ("The Fatal Attraction of Psychiatrist and Patient"), and the *New York Times* (". . . Dark Journey Leading to Death"). With the Board of Registration's upcoming hearing to be carried live on Court TV, Bean-Bayog had reason to fear a media circus. But she must have realized that failure to defend herself in public would be widely interpreted as an admission of guilt.

Bean-Bayog's surrendering her license had the effect of nullifying the board's proceeding, because its jurisdiction depended on her being a license holder. Shortly thereafter, Bean-Bayog got rid of the Lozanos' malpractice suit as well, by settling it before trial for $1 million—the limits of her malpractice insurance policy. As is customary in such settlements, Bean-Bayog didn't admit any fault.

The upshot of these legal maneuvers was that the disputed issues were never aired and resolved in any public forum—leaving, amid conflicting evidence, a melange of unresolved charges and countercharges about sex, suicide, and unconventional psychotherapy. Let's look briefly at the inconclusive record on the sex and suicide allegations, before focusing on Bean-Bayog's "nonabusive mom" therapy technique.

OPEN QUESTIONS ABOUT SEX AND SUICIDE

This may have been, as the Lozano family claimed, a case of sexual abuse by a therapist. Lozano told his sister Pilar, and others, about a sexual relationship with Bean-Bayog. The graphic sexual fantasies Bean-Bayog wrote about herself and Lozano raise questions, questions that linger after her explanation that she wrote the fantasies as a way of dealing with her own attraction to her patient, and that she never showed them to Lozano, who had stolen them from her office. Then there was the flash card that read: "I'm going to miss so many things about you, the closeness and the need and the phenomenal sex and being so appreciated." According to Bean-Bayog, this card had been dictated to her by Lozano and referred to sex with a former girlfriend.

Other evidence supports Bean-Bayog's story. If the diagnosis of Lozano as a borderline personality was correct (five psychiatrists agreed on that), his word may not have been worth much. Bean-Bayog's track record and reputation should have given her the benefit of the doubt. Bean-Bayog consulted other psychiatrists at least five times during her treatment of Lozano. Dr. Ralph Engle, a former president of the Boston Psychoanalytic Society who has been involved in many cases of sexual abuse by therapists, observed that "if there is abuse going on, the therapist never seeks consultation. That isn't the case here."

"We hold her completely responsible for his death," Pilar Williams said. But the law requires that malpractice be the "proximate cause" of death. There is documentary proof that Lozano was suicidal before he ever met Bean-Bayog. In the spring of 1986, a Mr. Thomson had come upon Lozano near Fenway Park. He was hanging by one hand from a chain link fence, some twenty feet above a sewage overflow. Thomson convinced Lozano to climb back over the fence, talked to him, and watched him walk away. Thomson came forward to supply an affidavit when he read about the malpractice case in the newspapers.

Bean-Bayog disputed the suicide claim, agreeing with the El Paso medical examiner that Lozano had miscalculated the dosages and caused his own death accidentally. The seventy-five injections suggest that Lozano may have been "skin popping"—injecting small amounts to prolong and intensify the high. If he really wanted to kill himself, it would have been simpler and quicker to mainline an overdose in a single injection.

In virtually all malpractice cases involving suicide, the deceased patient was seeing the defendant therapist at the time of death or had only recently terminated therapy. Lozano killed himself *ten months* after terminating with Bean-Bayog, after being seen by several other psychiatrists, and when he was in treatment with Dr. Gault, the Boston psychiatrist who had steered Pilar Williams to a malpractice lawyer. The case against Bean-Bayog for allegedly causing Lozano's suicide, if it ever got to a jury, would have been extremely weak.

Sexual innuendos and a bizarre death are part of the texture of this complex business. For our purposes, however, there is nothing new or particularly significant in those aspects of the case. What are both new, and significant, are the issues raised by Bean-Bayog's "nonabusive mom" treatment method: did it fail to conform to "the standards of accepted medical practice"—as the Massachusetts Board of Registration in Medicine charged?

There is no other reported psychiatric malpractice case involving standards of care for psychotherapy. Do such standards exist, and are they specific enough to be enforced? Even though the Bean-Bayog/Lozano dispute was never resolved on the public record, enough is known about her treatment, from records and public statements, to enable other psychiatrists to reach some informed assessments of its validity. Such assessments form part of the next chapter, which looks at the question of standards for psychotherapy in a broader context. We turn now to Bean-Bayog's belief that Lozano had been abused as a child—the rationale for her unconventional therapy.

CHILD ABUSE

In the spring of 1987, Bean-Bayog came to believe that the origin of Lozano's severe depression and strong suicidal tendencies was "horrendous" child abuse by his mother. Had Lozano actually been abused as a child? The available information suggests conflicting portraits of Lozano as a child.

Paul Lozano grew up in Upper Sandusky, Ohio, the youngest of six children in a Mexican-American family. He was a brilliant child who taught himself to read at age four. At age five, he tried to order a Mercedes-Benz by mail. This pattern continued through high school, where he was a straight A student. He wrote an essay on philosophy that won a state prize, even though he hadn't taken a course in philosophy. Lozano was bookish, but he made the varsity track team. He was listed in *Who's Who among American High School Students, 1978–79*.

Lozano continued to distinguish himself academically in college and graduate school. He graduated from the University of Texas at El Paso as a microbiology major and was courted by several medical schools. Despite his severe emotional problems, he did well in his first two years at Harvard Medical School.

By all accounts (except his own), Lozano had a happy childhood. According to Dr. Thomas Watkins, a retired pediatrician who saw him frequently during his teen years: "The family was a joy to know, and Paul was no exception. If there was anyone suicidal or depressed, it wasn't Paul." But happy children don't try to kill themselves. Lozano told Bean-Bayog and other therapists about two youthful suicide attempts. At thirteen, he tried to hang himself in the basement. On another occasion, he began to inhale gas. He stopped because he was afraid his father, a smoker, might walk in. Did these suicide attempts occur, or did Lozano make them up to manipulate his therapist?

Lozano's family has vehemently denied that he was subjected to child abuse—by his mother or his siblings. The family charged that Bean-Bayog had brainwashed Lozano into thinking he had been abused. According to a *New York Times* story, two weeks of interviewing Lozano's family and friends about his past did not turn up confirmation of the childhood he described to Bean-Bayog.

Lozano himself was Bean-Bayog's only source of information about child abuse. Her notes of their June 17, 1988, session contain the following exchange, with Lozano apparently in a regressed state.

BEAN-BAYOG: Think this has to do w/ mother?
LOZANO: I can't tell you. I can't tell you. I can't.
BEAN-BAYOG: What afraid of?
LOZANO: You'd do what happened then. You'd pick me up, all cozy but I'd know you wouldn't stop, you'd caress my head and then down my body. . . . And then she'd make me stay still and do whatever she wanted over and over and over, all those things moms just do.
BEAN-BAYOG: And you want me to be your mom?
LOZANO: Not like that. Not like that. I want to be 3 years old and have you be just my mom who'd never touch me. You'd just read to me and give me soup.

On another occasion, Lozano recalled: "When I was little my mom—I remember seeing her do it to my nephews—changing them or bathing them she would—kind of kiss—and fondle. . . . I could remember her doing it to me. . . . Pilar talks about her. . . hitting us with a belt, it wasn't just occasionally. . . . Pilar told me [Mother] used to like to make us laugh, make faces, then all of a sudden make us cry, yell and scream."

Bean-Bayog wasn't the only psychiatrist to whom Lozano reported being abused as a child. The staff psychiatrist in charge of Lozano's treatment during his first admission to McLean wrote in his discharge papers: "Paul says that he has actually felt rather depressed for all his life. He describes a childhood history of abuse by his older siblings, and perhaps by his parents." Later, Bean-Bayog sent Lozano to Dr. Gutheil at Harvard for consultation. Gutheil recalled Lozano telling him about his mother's "sexual intrusion in early childhood."

There is no way to resolve the conflicting evidence about child abuse. Maybe it happened, maybe it didn't. Or maybe it was innocuous—at least from the alleged abuser's perspective. An excellent book about the entire affair, *Obsession*, by Gary and Morris Chafetz, quotes a psychiatrist as saying that it's common for mothers in rural Mexico—the culture Lozano's mother came from—to pacify an infant son by massaging his penis.

Bean-Bayog's acceptance of Lozano's abuse stories is undercut to some extent by her assertion, made after suit was filed against her, that Lozano was "delusional" and a "sociopathic liar." On the other hand, experts agree that a history of abuse as a child is common among borderlines like Lozano. Furthermore, Lozano's recollections of abuse were detailed and seemed to have the ring of truth. On balance, Bean-Bayog seems justified in believing Lozano's accounts of abuse, even if he was lying.

THE "NONABUSIVE MOM"

Child abuse or no, Paul Lozano was a very sick young man when he first came to Dr. Bean-Bayog in July 1986. Judging from Lozano's repeated suicide threats during his first year of therapy—including two trips to the top of the Harvard School of Public Health, calculating his "free fall time," and two hospitalizations—Bean-Bayog's initial, conventional therapies weren't working. Bean-Bayog decided that she had to come up with a different approach.

In the spring of 1987 during Lozano's second hospitalization, Bean-Bayog came across an article in *Psychiatric Annals* by Dr. Alayne Yates titled "Psychological Damage Associated with Extreme Eroticism in Young Children: Evaluating Suspected Cases of Child Sexual Abuse." Dr. Yates is chief of child and adolescent psychiatry and a professor of psychiatry and pediatrics at the University of Arizona School of Medicine. The article stated that "[sexually abused] children need to develop intense non-sexual relationships that will serve as alternatives to the original, intensely sexual relationship. . . . For therapy to be effective, the therapist must form a close relationship with the child." Bean-Bayog wrote Yates's phone number and a note in the margin of her copy. The note read, "Article given to patient in early May, reviewed repeatedly while hospitalized and after." When Lozano was discharged in September 1987, Bean-Bayog began to nurture a "close relationship" with Lozano.

The essence of the new treatment strategy was to counteract the effects of the abuse Bean-Bayog believed Lozano had suffered as a child at the hands of his mother. She hoped that Lozano, through a healthy experience in therapy with a caring surrogate mother, would eventually be able to confront the abuses of his childhood and work his way to a healthier sense of himself. The means to that end was a fantasy "boy" Lozano created in therapy, with whom the adult Lozano could identify. As Bean-Bayog described it, "We invented a baby version of him. Maybe he could make friends with his 3-year-old self." Bean-Bayog, who had already befriended the Pound Puppy, began to play the role of "non-abusive mom" to the fantasy "boy."

The new approach was implemented primarily in Lozano's therapy sessions—four or five times a week. Bean-Bayog's voluminous notes in late 1987 and early 1988 reflect their close interactions. For example, the notes for July 31, 1987, shortly before Lozano was discharged from the hospital, describe him holding the Pound Puppy, saying that he wanted to be three years old, and "that's all. You wouldn't do anything else. You might read to me but I'd just be three years old and that's all."

Some passages in Bean-Bayog's notes, read out of context, imply that she wanted the adult Lozano to merge with the fantasy "boy," and to think of her as his real mother. That would have amounted to inducing a delusional state, possibly a psychosis, and would have been generally recognized as malpractice. As Dorothy A. Starr, a Washington, D.C., psychiatrist, put it: "We are stand-ins for people in real life. I find it important to keep clear that this is an artificial process. . . . I may look like a great mother, but I am not going to be the mother." Bean-Bayog denied any intention of "leading him toward a psychotic conviction that I was his mother," and other passages in the notes support her disclaimer. At one point, Lozano said, "When you were talking about how the boy wasn't real, just a fantasy, my heart started pounding." According to the authors of *Obsession*, "Bean-Bayog repeatedly reminded Lozano, the adult, that the boy was just a therapeutic tool." But it seems fair to ask whether Lozano was always able to keep that distinction in sharp focus.

Some therapy patients use "transitional objects" to comfort or calm themselves—like the security blanket Linus, the "Peanuts" character, is seldom without. Lozano had the Pound Puppy from the beginning. Bean-Bayog provided him with additional transitional objects, both during therapy sessions and to take home. Her note of July 22, 1987, envisioned a progression of objects: "Baby can have blanket and *Goodnight Moon*. Toddler can have *Owl at Home*. Boy can have *Alexander and the Terrible Day* . . . Medical Student can have *N[ew] E[ngland] J[ournal] of M[edicine]* articles." One book was inscribed: "For all of you, when someone loves you for a long time, and not just to play with, but really loves you, then you become real. Sometimes it hurts, though. Love, Dr. B."

As we've seen, Bean-Bayog also wrote flash cards for Lozano. She told him to read the cards every day until he knew them by heart and was "starting to believe them." As Bean-Bayog's lawyer explained: "Mr. Lozano would review these index cards as painful thoughts arose, and the constructive messages they contained helped to get him through the day." In addition to the "I'm your mom and I love you" card that caught Pilar Williams's attention at her brother's apartment, other cards read:

You can too act like a 3-year-old when you're 25.

You can curl up with a blanket, the sweater, and the Pound Puppy and all the notes I've written you and all the books and you can breast feed and be cozy.

If you begin to believe you can't be three years old, it's because you're losing contact with me.

When she was away from Boston for a few days, Bean-Bayog kept in touch with Lozano by phone. She was particularly concerned about his welfare during her extended Christmas vacation trip to the Philippines in December 1987. Hospitalization was considered and rejected as an option. But Bean-Bayog took several steps to keep Lozano going in her absence.

Before leaving Boston, Bean-Bayog wrote seventeen letters as the "nonabusive mom" to the three-year-old fantasy "boy"—one for Lozano to open each day that she was gone. In the first letter, she explained her itinerary and urged him to call her at the Manila Hotel. In the next letter, she said, "I'm thinking of you . . . I miss you. Separations are the worst." In a letter dated "Christmas," Bean-Bayog wrote:

You wake up early. It's Christmas. "Mama, wake up. Wake up. Can I go downstairs?" "Not 'til 6 my sweet."... You are dying for a puppy and I am braced for your reaction. You will get one, but it isn't under the tree. You dissolve into misery. "You promised." "Yes, but." "You promised," you wail. "You are getting one, but we have to go pick it out. And first we have to get it a bed and some food and a dish."

All the letters were signed "Love." In addition to the letters, Bean-Bayog loaded Lozano up with books, tapes, and more flash cards, one of which read: "Do I love you? Yes, absolutely. Lots. I'm keeping you in my heart all the time I'm away and afterwards."

It's unclear how long Bean-Bayog used devices like tapes and flash cards with Lozano. The family's malpractice lawyer conveyed the misleading impression that they were used throughout Lozano's four-year therapy. The authors of *Obsession* state that "they appear to have been employed, because of the particular circumstances of her three-week absence, only during the late fall of 1987." Bean-Bayog linked not only the flash cards and stories, but also "all of these mom things," to her trip to the Philippines.

The records of therapy don't yield a precise time frame. It's clear that the "mom things" began in the summer of 1987 and continued at least until March 1988, when Lozano said that he didn't "need to be three years old so much." Some transitional objects were used well before and for a time after the Philippines trip. In any case, it appears that the most intensive use of transitional objects, tapes, and flash cards did occur before and during the Philippines trip. Bean-Bayog saw it as "a life-saving, short term device so that he could stay alive until the next session after my three-week vacation. . . . I thought it would keep him quiet and alive. So did he. And it did."

So the *Bean-Bayog* case was left unresolved when she surrendered her license to practice medicine and settled the malpractice case in the fall of 1992. Several of her peers had spoken to the media, some of them implying that her "nonabusive mom" strategy had been malpractice, others making supportive comments. The next chapter discusses that malpractice question in the broader context of standards—more accurately, lack of standards—for psychotherapy generally.

CHAPTER 11
▼ ▼ ▼

In Search of a Standard of Care

We know we can help patients with psychotherapy, but it's difficult to know exactly what to do that helps. We don't have any accepted methods we're sure will bring about good results. Sometimes, you have to fly by the seat of your pants.

—PAUL CHODOFF, M.D.

In requiring a plaintiff in a psychiatric malpractice case to prove the applicable "standard of care," the law assumes there is a standard on which most therapists agree. That assumption is sound in sexual misconduct cases. And behind that professional consensus, one would expect to find some hard supporting evidence of its validity. That is sometimes true; for example, controlled studies have shown that antidepressant drugs are effective against depression. But neither a professional consensus on a standard, nor controlled studies supporting it, are present in the diagnosis and treatment of some mental illnesses.

DR. OSHEROFF'S CASE: DRUGS VERSUS PSYCHOTHERAPY

In the *Osheroff* case, the subject of chapter 9, there were well-qualified experts on both sides making markedly different diagnoses and advocating drug treatment versus psychotherapy; this amounted to a virtual standoff on the standard-of-care issues. The failure of Chestnut Lodge—an institution with a reputation for long-term psychotherapy and a bias against drugs—to obtain Dr. Osheroff's informed consent to psychotherapy without drugs probably tipped the arbitrators' decision in Osheroff's favor.

Dr. Osheroff's case touched off a heated controversy in the psychiatric community, with implications beyond Osheroff's particular problem. The traditional view is that mental illnesses are caused by environmental factors, particularly bad parenting, and that psychotherapy ("talk therapy") is the cure. That view has been under increasing challenge by biological psychiatrists advocating drug therapies for a growing list of illnesses. Some discoveries in drug therapies since the *Osheroff* case have had dramatic results. Dr. Gutheil described the effects of Clozapine on schizophrenic patients at the Massachusetts Mental Health Center: "Clozapine was a Lazarus drug around here. People who had been zombies got up from their beds and walked. It was just amazing."

Traditional and biological psychiatrists did not see the *Osheroff* case in the same light. Their differing perspectives were presented in a debate published in the *American Journal of Psychiatry* in 1990, with Dr. Gerald Klerman—a professor of psychiatry at Harvard Medical School—representing the biological school, and Dr. Alan Stone—a psychiatrist and professor at Harvard Law School—speaking for the traditionalists.

The biological school viewed the case as a vehicle to establish drugs as the standard of care for depression, the most prevalent mental illness. According to Dr. Klerman, *Osheroff* is a landmark case that "goes a long way toward establishing the patient's right to effective treatment." "Effective" is the operative word. For Klerman, it means treatment supported by "substantial evidence" of efficacy. The best evidence of efficacy comes from "randomized controlled trials"—the kinds of trials the Food and Drug Administration requires to demonstrate the efficacy of new drugs. There were no "controlled trials" on the efficacy of psychotherapy that met Klerman's standards. Therefore, Klerman argued, treatment by psychotherapy is "in question" where there is scientific evidence that some other treatment (read drug treatment) is effective for the particular illness. Klerman went on to suggest that in the absence of scientific proof of efficacy, the courts will end up setting standards for psychotherapy—standards that might limit or preclude its use.

Dr. Stone took Klerman to task for suggesting that the courts might step in to set standards for psychotherapy. As Stone pointed out, lack of consensus in the psychiatric community has been a main reason the courts have not assumed a regulatory role. Legalities aside, Stone argued that much so-called efficacy research, including controlled clinical trials, varies in quality, and he questioned whether "the science is good enough . . . to dictate to clinicians the clinical standards of care." Seeking to hoist Klerman by his own petard, Stone quoted Klerman's words from *The New Harvard Guide to Psychiatry*: "Individual psychotherapy based on psychodynamic principles remains the most widely used form of psychotherapy. Although systematic, controlled clinical studies do not exist, clinical experience supports the value of this form of treatment."

Is the *Osheroff* case a "precedent," and if so, for what? Stone was right in denying it that status in the narrow, legal sense. Legal precedents involve published opinions by appellate courts that can be cited for propositions of law, such as the *Tarasoff* decision and the duty to warn. The *Osheroff* case was settled after arbitration; it never went to a court trial or to an appellate court. No opinion was ever written, and even the arbitration panel, the lowest rung on the legal ladder, was divided on the case. In short, the case can't be cited for any proposition; all we can say is that it happened.

Nevertheless, Klerman might have been right in seeing the *Osheroff* case as a harbinger of other cases pitting biological against traditional psychiatry. The scale of Osheroff's challenge to Chestnut Lodge, a bastion of traditional psychiatry, was unprecedented. His financial settlement represented a victory of sorts—even if he had a net loss after paying his lawyers and experts—and may encourage others to follow his example.

While the *Osheroff* case created a stir in professional circles at the time, in the decade since there has been nothing like a revolution in the practice of psychiatry. The use of drugs has increased along with the supply, but psychotherapy remains a standard treatment for many illnesses. Few practitioners can be labeled purely traditional or purely biological in orientation. Dr. Gutheil believes that drugs and psychotherapy are "artificially dichotomized," and that "anybody who is any good works both sides of the street."

Dr. Robert Sadoff believes that the specific issue in the *Osheroff* case—use of drugs for depression—has been "pretty well resolved" in favor of drugs. Dr. Seymour Halleck agrees. "There is still some argument that some forms of psychotherapy, like cognitive or interpersonal therapy, are often as good as drugs. But nobody believes now that psychoanalytically oriented psychotherapy is better than drug treatment for depression."

MULTIPLE MINORITY VIEWS: NO SINGLE STANDARD OF CARE

Dr. Osheroff's case was atypical. There are, however, more common cases in which there is no clear-cut standard of care. Teenagers like Johnny Moore (chapter 3) are committing suicide in increasing numbers. Yet the treatment of suicidal adolescents remains a controversial area in which the American Psychiatric Association has never attempted to state a standard of care.

Dr. Halleck testified in a deposition in the Moore case that there are several different treatment philosophies today for suicidal adolescents, all of them legitimate and respected. Halleck described three of these philosophies: (1) keep adolescents out of the hospital, no matter what; (2) get them out of the hospital within two weeks, unless it's practical to keep them in for long-term care (six months to a year); (3) keep them in the hospital until all serious symptoms of suicidality are gone. Halleck added: "To talk about a 'standard of care' for when an adolescent should be hospitalized or discharged is . . . meaningless because you have to define whose standard of care you're talking about." Halleck himself subscribed to the philosophy that adolescents should be discharged in about two weeks.

Dr. Halleck wasn't called to testify as an expert in the *Moore* trial. After his deposition was taken, but before trial, the plaintiffs settled their claim against Dr. Barnhill and went to trial against the hospital. The settlement agreement included a provision that Halleck would not be a trial witness. As a result, no outside experts testified in support of what Barnhill did, and Barnhill himself failed to articulate the differing philosophies of care in one of his areas of specialization. For their part, the three experts for the Moores all subscribed to the philosophy—which they claimed was the standard of care—that suicidal adolescents should be kept in the hospital until their serious symptoms are relieved—for months, if necessary.

One wonders how the *Moore* case might have turned out if Dr. Halleck had been called to testify about the standard of care—or the lack of one. Barnhill's early discharge of Johnny Moore was most consistent with Halleck's view of the right approach. Halleck's view should have qualified as a "respectable minority," which could have insulated Barnhill from the charge of malpractice. The case illustrates the crucial role lawyers' tactics—like getting Halleck out of the case—can play in a malpractice trial. It bears repeating that trials are not a search for truth but a clash of adversaries.

NO STANDARD OF CARE

The standoff between opposing experts in the *Osheroff* case suggests there may be *no* standard of care, perhaps not even a respectable minority view, for some mental patients. The logical implication of present law is that no malpractice action may be maintained in such a case—

how can one breach a standard of care that doesn't exist? On the other hand, the courts haven't yet spoken to this issue, and logic should be tempered by fairness when they do.

Leonard Rubenstein, director of the Bazelon Center for Mental Health Law in Washington, D.C., argues that lack of a standard of care should not mean that therapists have complete discretion to choose among therapies, treating the patient like a guinea pig. He would require any treatment to be performed under an experimental protocol—similar to those that govern experimental surgery—including systematic data collection and peer review. Rubenstein's position seems calculated to protect the patient, but it's slow and bureaucratic. Dr. Gutheil suggests a more efficient approach: use your best judgment, be guided by analogy, and consult with several of your colleagues.

STANDARDS OF CARE FOR PSYCHOTHERAPY?

The term "psychotherapy" has no fixed meaning, beyond listening and talking to a patient. There are more "schools" of psychotherapy—perhaps over four hundred—than there are people who have tried to count them. In a *Washington Post* column titled "The Twilight of Psychotherapy," former psychiatrist Charles Krauthammer described a single conference at which more than two dozen schools of psychotherapy were represented, including Freudian, behavioral, and existential therapy—a "babble of conflicting voices."

The extraordinary diversity among schools is in part a reflection of the lack of standards of care for psychotherapy. Drs. Gutheil, Halleck, and Sadoff, who were interviewed in connection with chapters 5 and 8 (on suicide and violence), were also interviewed about standards for psychotherapy, and related issues. In addition, Drs. Paul Chodoff and Joseph Tarantolo, both practicing psychiatrists in Washington, D.C., talked with the author about those subjects. All five agreed that psychotherapy techniques should not be subject to mandatory standards of care. Dr. Halleck recalled working for a long time with Carl Whitaker, "[who] was a kind of genius, one of the first to do things like bottle feed patients. He was confrontive as hell, in ways that made you want to crawl under the table. But I never saw him hurt anybody, and most of his patients did very well."

Diversity in psychotherapies begins at the medical schools. Dr. Halleck described how psychiatry residents are taught at the University of North Carolina School of Medicine: "You'll learn one school pretty well. We teach our people a modified psychoanalytic way of doing it. Other people might teach a cognitive or behavioral approach. By the time you finish your training, you'll be exposed to four or five ways of doing it. You end up incorporating in your own style those of your favorite teachers." Psychotherapies are further differentiated by the temperaments of individual therapists, most of whom develop highly personal styles.

Psychiatrists don't necessarily feel bound by teachings in the professional literature. Dr. Halleck challenged the idea, common in textbooks, that therapists should never talk about themselves because it's exploitative and a preamble to getting sexually involved. He recalled Sid Jourard, a therapist in the 1960s who talked about self-revelation as one of the most helpful things. Halleck added, "In my work, I often talk about myself in terms of giving the patient another way of looking at things, which I think is useful and just simply human." Dr. Tarantolo saw self-disclosure as "part of the struggle for human intimacy, something you can't write a rule about."

The absence of a standard of care for psychotherapy doesn't mean the therapist is free of other legal and ethical constraints. For example, in obtaining informed consent, the therapist should tell the prospective patient that there is no single "right" way to do psychotherapy, describe the approach he proposes to take, what the alternatives are, and why he believes his approach is preferable. Some therapists do that, but many don't.

Dr. Chodoff, who chairs the Ethics Committee of the American Psychiatric Association's Washington Psychiatric Society, recently proposed a series of "Criteria for Standards of Care in Psychotherapeutic Practice." In general, Chodoff's criteria focus on the ethics of psychotherapy, rather than treatment results. Therapists would be subject to standards of training and competence and should refrain from exploiting the patient to gratify their own sexual, financial, or psychopathological needs. Under Chodoff's criteria, however, therapists wouldn't have to prove that their techniques work, and they would be free to resort to unconventional methods in difficult cases, so long as there is a reasonable supporting rationale or some precedent in the psychiatric literature.

CAN THE EFFICACY OF PSYCHOTHERAPY BE PROVED?

As noted earlier, Dr. Klerman cited randomized controlled trials as the way to demonstrate the efficacy of drugs that affect mental functioning. Such trials can provide evidence of efficacy but not conclusive proof. In testing a new antidepressant drug, for example, there is no way to measure improvement except by the subjective report of the individual patient. It's not like taking a temperature. It's also hard to distinguish those who were helped by the drug from those who experienced a spontaneous recovery.

Biological psychiatrists have long been putting pressure on their traditional colleagues to produce scientific evidence—controlled trials—showing that psychotherapy actually works. Columnist Krauthammer has suggested that "if psychotherapy is really an art, it should be supported by the National Endowment, not Blue Cross."

It's harder to apply scientific methods in measuring the efficacy of psychotherapy than in measuring drug efficacy. Psychotherapists work with unique minds, not identical fifty-milligram pills. And despite identical training for a trial, differences in individual therapists are bound to affect the results.

Nevertheless, controlled trials of psychotherapy have been growing in number and sophistication since the 1930s. Their central conclusion: psychotherapies, in general, have positive effects. And some have been shown to be either equal to or more effective than drugs for certain illnesses—including agoraphobia, panic disorder, and migraine headaches. However, comparisons of a wide range of psychotherapies have shown little or no difference between them. Dr. Lester Laborsky, a longtime researcher in this area, has suggested an analogy to the verdict of the dodo bird in *Alice in Wonderland*: "Everyone has won and all must have prizes."

Dodo bird verdicts from researchers are not useful in clinical practice. As Dr. Chodoff observed: "To the clinician, studies like these are of doubtful value or even relevance. . . . In dealing with the varied and complex problems of the usual practice load, it is not particularly helpful to be told that psychotherapy is a kind of chicken soup, generally and nonspecifically good for what ails your patient."

An ambitious study of alternative treatments for depression, sponsored by the National Institute of Mental Health in the 1980s, illustrates the state of the art. Three test groups were given different treatments: drug therapy (imipramine), cognitive-behavioral psychotherapy, and interpersonal psychotherapy (a kind of dynamic and humanistic therapy). A fourth group was given a drug placebo. Two hundred and fifty patients were randomly assigned to the four groups. In designing the study, the researchers made every effort to replicate the scientific model. For example, exclusion criteria were applied to leave the sample as free as possible of other disorders. The therapists—twenty-eight psychiatrists and psychologists—were specially trained and monitored.

As the study progressed, the interest of professional observers centered on the "horse race question": the comparison between the psychotherapies and drug treatment. The study did not produce clear-cut findings on that question, but the trend of the complex data indicated that drug treatment was slightly more effective than the two psychotherapies in reducing depression and restoring functioning. The data also suggested that the psychotherapies were about equally effective, and that the drug placebo was almost as effective as the psychotherapies.

"Everything is equal" findings from the National Institute's study and from other investigations have led researchers to speculate that common factors in virtually all forms of psychotherapy may be responsible for most of a patient's improvement, regardless of the therapist's orientation. Important common factors might include therapist empathy, warmth, genuineness, the patient's high regard for the therapist—traits one would hope to find in a good parent. Researchers will continue to look for "common factors" and other keys to the efficacy of psychotherapy.

In the meantime, however, psychotherapy can't be judged against the scientific model. Indeed, as one critic remarked, "The more rigor you apply to research in psychiatry, the less interesting the results are." But psychiatrists needn't apologize for that. According to Dr. Tarantolo: "We're doing in therapy pretty much what shamans and priests and wise men have been doing through the ages. There was always somebody in the clan who you went to and told the most terrible things. To say you need science or statistics to prove the worth of that would be like trying to prove what a human being is."

There is another reason to question whether psychotherapies are fairly evaluated by scientific standards. In cases of severe depression, everyone would agree on the treatment goal: to alleviate the depression. When a patient goes into psychotherapy with symptoms of neurosis or character disorder, however, it may be unrealistic to expect those symptoms to go away, that psychotherapy will "cure" them. But the patient may come away with something more valuable—if harder to measure—than relief from symptoms. As Dr. Halleck described his own experience in several years of psychoanalysis: "My analysis didn't help me one bit with my symptoms. I ended up just as crazy as I was before. But it really made me like myself a lot better; it made me more confident and comfortable with myself. That was worth every penny. And that's as successful as analysis gets."

The absence of standards and variable treatment goals help to explain why there have been so few malpractice cases involving allegedly "bad" psychotherapy. The case of the *Massachusetts Board of Licensing in Medicine v. Margaret Bean-Bayog, M.D.* is the most notable exception.

IRRESPONSIBLE PSYCHOTHERAPY OR COURAGEOUS ATTEMPT TO SAVE A PATIENT?

In the disciplinary proceeding by the Massachusetts Board of Registration in Medicine and in the malpractice case brought by Paul Lozano's family against Dr. Bean-Bayog (chapter 10), the core issue was Bean-Bayog's treatment strategy of presenting herself to her patient as a caring, "nonabusive mom." The Massachusetts board charged that Bean-Bayog's treatment "did not conform to accepted standards of medical practice": a clear charge of malpractice in psychotherapy. The board didn't elaborate on what it meant by "standards of accepted medical practice." When the case was dismissed before trial, the board's prosecutor was relieved of the burden of trying to prove "accepted standards."

The Massachusetts board might well have had problems demonstrating what the "accepted standards" were. Before the board's allegations were issued, the board's investigative attorney had tried unsuccessfully for months to locate a Boston-area expert witness to represent the board's position. Months after the allegations were filed, the board finally hired Paul R. McHugh, M.D., chairman of the Johns Hopkins Department of Psychiatry, who is strongly oriented to biological psychiatry. Dr. Gutheil, who was the principal expert for Bean-Bayog and played a major role in developing her defense, commented that "for [McHugh] to discuss psychotherapy is tantamount to having a Christian Scientist discuss the indications for surgery."

Three years later, both Dr. Gutheil and Dr. Halleck, when interviewed about the malpractice issues raised by Bean-Bayog's "nonabusive mom" treatment strategy, expressed the opinion that Bean-Bayog had not committed malpractice.

Gutheil and Halleck agreed that, contrary to the board's allegation, there are no "accepted standards of medical practice" for psychotherapy. They thought there might be such a thing as malpractice in psychotherapy, despite the lack of standards, if the therapist were to do something truly bizarre—for example, use therapy that had *no* theoretical justification, that was not endorsed by other therapists, and that injured the patient.

Halleck thought Bean-Bayog's therapy had been unusual but not "beyond the pale." There was respectable minority support for what she had done, as well as ample support in the literature. Halleck was reminded of Frieda Fromm-Reichmann, an internationally famous interpersonalist therapist and "a very warm person who could get people into childhood relationships with her very quickly."

Gutheil essentially agreed with Halleck. To the charge that Bean-Bayog had "regressed" Lozano, Gutheil pointed out: "If she had really regressed him, he would have stayed with that stuff and become dependent on it. It's like you give him heroin, he wants more heroin. For a brief period she used these gimmicks. As he recovered, he threw the crutch away." Gutheil referred to precedents in the medical literature, some of them more unconventional than anything Bean-Bayog did with Lozano. He cited a case of a Swiss therapist who gave her patient two apples when she went on vacation, encouraging the patient to think of them as the therapist's breasts. If the patient felt needy while the therapist was away, she was to take a bite. Gutheil was confident the case "would have been won, based on the records alone."

RECOVERED MEMORIES

"Recovered memory" cases are a growing trend in psychiatric malpractice litigation. A recent California case, *Ramona v. Isabella*, resulted in a $500,000 verdict for the father of bulimia patient Holly Ramona, who "recovered" memories of sexual abuse by her father, Gary Ramona, during therapy. Gary Ramona charged that the defendants, a family counselor and a psychiatrist, had falsely told Holly that 80 percent of all bulimia patients were sexually abused during childhood, fostering a suggestive environment that induced the memories. The defendants allegedly described sodium amytal as a "truth serum," which induced her to submit to the drug. As a result of his daughter's charges of abuse, Gary Ramona lost a $400,000-per-year vice presidency of Mondavi Wineries, his marriage failed, and he became estranged from his three daughters.

Ramona and other "recovered memory" cases may involve the quality of psychotherapy because they may fault the psychotherapist for probing certain kinds of recollections, for *creating* false memories that can be damaging to relationships and reputations, and for recommending action by the patient, such as confronting an allegedly abusive parent. Ironically, probing unpleasant and often repressed memories lies at the heart of traditional psychoanalytic psychotherapy.

It's too early to reach conclusions about recovered memory litigation. Numerous cases are in various stages of preparation, but only a few have been tried. Most of the cases may turn on undue suggestions of abuse by therapists and stop short of faulting them for probing the possibility of abuse where there are indications of it.

THE FIFTY-MINUTE HOUR AND THE
WORRIED WELL

Serious mental illness like Paul Lozano's represents only a part of the work of practicing psychiatrists, who spend much of their time with neurotic but functioning patients—a population sometimes patronizingly referred to as the "worried well." These, the principal consumers of psychotherapy, are people who have real emotional problems but still manage to hold jobs, raise children, stay married, or survive a divorce. Clinical psychiatrists and social workers spend most of their time in fifty-minute psychotherapy sessions with troubled people, most of whom lead more or less normal lives.

There are no reported court decisions about people who have taken their unhappiness into therapy, left therapy still (or even more) unhappy, and sued the therapist for not making them better. This suggests that such cases would be losers. As we have seen, there is no generally accepted standard of care for psychotherapy, whether for the desperately ill or the worried well. There are other reasons such a suit would fail.

For one thing, you can't compare tuning a Pontiac with tuning a psyche. The Pontiac is an inert piece of metal; everything is up to the mechanic. In therapy, most of the work has to be done by the patient. Partly for that reason, ethical therapists don't promise any particular result—certainly not happiness. If, for whatever reason, the patient isn't ready to work, nothing will happen, no matter what the therapist does.

Patients who begin to work in analytic therapy will find themselves revisiting the most unpleasant and difficult parts of their lives. Working with the therapist, they begin to dismantle defenses they've erected; they look at, and deal with, their personal demons. This is a painful part of therapy. Some patients become discouraged and angry and stop coming. Should a disgruntled patient go to court at that point, the therapist could credibly claim that the former patient was just beginning to get somewhere.

There is little or no record of what happened in therapy, only the recollections of the participants. Sessions are not recorded, and most therapists' notes are fragmentary or nonexistent. There is nothing comparable to the before-and-after photos in a weight-reduction ad, no happiness meter readings.

A "happiness" case, if it ever got to a jury, would probably get a cool reception. Jurors can sympathize with a victim of seduction or a psychotic patient given the wrong drug. But when it comes to the "slight hurts of life" (as one judge termed them), the average juror is a bullet biter who has never been in therapy, and who probably regards those who have with skepticism, if not disdain.

That psychotherapy is more art than science is not necessarily a bad thing, but it does lead to an anomalous result: dissatisfied customers can sue their doctors, their lawyers, or their auto mechanics, but their therapists are not accountable in court for the quality of their work. Except for potential suicide situations, one wonders why therapists for the worried well buy liability insurance.

Dr. Halleck expressed regret that psychotherapy is too much science and not enough art. "The early days of analysis were very exciting. There were a lot of creative people in it. In the 50s and 60s, it was still a very vibrant, experimental field. It's become very standardized and medicalized now. And in some ways, that's too bad." Dr. Tarantolo joined Halleck in questioning medicalized psychiatry—with its emphasis on standardized diagnoses and formal treatment plans. "More often than not . . . you don't know what's coming. You're on the horse and you're holding on. Hopefully you're holding on in some way that's fairly humane and somewhat intelligent. And you're not too terrified of making mistakes."

PART IV

SEXUAL MISCONDUCT

CHAPTER 12
▼ ▼ ▼

Mrs. Barkley,
Twice a Week

> You were just fantasizing. Patients always fantasize about
> their therapist. I'll just deny it.
> —JONATHAN FOX, M.D., upon terminating therapy with
> his patient Joan Barkley

Dr. Jonathan Fox, a psychiatrist with a distinguished career as an army
medical officer, found himself in an unaccustomed position: in the dock,
charged with adultery, sodomy, and indecent acts with his patient, Joan
Barkley, the attractive blond wife of an army major. Seven army colonels sat across from Fox in the court martial jury box, ready to pass
judgment on his conduct. If convicted of all the charges, Fox faced a
maximum punishment of fourteen years' imprisonment, plus dismissal
from the army with forfeiture of all benefits.

Joan Barkley was the prosecution's lead witness. She described the
first time Fox had sex with her in his office at Brooke Army Medical
Center, Fort Sam Houston, Texas. "He then pulled me up from where I
was sitting and started kissing me. He was french kissing me. He started
fondling my breasts, and then he led me over towards the couch and
told me to get undressed." Their next therapy session included intercourse and fellatio. At the end, Barkley recalled, "He stood up and started
masturbating himself, and it ended with him ejaculating on my breasts."
Barkley went on to testify that Fox had sex with her in every therapy
session, except one, for the next two years.

Up to that point, Jonathan Fox's life had unfolded like a Horatio Alger
story of hard work, driving ambition, and repeated successes. Born to a
poor family in Brooklyn, the son of an office clerk and a schoolteacher,
he won academic scholarships that enabled him to earn undergraduate
and medical degrees from Columbia University.

MODEL SOLDIER, TROUBLED WIFE

Fox volunteered for army service in 1961 and entered an army residency program in internal medicine. During the mid-1960s, he was commanding officer of a hospital in Korea. He completed a fellowship in gastroenterology in 1969 and left the army for private practice in 1972. Although successful in practice, he returned to the army in 1980 to begin a three-year residency in psychiatry at Fort Sam Houston. He completed that residency at the top of his class.

Jonathan Fox loved the army. An intensely physical man, Fox was a tennis instructor and held a black belt in karate. He was one of few doctors to complete Army Ranger School, for which he received a commendation. Fox was also an honor graduate of Airborne School and of Flight Surgeon's School. In sixteen years of service, he rose to the rank of colonel.

When Joan Barkley became his patient in 1981, Dr. Fox was forty-six years old. He had been married to his college sweetheart for over twenty years. Both had gone on to medical school, marrying immediately after graduation. Marcia Fox became a pathologist. They had two children, a son who also became a doctor, and a daughter who became an accountant. The Foxes owned a home in a middle-class suburb of San Antonio.

There is little in what is known of Dr. Fox's background to explain why this mature, intelligent, and ambitious man should have jumped the tracks with Barkley, wrecking his career and jeopardizing his marriage. Fox's brother testified at the trial, "The family relationship is just out of this world." Longtime colleagues and friends also described the family in glowing terms and the Fox marriage as "excellent." While Fox's lawyer would tell the jury that his client "was having some problems at home" and possibly a "mid-life crisis," he provided no specifics.

In contrast to Fox's straight-arrow background, Joan Barkley's was littered with signs foreshadowing a relationship with someone like Fox. Joan Barkley had met her high school sweetheart, David, when she was fourteen and a freshman in high school. She was a cheerleader. David was seventeen, a senior, and an athlete. David was the only person she ever dated. They married five years later, while attending college. He finished college; she dropped out to have their first child, a girl. Two sons followed. When the children were small, Joan Barkley didn't work outside the home. Life as an army wife was not conducive to career development.

After her first pregnancy, Barkley experienced painful muscle spasms, for which her doctor prescribed Darvon, a painkilling drug. She became addicted to Darvon, not so much for the relief it gave from pain as for the "high" that came with it: "It made me feel very powerful and able to function. I liked that feeling because I was able to get up and clean my house and take care of the kids." Barkley fed her increasing addiction to Darvon for the next decade—getting simultaneous prescriptions from different doctors and through cooperative friends—until she came under Dr. Fox's care at Fort Sam Houston.

Joan Barkley's dependencies were not limited to drugs. She had always had an unusually close attachment to her father, whom she described as "very strong and successful." When it came to a husband, she "wanted someone like my dad . . . someone that I respected." Major Barkley described how his wife's dependence on her father continued even after they were married. "Many things that I felt we couldn't afford in our marriage, she would say, 'Well, my daddy would have gotten it for me.'" For example, when Major Barkley balked at the price of a new car his wife wanted, her father bought it for her.

THE BARKLEY MARRIAGE

The Barkley marriage was rocky. They had loud arguments, during which Major Barkley sometimes hit his wife. They shared the same bed but had sex only occasionally. Joan Barkley suspected her husband of infidelities, including an affair with his commanding officer's wife. She herself had a series of affairs. Before Dr. Fox, she had had an affair with a neighbor who combined sex with sympathetic advice to "try to keep the family together." The neighbor was a dentist, and, as with Fox, they had sex in his office.

Major Barkley found it hard to support a family of five on his military pay. So Joan Barkley went to work at a medical laboratory as an assistant supervisor. Her supervisor was a Mr. Martinez. They worked the graveyard shift, from 8 P.M. until 4 A.M., or later. Barkley and Martinez would sometimes have breakfast together after their shift. She would tell him her troubles, and he would sympathize. In the middle of her relationship with Dr. Fox, Barkley began a simultaneous affair with Mr. Martinez. Her affair with Martinez continued through the court martial two years later, with (according to Barkley) the acquiescence of her husband and Martinez's wife.

Joan Barkley described Martinez as in his early fifties, tall, thin, bald, with a beard and glasses—not attractive but "very supportive. . . . When I leave him, he checks my gas and my tires to make sure everything is okay. If I don't call him when I get home, he will come looking for me. . . . He just watches over me. . . . He's a lot like a father type." Barkley claimed that she didn't look upon Martinez "as a sexual outlet." She acknowledged, however, that they had an ongoing sexual relationship, which included intercourse and fellatio.

You don't have to be a psychiatrist to see that Barkley was an extremely dependent person. She seemed to lack a solid sense of her own identity. Barkley typically began her diary entries by describing what she had worn that day, as if she were trying to convince herself that she was real. Her diary entry for January 12, 1983, begins "beige pants, tan print blouse"—clothes she had taken off earlier that day to have sex with Fox. As one of the psychiatrists who examined her put it, "It's like her plus another person is a whole person. . . . Her plus Fox is another person; her plus her dad is another person. She needs that kind of thing." As Joan Barkley herself put it, "I don't know who I am."

Trouble began to brew in December 1981 when Barkley went to Brooke Army Medical Center seeking help for her addiction to Darvon. The hospital setting seemed to promise a safe, quiet place to be healed. Barkley was thirty-one years old, and her addiction to Darvon had escalated to some thirty-five capsules per day—a life-threatening level if continued for long.

Barkley was referred to Dr. Fox, then in his second year of residency in psychiatry. Following a brief period of detoxification as an inpatient, she entered outpatient psychiatric treatment with Fox at his Fort Sam Houston office. A combination of psychotherapy and antidepressant drugs enabled Barkley to overcome her addiction to Darvon in a few months. Psychotherapy with Fox, focusing on her personal and family problems, continued twice a week.

Early in the course of therapy, Dr. Fox presented a treatment plan to Barkley. He told her how important her father had been to her, and that Darvon had become a substitute for her father after she married. Fox proposed to substitute himself for the Darvon, so that she would become dependent on him instead. After that, he proposed to break her dependency on him, so that she would no longer be dependent on anyone.

MIXING THERAPY AND SEX

From the first session, Fox asked Barkley detailed sexual questions about her sexual preferences and behavior. She had answered such questions because "he could have asked me anything. I was in the position where I . . . was scared all the time that he would refuse the treatment or tell me that he could no longer see me, and I needed him at that point."

After seeing Barkley for about a year, Dr. Fox asked her if she thought she "could have sex with him and keep it separate from the therapy." She replied that she didn't know, and Fox stared at her, "it seemed like forever." During their next session, on December 20, 1982, Barkley gave Fox some lottery tickets. Fox then led Barkley to his couch and told her to undress, which she did.

After that, a virtually unbroken sequence of intense sexual encounters occurred, twice a week, in Fox's office until he completed his residency in psychiatry, with honors, in June 1983—about six months (some fifty therapy sessions) later. Joan Barkley's diary for December 21, 1982, describes fellatio, intercourse in "a few new ways," and Fox's wrapping up the session by masturbating and asking her whether she wanted him to ejaculate in her mouth or on her breasts. She had replied, "either way, whichever he wanted," and Fox had given her a "little of both." They had also talked about her work hours and Christmas shopping.

On some occasions Fox would dispense with "therapy" altogether—initiating sex at the beginning of the session and then leaving because he "had to run." There was only one session in which sex did not occur. That time, Dr. Fox learned that his son had broken his leg and he left to attend to him. Another time, Fox had been out of town for two weeks and Barkley had been hospitalized at Brooke Army Medical Center for painful muscle spasms in her legs. Nevertheless, at Fox's request, Barkley went to his office in her hospital gown and a housecoat. He explained that her leg problem was a neurotic response to his absence, and they had sex in his office.

When he completed his residency in psychiatry, Dr. Fox was assigned to a hospital for U.S. forces in West Germany. After vacating his office at Brooke, Fox phoned Barkley and they met at several motels before Fox left for Germany in July 1983. According to Barkley, the motel sex was "louder . . . more vocal and demanding" than in the muted hospital corridors of Brooke Army Medical Center.

Dr. Fox's tour of duty in Germany lasted a year. During that time, he flew back to Texas about once a month. Upon his arrival, he would call Barkley and ask her to meet him at a motel. Their sexual activities were as before, but Fox continued to tell her that he was providing therapy as well.

While he was overseas, Dr. Fox asked Barkley to write him letters about her sexual fantasies. One letter began, "Dear Sexy, Right now my pussy is all wet and juicy and throbbing so much I have to let myself come." Barkley claimed at the court martial that she never sent this letter to Fox, but she admitted authorship.

One night in April 1984, Major Barkley was cleaning out the basement when he found the "Dear Sexy" letter in a suitcase with his wife's diaries. She was at work at the time. Major Barkley opened one diary, recognized his wife's handwriting, and "I went berserk. I went in and got my shotgun . . . and I wanted to shoot [Fox]. . . . It was just the most perverted sex acts . . . with biting and hurting along with the perversion and masturbation. . . . I just couldn't believe it. I went crazy." Barkley went through his wife's closet looking for other incriminating evidence. He found motel keys and a "Please Call" slip for Dr. Fox, with a four-digit phone number written on it matching the number on one of the motel keys.

There was no hard liquor in the house, but Major Barkley managed to get drunk on a bottle of crème de menthe. When Joan Barkley came home from her job late that night, the situation deteriorated rapidly. He went into a rage, accusing her of doing what she had written. Seeking to reassert his marital rights, he demanded that she perform fellatio on him, as she had with Fox. His wife denied everything. Major Barkley threatened to shoot himself, and Joan Barkley called the police.

Then she took the shotgun outside to hide it. Major Barkley pursued her angrily, and she ran for the back fence. Major Barkley caught up with her and pulled her back, ripping her blouse off. She cut her neck on the fence, drawing blood. Amid the commotion, the Barkleys' thirteen-year-old daughter came out of her bedroom, stunned and crying. Joan Barkley called a friend of the family, who came and sat with them until 5 A.M. The police eventually responded to Barkley's call. An officer took possession of the shotgun and, upon his departure, noted that "all seems copacetic."

Discovery didn't end the affair. Dr. Fox continued to invite Barkley to local motels on his return visits to Texas, and she went.

Despite his first impulse, Major Barkley didn't confront his wife's lover. He did take to sleeping on the living room couch, but his motives are unclear. He had every cause for righteous anger and for considering divorce. But he also knew that under Texas law, he wouldn't have to pay alimony if he didn't "condone" his wife's adultery by sleeping with her.

In July 1984, Dr. Fox completed his overseas assignment and returned to Brooke Army Medical Center to become assistant chief of Outpatient Psychiatric Services. He resumed seeing Joan Barkley in his office at Brooke about once a month, through March 1985. Barkley claimed that she saw their relationship as one of "patient and therapist" but, as before, almost every session included intercourse, fellatio, and masturbation. Dr. Fox would sometimes call Barkley at home and ask her "to say sexual things to him over the telephone."

Finally, in March 1985, Barkley came to Dr. Fox's office for a last appointment, had sex with him, and told him—about a year after the fact—that her husband had discovered their sexual relationship. Fox falsified the record of the last appointment by noting in Barkley's chart that her diaries referred to sexual fantasies about him. Barkley did not see Fox again until she confronted him as a witness for the prosecution.

In November 1985, Dr. Fox's attempted cover-up began to unravel. Barkley had become addicted to Florinal 3, a drug containing codeine that Fox had been liberally prescribing for her, ostensibly for headaches. Barkley was admitted once more to Brooke Army Medical Center for drug addiction. She told a staff psychiatrist that she had had sex with another army psychiatrist whom, however, she declined to name. But the list of suspects was short; Barkley's only long-term therapy had been with Fox.

About the same time, Barkley finally admitted to her husband that she and Fox had indeed had a sexual relationship and that the relationship had continued even after his discovery of the diaries. These disclosures apparently exhausted Major Barkley's capacity for denial, and he reported the matter to a senior officer at Fort Sam Houston, who started a formal investigation.

THE COURT MARTIAL TRIAL

In December 1985, Dr. Fox gave a sworn statement to an investigator for the army's Criminal Investigation Division. He denied engaging in any form of sexual activity with Barkley. Fox continued to stonewall Barkley's allegations as his court martial approached. His only lapse occurred in a conversation with his commanding officer, when Fox remarked that a court martial "was a hell of a price to pay for a minor indiscretion."

As the trial began, however, it became apparent to Fox and his lawyers that the prosecution had an overwhelming case. It wasn't—as in many sexual misconduct cases—merely a matter of her word against his. Her very detailed diaries had the ring of truth. Qualified experts were prepared to testify that Barkley had been sexually abused. Perhaps most damning of all were the motel records, keys, and phone call logs linking Fox to Barkley in a way that had only one explanation.

If he continued to maintain his innocence in the face of the case against him, Fox would have risked alienating the jury into returning a more severe sentence. Fox opted not to take the risk and accepted a plea bargain: he admitted the allegations of sexual misconduct and pled guilty to adultery, sodomy, and indecent acts, in return for a limit on his maximum sentence.

Following Fox's guilty plea, his trial went forward so that the jury could determine the appropriate punishment—not, however, to exceed the limit in the plea bargain. The prosecution and the defense presented their differing versions of the facts through the testimony of the Barkleys, Dr. Fox, and a parade of expert and character witnesses.

Winston Churchill once summoned a waiter, saying: "Pray, remove this pudding. It has no theme." Like a good pudding, a good court case has to have a theme. Here, the prosecution's theme was that Dr. Jonathan Fox had ruthlessly exploited an especially vulnerable patient, causing irreparable damage. But according to the defense, Joan Barkley was a temptress who had seduced a neophyte psychiatrist; she had, the defense claimed, been sleeping around and abusing drugs for years, and her psychological injuries were self-inflicted. These opposing themes were sounded throughout the trial.

The prosecution presented its case first, beginning with Barkley. She told her story of sex on the couch, in motel rooms, and on the telephone—all of which she submitted to because she needed Dr. Fox for therapy or for pills. He never told her that he loved her. He had exploited her. "It was very, very cold. . . . It was turn this way and bend that way, sit up and sit down. It was always like orders."

Barkley also testified about the impact of her relationship with Dr. Fox on her marriage and her children. She claimed that before Fox came into her life, she had been a "very good mother" and that, despite problems, she and her husband were sleeping together. After Fox, she suffered from continuing depression and was unable to function as wife and mother. As she summed it up, "I really and truly haven't done anything."

The Barkley children had suffered as a result. Joan Barkley was called in for counseling when their now sixteen-year-old daughter, formerly a good student, began to fail most of her subjects. Their two sons, ages thirteen and seven, began to have "behavior problems." One son went into therapy when he began destroying things in the house, including things he had made for Mother's Day.

Major Barkley took the stand to describe his discovery of the diaries in the basement, the stormy aftermath, and the impacts of his wife's relationship with Fox. He was effusive in his praise of her pre-Fox homemaking and mothering skills. She was an "excellent mother"; everything she did "was devoted to the children." Their sex life was "normal." Dinner was always on time, and the house was always clean. Post-Fox, his wife had stopped caring for the children or the house. "She has not washed a dish . . . cooked a meal . . . or done anything other than sleep or cry."

Major Barkley's testimony had a strong sexist tinge, perhaps not surprising in a career army officer. As he saw it, his wife's duties were as a mother, homemaker, and sexual partner. He pointed to her failure to cook and wash the dishes as evidence of psychological impairment—a standard he presumably wouldn't apply to himself. Joan Barkley got no credit for holding down a job from 8 P.M. to 4 A.M.

Both Barkleys' testimony about psychological injuries was hardly disinterested. Before the court martial began, the Barkleys had hired a lawyer to file a civil malpractice suit against Dr. Fox and the army. As the court martial trial began, their malpractice suit was pending, claiming damages of $1 million. That suit was settled after the court martial for an undisclosed, but substantial, amount. As a practical matter, the value of their civil settlement would be strongly affected by the injuries proved in the court martial.

After the Barkleys, the prosecution's case was presented through the testimony of Colonel William Grant, an air force psychiatrist, and Jacqueline Bouhoutsos, a clinical psychologist. Dr. Grant emerged as the most effective witness called by either side, an effect undoubtedly enhanced by the presence of seven other colonels in the jury box. A practicing psychiatrist for twenty years, Grant was then chairman of the Department of Psychiatry at Andrews Air Force Base in Maryland.

Dr. Grant began by endorsing the Hippocratic Oath's ancient prohibition of sex with patients, tracing it to the present-day ethical prohibition by the American Psychiatric Association. The prohibition is absolute—"with no equivocation; no hedging; no way to get around it."

Grant next described the dynamics of the relationship between the female patient and male therapist. The patient typically comes into therapy depressed. She sees the therapist as strong and in control, the one "who's going to tell her how to manage her life." The therapist encourages her to reveal her innermost thoughts, assuring her that her trust will not be betrayed.

"Transference" and "countertransference" are concepts Freud originated to describe critical interactions between patient and therapist. Grant explained that transference involves the patient's projecting onto the therapist unresolved feelings she has had for other people, usually a parent. There are three general types of transference: erotic, idealized, and hostile. In an erotic transference, the patient may develop a strong sexual attraction for the therapist, even fall in love with him. In an idealized transference, the patient comes to see the psychiatrist as powerful and all-knowing and becomes highly dependent on him.

Transference is the vehicle through which the patient, with the therapist's help, works through earlier emotional conflicts, gains greater self-knowledge, and has a better-adjusted life. It is the therapist's job to recognize when transference is occurring and to handle it appropriately.

"Countertransference" refers to the therapist's feelings for the patient as therapy progresses. As with the patient, the therapist's counter-transference can be erotic, idealized, or hostile. But the therapist is supposed to control his feelings and not allow them to determine his actions. He should maintain a position of objectivity, from which he can interpret the patient's feelings and lead her to greater understanding.

Barkley had experienced a predominantly idealized, partly erotic transference with Fox. Grant stated that she would be dependent and vulnerable in such a transference, having "almost the vulnerability of a child." Driving his point home, Grant paraphrased a statement of the sexologists Masters and Johnson: a psychiatrist who has sex with a patient shouldn't be sued for malpractice; he should be tried for rape. Grant added a refinement by the dean of the Yale Medical School: the prosecution should be for statutory rape, "as if an adult had raped a child."

Dr. Grant had spent some twenty hours with Mrs. Barkley before the trial to review her experience with Fox, and to assess the injuries he had caused. Grant found that Barkley had a mixed personality disorder, with borderline and hysterical traits that reinforced her unhealthy attraction to father figures. Grant explained that such a person wants somebody to shelter her through life. She, in return, gives a kind of "sexualized dependency": she will let you know that she finds you attractive; but she doesn't want sex, she wants to be protected. Grant noted that during his interviews with Barkley, she had been "coy" with him.

Dr. Grant concluded that Fox had been guilty of "gross malpractice" and that his treatment had made Barkley much worse, instead of better. Far from resolving her inappropriate attachment to her father, the treatment left Barkley thinking, with her marriage in a shambles, that "if she goes back home, daddy will take care of her."

After Fox, Barkley had gone into therapy for about a year with another therapist. According to Grant, however, that therapy hadn't "gone anywhere" because of her impaired ability to trust a male therapist. All things considered, Barkley's prognosis, both for the short and long term, was "quite poor."

Dr. Grant was cross-examined by a lawyer for the defense. Not only did he fail to blunt Grant's testimony, he brought out more evidence damaging to Fox. Grant was asked, for example, whether Fox had experienced a romantic countertransference with Barkley. For if Fox had fallen in love with Barkley—even the artificial love of countertransference—his actions would have been cast in a more sympathetic light. Grant doubted that countertransference had occurred.

> The relationship lacked the personal quality [of erotic countertransference]. It was not as if Dr. Fox enjoyed spending time with her as a person. . . . He didn't make lunch dates with her. He never sent her flowers. There were no stolen hours just to talk, just to be with each other. The nature of the sexual relationship was degrading. I find it hard to conceive of someone ejaculating in the face of someone he loves.

The point was reinforced by the prosecution's second expert, Dr. Jacqueline Bouhoutsos, a prominent authority on sexual misconduct, co-author of the book *Sexual Intimacies between Therapists and Patients*, and a longtime practicing psychologist. She was called to testify about injuries typically resulting from sexual exploitation of therapy patients and about the injuries to Joan Barkley in particular.

Dr. Bouhoutsos was the senior author of a study on sexual exploitation that had involved sending questionnaires to all 4,385 psychologists then licensed in California. Each was asked to report about patients who told them they had been sexually involved with a previous therapist, and about the consequences for the patient. Possibly reflecting some reluctance to discuss the subject, the response was poor: only 704 psychologists returned the questionnaire (a 16 percent return rate). However, those 704 returns reported 559 cases of sexual misconduct. Although, as Bouhoutsos conceded, the study did not represent a valid statistical measure of the problem (there probably is no way to get such a measure), it suggests that the problem is disturbingly widespread.

Based on the questionnaire data, the study identified nineteen symptoms commonly found in victims of sexual misconduct in therapy. These included guilt, feelings of isolation and emptiness, inability to trust, suppressed rage, bondage to the therapist, fear, anxiety, and increased suicidal risk. Such symptoms are not recognized as a separate disorder in the American Psychiatric Association's *Diagnostic and Statistical Manual of Mental Disorders*. However, Bouhoutsos labeled them, collectively, the "therapist-patient sex syndrome." She considered any victim of sexual misconduct who displayed half or more of the nineteen symptoms to be suffering from that syndrome.

Dr. Bouhoutsos interviewed Joan Barkley for eight hours to assess the injuries inflicted on her by Jonathan Fox. She found in Barkley seventeen of the nineteen symptoms of therapist-patient sex syndrome. She noted, for example, Barkley's feeling of emptiness "because she cannot exist without someone else to lean on." There were feelings of bondage: Barkley thought Fox "was God, and that without him she could not continue to exist."

Now it was the defense's turn to make a case for mitigation of Fox's punishment—not an easy task after Fox had pled guilty to multiple sexual felonies, admitting a lot of kinky details. In his opening statement to the jury, Fox's defense lawyer promised to show that Fox is "a warm, caring man," that he had been inexperienced in handling the transference phenomenon, and that Barkley "came on very strong" to him. The affair was something Fox hadn't planned or wanted; it was "something that just happened to him." Unfortunately for Fox, the defense case did not live up to its advance billing.

Foreclosed by the guilty plea from claiming Dr. Fox didn't do it, the next best thing was to claim he wouldn't do it again. The defense called to the stand Dr. Thomas Drummond, a psychologist retained by the defense to administer a series of tests to Fox, including the Rorschach Inkblots test, a "multiphasic sex inventory" test, and the Minnesota Multiphasic Personality Inventory (MMPI) test.

Based largely on the test results, Dr. Drummond found that Dr. Fox was "no more exploitive of other people" than the average adult, that he lacked the "thought patterns and behavioral history" of a sociopath, that his sexuality was that of "a normal heterosexual adult male," and that he was not a "sexual predator." Dr. Drummond concluded that the affair with Mrs. Barkley "was an isolated instance, and did not emanate from the insistent needs of a disordered personality."

But the tests didn't carry much weight. It would have been possible for Dr. Fox to take advantage of his professional knowledge to skew the results. More important, the psychological tests used on Dr. Fox cannot identify even ordinary sex offenders, let alone more sophisticated ones. Experts consider behavioral history to be the most significant factor in evaluating sexual misconduct. In this case, Fox's behavior with Barkley over a two-year period spoke for itself.

The defense relied heavily on character witnesses. Colonel Albert Cuetter, a neurologist who knew Dr. Fox socially and professionally, stated that he was "a helluva good doctor" and "a great father." Cuetter was asked a hypothetical question later posed to other defense witnesses: He was to assume that his daughter was beautiful, flirtatious, prone to illicit sexual involvements, and badly in need of therapy. Knowing what he knew about Fox's admitted sexual misconduct with Barkley, would he have any reservation in referring his daughter to Fox for therapy? Cuetter's answer was no. Other character witnesses testified in the same vein.

Dr. Fox took the stand as the last witness. He described Barkley, his first long-term patient, as "blossoming" in front of him. Her dress had become "more explicit." He recalled being aware of transference as it began to occur in her, and he had thought he was maintaining the proper therapeutic distance. According to Fox, Barkley had described longings for "passionate erotic encounters" with him. But he had rejected her over-tures, as he had been taught to do, saying, "How productive could this be?" or "Would this be of any help to you?"

Then came the fateful day when Barkley handed Fox the lottery tick-ets. "From there, it just happened. . . . Before you knew it, we were hav-ing sex in the office. It was a very passionate affair." After that, Fox "just wanted more." He found himself "addicted" to sex with his patient, which he continued in a "compulsive way." But Fox denied exploiting Barkley. He testified that their relationship had been mutual and "strictly sexual"— that there had been "no romance or expectations of it from either side." He believed that Barkley had enjoyed their sexual relationship, as he had.

Did Joan Barkley enjoy the affair? Despite her repeated denials, there are strong indications that she did. She wrote the "Dear Sexy" letter of her own free will when Fox was in Germany. Her diary entries are any-thing but passive. For example, the entry for January 12, 1983, describes fellatio with Fox in glowing terms, and how she "wanted to fuck."

What difference does it make whether Barkley enjoyed sex with Fox—even sought it—or whether, as she claimed, she complied passively with his demands? According to the prosecution's experts, the responsi-bility for avoiding sex is entirely the therapist's, who is ethically bound to resist temptation, even if the patient begs for it.

On the other hand, it made sense for the defense to put as much responsibility on the victim as possible. While the jury of seven army colonels might accept, in principle, an absolute bar as the ethical stan-dard, they would nonetheless relate to a come-on from an attractive woman and the idea of consenting adults.

At the conclusion of the defense case, the lawyers made their clos-ing arguments, and the judge instructed the jury on the range of punish-ments they could impose. After hearing four days of testimony, the seven colonels took just forty-five minutes to decide on Fox's punishment:

dismissal from the service with forfeiture of benefits. Fox's decision to plead guilty probably saved him from a prison term. After Fox had exhausted his avenues of appeal, the secretary of the army ordered that Colonel Jonathan Fox "cease to be an officer of the United States army."

Joan Barkley went back home to Louisiana. Dr. Fox left the San Antonio area. His present whereabouts and line of work are unknown.

CHAPTER 13
▼ ▼ ▼

One Doesn't Just
Say Goodbye

Nothing in your fantasy would ever prepare you to find your psychiatrist in bed with your wife.

—ELISSA BENEDEK, M.D.

Bill Jackson was concerned about his estranged wife, Jenny. It had taken her a long time to answer the phone, and when she did, her tone seemed strange. Deciding to check on her, he drove over to the family home they had shared until the month before. Everything looked normal as he drove by the house at about 11 P.M.: Jenny's car was in the driveway, and there were lights in the family room and master bedroom. But when he drove a half block past the house, he saw a blue Karmann Ghia pulled off the road and into the bushes. A bumper sticker—"Go Fly a Kite"—was visible through the bushes. Jackson had seen the Ghia three times a week for years. It belonged to his psychiatrist, Dr. Philip Winston.

Bill Jackson parked his car and walked around to the back of the house to look in the windows of the family room. Through a crack in the curtains, he could see a pair of men's black loafers and a green velour sweatshirt. He recognized the sweatshirt as one Dr. Winston sometimes wore during therapy sessions. Jackson looked up, saw light in the bathroom of the master bedroom, and said to himself, "Something is rotten in Denmark around here."

Jackson returned to his car, took his Sears Roebuck, 12-gauge shotgun out of the trunk, loaded it, and stuffed his pockets with shells. He let himself in the house, reconnoitered the downstairs, and, finding no one, went upstairs. He saw his elder son asleep in his bedroom. Then he walked to the master bedroom door, found it locked, and kicked it open. As Jackson later recalled the scene:

177

I saw my wife sitting up in bed naked except for a light housecoat she was putting on. And I could see her breast and her pubic hair and I could see Philip Winston sitting up in bed next to her pulling on his undershorts. . . . I raised the gun and aimed it above the bed . . . and as I did that, Dr. Winston said: "Now Bill, don't be irrational, Bill. Jenny loves me."

Jenny and Winston got out of bed and began to edge toward the bathroom. Jackson waved the shotgun in their direction, Winston sank to his knees, and Jackson fired over his head, the buckshot ripping a ragged hole in the bedroom wall and through the outside brick. As Jackson began to reload, Winston jumped him, trying to take the shotgun away, and a struggle ensued. Winston hit Jackson with a splintered bannister railing, breaking a front tooth. Jackson bit Winston on the shoulder after attempting unsuccessfully to gouge his eyes out. The combatants tumbled down the stairs, broke a glass door, and ended up, still struggling, on the front lawn.

In the midst of the melee, Jenny threw the shotgun in the shrubbery and called the police. Still holding on to Winston, Jackson grabbed Jenny by the hair and shouted to the neighborhood at large, "I just caught my psychiatrist in bed with my wife." Winston shot back, "Oh, yes, Bill, go ahead and tell the whole world about it. It must hurt a lot, doesn't it?"

A neighbor came over to investigate the commotion. When police cars and a rescue-squad truck arrived soon after, Jenny was still clad in her light housecoat, and Winston was on the Jacksons' front lawn in his undershorts. Everyone went inside. Jenny flopped down on the couch, her head in her hands. Bill went to her and said, "I'll get you for this. I'll kill you."

The police took Jackson before a magistrate in handcuffs. Winston accompanied them as the complaining witness. He thought Jackson was "irrational and dangerous" and "needed to be off the street." After Jackson agreed to go voluntarily to a psychiatric ward for observation, Winston didn't press assault charges.

When Bill Jackson found Philip Winston in bed with his wife, on July 6, 1979, he had been Winston's patient for four years. Jackson thought of Winston as his best friend. In hundreds of therapy sessions, Jackson had opened up to Winston, revealing his thoughts, feelings, hopes and fears, and the intimate details of his marriage. He trusted him completely.

Jackson's reactions to finding Jenny and Winston in bed together may seem extreme. But even apart from the therapy relationship, when a husband finds his wife in bed with another man it stirs primal feelings of rage, betrayal, and a consuming desire for revenge. It is hardly surprising that the husband's first impulse would be homicidal. (In Texas, shooting the paramour caught in flagrante delicto was long regarded as justifiable homicide.) When betrayal of a therapy relationship is added to the mix, those feelings are magnified, particularly when the spouse is as volatile and vulnerable as Bill Jackson.

THE YOUNG COUPLE

Bill and Jenny Jackson had attended high school together in Minnesota, had started dating at sixteen, and had gotten married at twenty-one, when Bill was in veterinary school at Iowa State University in Ames. Bill graduated in 1970 and went into veterinary practice near Cedar Rapids, Iowa. Jenny earned a B.A. degree from Iowa State and an M.A. from the University of Iowa.

The Jacksons' life in Cedar Rapids was pleasant, if uneventful, for several years. Bill's practice grew, they bought a home, they took trips together, and sons William Jr. and Robert arrived. They had "a very stable and good marriage," according to Bill. But in 1974, after the birth of their second son, Bill began to display some unusual behavior. There was excessive spending—six stereo systems and two sailboats. As Jenny recalled, there was also "incessant talking and jumping from one subject to another, without much coherence." Bill didn't sleep much and kept a lot of balls in the air. "It was sort of exhausting to be with him."

In October 1975, Bill entered a mental hospital in Iowa City voluntarily. He left after a few days, against medical advice. On his return home, he discovered that Jenny had locked him out of the house. Bill forced the front door to find that Jenny had locked herself in the bedroom. Then he forced the bedroom door to get (he said) his checkbook to pay the cab driver. Jenny hired a lawyer to try to get Bill committed to a mental hospital—involuntarily, if necessary. Bill responded by hiring a lawyer of his own.

The lawyers negotiated, and Bill eventually entered a second mental hospital for evaluation. He insisted, however, that Jenny not stay in the house while he was in the hospital, so she took the kids to her parents' home in Minnesota. When Jenny returned, she phoned Bill, who told her she had come back to Cedar Rapids three hours early, and demanded that she go back to Minnesota. She ignored his demand. Following tests and observation, the psychiatrists reached a diagnosis: manic-depressive illness.

DR. WINSTON'S THERAPY

When Bill Jackson was discharged following his second hospitalization, his hospital psychiatrist referred him to Dr. Philip Winston. Winston had graduated from Cornell College and the University of Iowa Medical School, had served as an army doctor, including a tour in Vietnam, and had completed a residency in psychiatry at the University of Wisconsin. When Jackson's therapy began, Winston was forty and his patient was thirty-one. Winston was married, with two children. Not coincidentally, Winston and his wife were to separate in late May 1979, within days of the Jackson separation.

Jackson began treatment with Winston in the fall of 1975—two or three times a week in the beginning, tapering off to once a week in 1976, and increasing to thrice weekly in 1977 until its abrupt ending on July 6, 1979. Winston used the records and test results from Jackson's hospitalizations to develop a treatment plan. Among other things, they indicated that "his sexual preoccupation borders on the morbid, and it would seem to derive from underlying feelings of inadequacy, inferiority and insecurity. . . . Apparently he tends to see himself as something of a martyr who had been crucified to meet others' expectations. . . . Considerable evidence of underlying psychopathy was noted on the tests, in addition to the mood disorder."

Winston concluded that Jackson had "very severe emotional problems"—a personality disorder in addition to manic depression—and that his treatment goal would be to "try to stabilize" the manic depression and "work with the personality disorder." Jackson's principal medication was lithium, the standard treatment for manic depression. His moods continued to fluctuate, however; during his manic phases, Winston added tranquilizers. Yet Jackson's mood swings were never fully stabilized.

During 1976, the Jacksons began having occasional joint sessions with Winston. The main purpose was to help Jenny adjust to Bill's illness. They also discussed money problems and tensions created by pressure from Bill for anal sex, which Jenny refused. At the same time, Jenny began to see Winston individually from time to time.

In the spring of 1977, Winston recommended that Jackson undertake a course of "insight therapy" to deal with the personality disorder underlying his manic depression. Winston proposed that they meet three times a week for an indefinite period. Jackson would lie on the couch and be encouraged to fantasize and free-associate—about his childhood, his parents, and especially his dreams. Jackson agreed, and insight therapy was undertaken for the next two years.

In April 1978, Jackson hired Ann Costa as an assistant. Jackson began having erotic dreams about Costa, which he transcribed in a bedside notebook. Jenny Jackson, without her husband's knowledge, read his description of a sexual encounter with Costa and confronted him about having an affair. He denied it, saying it was only a dream.

The following August, Jenny returned with the kids from a trip to Minnesota to find strands of blond hair on the couch, champagne bottles and burned-down candles in the garbage. She again confronted Bill about an affair. This time, he admitted that he had been having an affair with Ann Costa during the summer and that she had been in their home while Jenny was away. Jenny demanded that Bill phone Costa immediately—that Sunday evening—and fire her while she listened on the other line. Bill complied with Jenny's demand. So Ann Costa was out of the picture, but not out of Bill Jackson's mind. Jenny would later tell the jury: "[Bill] indicated that he found Ann more pleasurable as a sexual partner because she had not had children and . . . her vagina was tighter. . . . He suggested that there was an operation I could have to tighten me up."

The Jacksons discussed Bill's affair with Winston in joint therapy sessions. Bill agreed that if he were contemplating another affair in the future, he would tell Jenny about it, but he would not promise not to have another affair. With that, the Jackson marriage took a turn for the worse, and Jenny began to see Winston twice a week in therapy.

In April 1979, Jenny told Bill that the marriage was over and asked for a separation. Bill put a fist through the bathroom wall, threw the mattress Jenny was sitting on across the room, threatened to destroy her, abandon the kids, and burn the house down. He then loaded the family silver and her jewelry into his car and drove over to Ann Costa's house. He was chagrined to discover that Costa was not interested in renewing their relationship. (At the trial, Costa would deny that there had ever been a sexual relationship between them.)

Winston's bills were beginning to strain the Jackson budget. Between the two of them, Bill and Jenny were in therapy five times each week at $50 per session, generating monthly bills of about $1,000. Bill Jackson's income had suffered from his struggle with manic depression, and Jenny was unemployed. They now faced the additional expenses of separation and divorce.

Jenny Jackson had her last paying session with Winston in late April. On May 4, Bill Jackson stopped going to thrice-weekly insight therapy, citing financial reasons. On May 28, at Jenny's insistence, Bill moved out of the family home. Although formal custody arrangements had not yet been worked out, the children lived in the family home with Jenny and visited Bill.

FIREWORKS AND FALLOUT

At about the same time, things began to heat up between Jenny Jackson and Philip Winston. Jenny expressed warm feelings for him in her final therapy sessions in April. According to Winston, they discussed how she felt and decided she was not in transference with her psychiatrist, but that she was experiencing true feelings for the real Philip Winston. For his part, Winston stated that "she was still my patient. I did not have the feeling of wanting her then."

A few weeks later, however, Jenny was in Winston's office "as a friend" when he told her he "loved her and wanted to reach out to her." Shortly after that, and only days after Bill had moved out, Winston started going to the Jackson home in the evenings after the children were in bed, and going to bed with Jenny. They cemented their relationship in early June, when they spent four days at a resort lodge in the Ozark Mountains. Their affair progressed smoothly until Friday night, July 6, when Winston got careless parking his Karmann Ghia.

After the shotgun blast, the handcuffs, and the trip to the magistrate, life continued to be difficult for Bill Jackson. He went voluntarily to the psychiatric ward of a local hospital, where he stayed for three days. On the Sunday morning after the Friday-night fracas, Jackson recalled, he was standing with a nurse, looking out a window of his ward, when he saw a familiar car approaching. "And I said 'Hey, that's my wife,' and sure enough, there was my wife driving my old Buick, coming up to the turn to the hospital. As she drove by, I could see in the back seat Philip Winston with his arms around my two children." Jenny Jackson appeared on the ward later with Bill's hospital psychiatrist. She told Bill that she loved Winston. She gave him get-well notes from their two boys, written on Winston's prescription pad.

Discharged the next day, Jackson was intent on revenge. A friend tipped him off to the whereabouts of Winston's Karmann Ghia. Jackson found the car unlocked, removed a suitcase and briefcase, and slashed two of Winston's tires. Jackson then drove to Winston's office. Winston wasn't there, so he uprooted Winston's rosebushes. He opened Winston's briefcase and found BankAmericard charge slips dated the preceding weekend from a Holiday Inn in Davenport, Iowa, and a Robert's Restaurant in Clinton, Iowa. He also found a towel from his home wrapped around four Oriental silk prints. The prints had been given to him and Jenny twelve years earlier as a wedding gift.

Jackson left the suitcase and briefcase on the doorstep of Winston's office and, following the trail from the restaurant charge slip, drove to

Clinton, Iowa. He found Robert's Restaurant directly across the street from a motel, and in the motel parking lot he saw his 1955 Buick. It was 1 A.M. Jackson stayed up all night. He called his lawyer and his parents, who agreed to drive up from Florida to help. He let the air out of the two back tires of the Buick and removed its distributor cap. About 7:30 A.M., Jenny and the two boys came out of their motel room. The boys ran to him.

Jackson took his boys back to the family home and found it in disarray. There were dirty plates and trash scattered in the kitchen. In the boys' rooms, the drawers had been pulled out and clothes were strewn about. The bed in the master bedroom was unmade from Friday night; there were black hairs, semen stains, and candle wax on the sheets. Winston had left a *Treasury of Great Poems* behind.

Jackson's parents arrived as promised, and the boys lived with them in the family home for about a year. The Jacksons were divorced in January 1981. When they couldn't agree on custody, there was a contested hearing, after which Jenny was awarded custody and occupancy of the family home. Jenny later moved the boys back to Minnesota, making it hard for Bill to visit them.

Bill Jackson's losses were economic as well as emotional. His income from his veterinary practice declined substantially in 1979, compared with prior years. The incident and subsequent events had impaired his ability to concentrate. Jackson had paid Winston $17,396.50 for therapy, mostly for himself.

In the meantime, life was difficult for Dr. Winston, as well. Over the weekend, he and Jenny had fled to motels with the kids, remembering the shotgun and fearing for their lives. When he returned to Cedar Rapids on Monday, Winston met with his partners in his group practice. They decided that Winston should withdraw from the practice, and recommended that he enter the Menninger Clinic program for impaired therapists. Unfortunately, the program was full.

Winston flew to Colorado Springs the next day, intending to enter another psychiatric facility, but it, too, was full. Winston entered outpatient therapy. He also obtained a license to practice in Colorado and got a job on a hospital psychiatric ward.

JACKSON V. WINSTON

Bill Jackson sued Dr. Philip Winston for malpractice in August 1979, almost before the shotgun smoke had cleared. The thrust of the case was that the defendant Winston had caused the plaintiff's wife to commit adultery with him; that the defendant should have known that the plaintiff, his patient, would discover the adultery; and that it would cause him "severe psychological damage." Plaintiff Jackson demanded a judgment against defendant Winston for $1 million, plus $17,396.50 in fee refunds.

Like most psychiatrists, Winston carried malpractice insurance. Not only did the insurance company lawyers contest Jackson's suit, they filed a counterclaim based on the shotgun incident and the slashed tires. According to the counterclaim, Bill Jackson had "wantonly" pointed a shotgun at Winston and "discharged the aforesaid shotgun," putting Winston "in apprehension and great mental anguish and distress." (The counterclaim did not mention that the defendant had just climbed out of bed with the plaintiff's wife.) The counterclaim alleged that the tires on the Karmann Ghia were worth $85 and that their slashing had caused "mental anguish to the defendant Winston."

Two years later, after depositions and the usual delays, the case went to trial before a judge and jury. The following facts were undisputed: Bill and Jenny Jackson had been Winston's patients; Winston had started sleeping with Jenny in June 1979, a week or so after both the Jacksons and the Winstons had separated. In addition, and somewhat surprisingly, the defense conceded that it was unethical for a psychiatrist to sleep with his patient's wife.

Sex with the Patient's Wife

Jackson v. Winston was a landmark case when it was tried in 1981 and affirmed by an appellate court in 1983. By that time, it was well established that a psychiatrist could not ethically have sexual relations with a patient and that such an ethical violation could also serve as the basis for a damage suit. But until the *Jackson* decision, there were no precedents for a malpractice suit against a psychiatrist for seducing the spouse of a patient.

Despite the lack of such precedents, Winston and his lawyers apparently made a tactical decision not to argue that psychiatrists are free to bed their patients' wives. They might have surmised that the jurors would find wife-of-a-patient seduction even more offensive than patient seduction—where, transference aside, the patient at least appears to be a willing participant. But even with Winston's concession, Jackson's lawyers were determined to put their position on the record.

Experts are chosen for their credentials, their knowledge, and, above all, their ability to impress a jury. Jackson's lead expert, psychiatrist Elissa Benedek, was a good choice. Dr. Benedek was employed by the Michigan Department of Mental Health and had practiced privately for more than twenty years. She had taught at the University of Michigan and served as a consultant to the National Institute of Mental Health. She had written three books and numerous journal articles. Being married and the mother of four added a human dimension to her professional standing.

Dr. Benedek roundly condemned sex with a patient's wife. "The whole foundation of psychiatric treatment is trust and confidence. If the psychiatrist is having sexual relations with your wife, it is absolutely impossible to ever trust him again. That's a violation of every single part of the treatment contract." Moreover, Benedek thought, the patient's ability to form the trust necessary to benefit from psychiatric treatment would be undermined, rendering previous and future therapy useless.

Having conceded that sex with a patient's wife is wrong, Winston and his lawyers didn't have much room to maneuver. But they thought they saw an opening. They would claim that Winston had terminated his therapy, and his doctor-patient relationship, with both Bill and Jenny Jackson—in May and April, respectively—*before* he began his affair with Jenny in June. Since the Jackson couple was no longer in treatment with him, it was permissible for him to have an affair with Jenny.

Bill Jackson's position was that his doctor-patient relationship with Winston had not been terminated until he caught Winston in bed with his wife. As a fallback, Jackson contended that even if the relationship had terminated earlier, Winston could not ethically seduce his wife so soon after terminating therapy with him. Much of the trial testimony focused on when Winston had terminated therapy with Bill Jackson.

Termination

By May 1979, Bill Jackson had been in insight therapy thrice weekly for about two years. At the same time, Winston had been giving Jackson prescriptions for manic depression medication and monitoring his lithium level by blood testing. Jackson was having a hard time paying his therapy bills, the therapy didn't seem to be going anywhere, and he had just learned that he faced the added expenses of a separation. The Jacksons had not yet signed a separation agreement, but at that point, Jenny was asking for the house, the kids, and $1,000 a month in alimony.

On May 4, Bill Jackson kept his next-to-last appointment with Winston. As he recalled the session, he had been "torn apart" by Jenny's surprise separation request and had "poured out his heart" to his therapist about it. Since Winston had been seeing Jenny in therapy for months, Bill wanted to know what was going on, and why, all of a sudden, his wife of twelve years was asking him to leave. Winston only commented enigmatically, "Jenny keeps her own good counsel."

Jackson told Winston that he had decided to terminate thrice-weekly insight therapy for his personality disorder because he couldn't afford it any longer. (Winston later testified—without any apparent irony—that Jackson's personality had prevented him from benefiting from therapy for his personality disorder.) At a minimum, however, Jackson would have to keep seeing a psychiatrist to have his lithium medication monitored. If he were to stop taking lithium, he would risk another manic episode, with possibly serious consequences. According to Jackson, he told Winston that he wanted to continue with him on an every-other-month basis for lithium monitoring. Winston concurred in that approach, wrote an appointment in his book for two months later, and gave Jackson a prescription to help him sleep.

Winston recalled the session differently: Jackson had told him that he was unhappy with Winston for failing to keep the Jackson marriage together, and that he wanted to terminate therapy with Winston altogether. Winston had agreed to a complete termination, saying he could no longer see a couple in the Jacksons' situation because his marriage was breaking up, too.

A week later, Winston wrote a peculiar letter to Jackson.

Dear Bill:

I have told Jenny, as I had mentioned to you, that I don't feel I can be an unbiased and objective therapist to either of you at present, but had hoped to wind the therapy down a bit more gradually than just stopping all at once as you felt was necessary. I also offered to continue to see either of you as a friend, rather than a therapist, and I suspect Jenny will take me up on that for awhile. . . . I would like to be on hand to refill your medication when needed and at some time in the future months discuss therapy options with you, if you wish. Meanwhile I will be interested in hearing from you and keeping up with you as a friend. . . .

Sincerely,
Philip Winston

Winston's letter didn't fit the facts. The Jacksons' needs for joint therapy were separate from the manic depression problems Bill Jackson had brought to Winston in the first place. While it might have been understandable that Winston—with his own marriage falling apart—would not want to do joint therapy with another troubled couple, there was no reason that he couldn't continue to treat Bill individually for manic depression.

Jackson didn't view Winston's letter as a termination of their relationship. Dr. Benedek agreed: "We have a duty not to abandon patients." Once a relationship is established, the doctor is obliged to continue treatment or to help the patient find another doctor. Termination must be done thoughtfully, over a period of time, so that patients can work through their feelings about leaving. And once termination is completed, the relationship is over completely. According to Benedek, "A doctor does not terminate a relationship by saying to a patient . . . I will continue to see you as a friend."

Dr. Alan Roses, Jackson's other expert, also had strong credentials. Roses was a professor and chief of the Division of Neurology at Duke University School of Medicine and a fellow of the American Boards of Psychiatry and Neurology. Roses summed up the termination concept succinctly: "One doesn't just say goodbye." He agreed with Dr. Benedek that Winston's letter to Jackson had not been adequate as a letter of termination. "He didn't terminate the care. The writer of the letter . . . 'would like to be on hand to refill your medication as needed and discuss therapy options.' That is not a termination of care. It's a continuation of care."

Defendant Winston also produced an expert, Dr. Jason Winters. Although Winters was well qualified—he had psychoanalytic training and teaching experience at the university level—as one of Winston's former partners his objectivity was open to question. Winters testified that it was possible to terminate a patient by letter. But Winston's lawyer didn't ask Winters the logical follow-up question—whether Winston's letter to Jackson had terminated their doctor-patient relationship. He may have been afraid of what the answer would be.

Apart from its literal terms, the Winston letter to Jackson is understandable in context: Winston knew when he wrote it that he intended to embark on an affair with his patient's wife. He had already terminated therapy with the wife and wanted something in writing to show that he had terminated with the husband as well. And with knowledge of the Jacksons' plans for an imminent separation, Winston had agreed with his wife to separate at the same time, opening a clear path for him to Jenny Jackson. Seen in that context, Winston's letter was a self-serving device to cover his own flank.

On July 5, Jackson kept the appointment he had made with Winston on May 4. Jackson recalled commiserating with Winston about the latter's separation. He also recalled Winston's saying he had a problem being a therapist both for him and for Jenny, and that he had suggested Jackson seek psychiatric care elsewhere. By that time, however, Winston had been sleeping with Jenny for about a month.

Winston had different recollections of the July 5 session. Jackson had called a few days before July 5 for an appointment, and he happened to have time open. Winston thought it was a coincidence that July 5 was two months after the May 4 appointment—two months being the recommended interval for lithium monitoring. Winston testified that he had not known why Jackson wanted to see him and that they had spent the time discussing other therapists for Jackson. Winston's notes and appointment book should have shed some light on whether Jackson had terminated on May 4. Winston undermined his own credibility by testifying that he had lost his notes and book.

Although the jury did not make an explicit finding that a doctor-patient relationship between Winston and Jackson had continued into July 1979, such a finding is implicit in their verdict. But even if the jury had found—against the weight of the evidence—that Jackson had been terminated in May, there was an alternative basis for awarding damages to him.

Sex after Therapy?

In the past, it has not been unusual for psychiatrists to become involved with, and sometimes marry, former patients. More recently, such relationships have become controversial, and the American Psychiatric Association has taken the position that they are always unethical. Some fourteen states have enacted some form of criminal sanction against therapist sex with a former patient.

Dr. Paul Appelbaum, director of the Law and Psychiatry Program at the University of Massachusetts School of Medicine, expresses a minority view, opposing a total ban on sex with former patients. Appelbaum agrees, however, that there should be a one-year "cooling off" period during which there would be no contact between therapist and former patient. Winston waited about one month after termination before having sex with Jenny Jackson. At the trial, he conceded that "when I look back on it, I understand how very premature all of that was."

Dr. Glen Gabbard, a psychiatrist at the Menninger Clinic, explained the dangers of sex with an ex-patient. "Termination of treatment does not make intimacy safe. . . . Several studies have suggested that sex with a former patient instantly reactivates the transference and intensifies it. . . . Accepting post-termination intimacy would drastically change the therapeutic process. Therapists would be free to use their practices as a dating service."

Dr. Gabbard's reasoning would have made a malpractice case for Jenny Jackson against Winston, but probably not for Bill. It was her transference, not his, that would have been "reactivated" when she and Winston went to bed together. For different reasons, however, a ban on sex with the spouse of a former patient is equally justifiable. As Dr. Benedek explained at the trial, "There are a whole range of consequences to discovering . . . your psychiatrist in bed with your wife. . . . There's humiliation, there's emasculation."

Winston's lawyers didn't attempt to counter Dr. Benedek's testimony directly. Instead, they tried to convince the jury that Winston's love for Jenny was true and that the Jackson marriage had been "completely broken" before he expressed his feelings for her. Winston declared from the witness stand, "I love her very much. I wish to marry her." Jenny appeared as a witness for Winston. "I love him very much," she said.

The jury may have been convinced that Philip Winston and Jenny Jackson loved one another. But that was no comfort to Bill Jackson, even assuming that Winston had terminated Jackson as a patient about a month before their affair began. A former patient has a right to expect his psychiatrist to stay away from his wife for a lot longer than that.

A Porous Defense

Winston's lawyers called only three witnesses, in addition to Winston. Their testimony leaves one wondering why they were called. The apparent reason for calling Ann Costa, Jackson's erstwhile assistant and occasional lunch companion, was to portray Jackson as a philanderer, thereby tarring him in the eyes of the jury. In a previous deposition, however, Costa had denied ever having sex with Jackson. The most she would admit on the witness stand were two chaste kisses, on separate occasions, and some reciprocal commiseration over their marital difficulties. Costa stuck to her story on the witness stand.

Dr. Winters, Winston's former partner, testified about several abstract points, but he had little to say about the concrete case before the court. His principal contribution probably helped Jackson more than Winston. Winters described a meeting of their group practice on July 9 in which Winston was asked "not to see any patients until he had a full evaluation." Winters expressed his opinion that Winston may have needed psychiatric treatment at that time and that his judgment had been impaired in the period May–July 1979. Winters, the only expert witness for Winston, all but admitted by this testimony that Winston had committed malpractice by seeing patients while he was impaired.

Winston took the stand in his own defense. Having already conceded most of the case, he did little to help his own cause. Jenny Jackson was the last witness for Winston. Apparently, she was called for the same reason as Ann Costa—to make Bill Jackson look bad. She did a better job of it. Jenny went over Bill's manic behavior, the alleged Costa affair, pressure from Bill for anal sex and to have her vagina tightened, Bill's threat to kill her when he found her with Winston, even some ancient history—an affair Bill had while in veterinary school. Her message: the Jacksons had a bad marriage, so Philip Winston shouldn't have to pay heavily for breaking it up.

Bill Jackson undoubtedly was a difficult man to live with. He had a serious mental illness, manic depression, which in his case was only partly controlled by medication. He was quick to anger, insensitive, and impulsive. He cheated on his wife. But Bill Jackson had some good qualities, too. He worked hard. He appeared to be a good father. He could acknowledge his problems, and he went into therapy to gain better understanding and control of himself. Winston owed his patient—with all his flaws—conduct worthy of his trust. Instead, Winston betrayed his patient by taking his wife. The jury understood that.

The Jury's Verdict

After six days of testimony, the judge instructed the jury and sent them to deliberate. The jury returned a verdict for Bill Jackson and awarded him a substantial amount of money: for his claim of "criminal conversation" (adultery), $50,670; for that of medical malpractice, $102,000; and an additional $500,000 in punitive damages—for a total award of $652,670. The jury also returned a verdict for Winston on his counterclaim. For personal injuries, he won $3,000; for his damaged tires, $85.

POSTSCRIPTS

Winston appealed the trial court's decision, which was affirmed. While the first appeal was pending, Winston's malpractice insurance company refused to pay the trial court's judgment. The company argued that its policy didn't obligate it to pay punitive damages, representing the bulk of Bill Jackson's award. Jackson sued the insurance company and won. The insurance company appealed, and, once again, Jackson won on appeal. So Jackson and his lawyer finally got their money, five years after the fateful night.

Dr. Winston's relationship with Jenny Jackson cost him his license to practice psychiatry in Iowa, but he later managed to obtain another license in a western state (a practice now made difficult by required reporting to the National Computer Bank). After his insurance company paid the judgment and Jenny joined him in the West, it appeared that his life was taking a turn for the better. Then one day, one of his patients walked into his office with a 9-millimeter pistol and shot him several times before turning the pistol on himself. Winston was taken to the hospital in critical condition but somehow survived.

CHAPTER 14
▼ ▼ ▼

Sex as "Part of the Therapy"

> The necessary intensity of the therapeutic relationship may tend to activate sexual and other needs and fantasies on the part of both patient and therapist, while weakening the objectivity necessary for control.
> —American Psychiatric Association,
> *The Principles of Medical Ethics*

Psychotherapists, more than other healers, have to struggle with intense emotions between themselves and their patients. Erotic feelings between therapist and patient arose in the very first psychotherapy. In 1880, Joseph Breuer was treating Anna O. (to whom the phrase "talking cure" is attributed) by hypnosis. Breuer became, as therapists would say today, "overinvolved." Ernest Jones, Freud's biographer, reported Freud's description of what happened.

> Breuer developed a strong countertransference to his patient. His wife became bored at listening to no other topic. Perhaps compounded of love and guilt, he brought the treatment to an end. That evening he was fetched back to find [Anna O.] in the throes of an hysterical childbirth. He managed to calm her down and then fled the house in a cold sweat. The next day he and his wife left for Venice for a second honeymoon.

Doctors since ancient times have taken the Hippocratic Oath to abstain from sexual relationships with their patients—"with women or with men, be they free or bonded." Recognizing that "a kiss signifies a certain erotic intimacy," Freud endorsed the Hippocratic ban on sex with patients. Nevertheless, some of the early psychoanalysts had sex with their patients, including Carl Jung, Otto Rank, and Ernest Jones. Sandor Ferenczi, a member of Freud's inner circle, took as a patient the daughter of a woman he was having an affair with, and then fell in love with the daughter. Predicaments like Ferenczi's have generated ironic jokes, like the story of a judge who allowed a psychiatrist to continue having sex with his patient—if he promised not to enjoy it.

Freud's position eventually prevailed. The American Psychiatric Association's code of ethics states unequivocally, "Sexual activity with a patient is unethical." The ethical codes of the other professional associations—the American Psychological Association, the National Association of Social Workers, and the American Association for Marriage and Family Therapy—also prohibit sexual contact with patients. Although rumor had it that a few therapists defended sex in psychotherapy in the 1960s and early 1970s, that position has never been embraced by any identifiable school of psychotherapy.

HOW PREVALENT IS SEX IN THERAPY?

Ethical bans on sex in therapy are backed by the threat of license revocation, malpractice suits for damages, ruinous publicity, and, in a growing number of states, criminal penalties. Despite all that, some therapists do it anyway—often explaining that sex is "part of the therapy." A cynical inside joke has it that "you can get away with having sex with your patient, if you keep on having sex with your patient. The trouble starts when you stop."

No one knows how many therapists abuse their patients sexually. It would be hard to conduct systematic research into behavior that is both illegal and unethical. Most offenders wouldn't risk jeopardizing their careers by admitting it. Out of fear or shame, most victims don't come forward.

The most commonly cited data come from a series of self-report studies in which various groups of professionals were mailed anonymous questionnaires and asked if they had had sexual contact with patients. From the first study, published in 1972, to more recent ones, return rates ranged from 16 to 50 percent. The questions varied considerably, so the data are hard to compare. Some surveys asked about sexual intercourse, some asked about sex "with a patient," while others clearly differentiated current and former patients.

The results of all these studies were wide-ranging and of limited value. Between 2 and 18 percent of male therapists acknowledge having sex with a current or former patient, compared with 0 to 4 percent of female therapists. The psychologists produced the highest numbers, the psychiatrists were close behind in second place, and the social workers came in a distant third.

A 1985 national survey of psychiatrists by Dr. Nanette Gartrell and others points up the limitations of such surveys. In the Gartrell survey, an anonymous questionnaire was mailed to 5,574 randomly selected psychiatrists; 1,423 (26 percent) were returned. Survey results were based on 1,316 respondents who answered the question about sexual contact. Eighty-four (6.4 percent) of those respondents admitted having sexual contact with 144 different patients.

There are several reasons to believe that, in the real world, more than 6.4 percent of psychiatrists have sex with their patients. Given the self-incriminating nature of such questionnaires, even with anonymity, complete candor can hardly be expected. Turning to specifics, 107 survey respondents (7.5 percent) answered other questions but not the sexual contact question. If most of them had answered that question with admissions of guilt, the percentage of offenders might have doubled. And among those who did return the questionnaire but denied sexual contact with patients, some might have been lying. Assuming that psychiatrists who have sex with their patients are as apt to lie about this as lawyers or clergymen who do likewise, that number could be significant. But the offender-therapist confronted with this question doesn't have to duck it or give a dishonest response. The easiest way out, of course, is to throw the questionnaire away, as more than four thousand psychiatrists—72 percent of the survey sample—did.

Most of the sexual contacts (63 percent) reported in the Gartrell survey were with *former* patients, and most of those contacts (also 63 percent) were initiated within the first six months of termination. As we saw in chapter 13, it hasn't been uncommon for therapists to become involved with and later marry former patients, but the ethics of sex after treatment, in or out of wedlock, are controversial. An anonymous psychiatrist, a thirty-two-year-old divorced man, endorsed the American Psychiatric Association's position: "Once someone walks through the door as a patient, they can *never* be a friend, lover, etc. That still leaves me with about 5 billion other people to be involved with."

The Gartrell survey was reported in the *American Journal of Psychiatry*, giving it credibility and wide circulation in the profession. Acknowledging some of the survey's limitations, the survey investigators nevertheless offered the "conservative" estimate that "6%–10% of psychiatrists have had sexual contact with patients." Those limitations, and the results of other surveys, indicate that 10 to 15 percent would be a more reasonable estimate. Some investigators have gone farther, suggesting that a more accurate figure would approach 20 percent.

Three surveys conducted since the late 1970s have looked at sex between psychologists and their clients. The first two yielded almost identical results: about 12 percent of male psychologists and 3 percent of female psychologists admitted having sex with one or more patients. The most recent survey, conducted in the late 1980s, indicated only a slight decline—10 percent of male and 2.5 percent of female psychologists—despite educational campaigns by the American Psychological Association.

A survey of one thousand social workers indicated that only about 4 percent of male, and virtually no female, social workers have sexual contact with clients. These comparatively modest statistics may be due to factors other than superior virtue. Most social workers are women, and, for whatever reason, female therapists are less likely to seduce their clients. Apart from that, most social workers do traditional social work, not therapy, and they work for agencies where opportunities for sex would be limited.

The more repeat offenders there are out there, the bigger the problem—particularly since most offenders don't get caught. The Gartrell survey of psychiatrists is deceptively reassuring on that score. It found that two-thirds of the admitted offenders had been sexually involved with only one patient, and most of the remaining third with two. Only 13 percent admitted involvement with three or more.

Other evidence points to a more serious repeat offender problem. Another study found that 80 percent of offender-therapists—more than double the 1985 survey finding—abuse more than one patient. The Gartrell survey itself found that *two-thirds* of responding therapists had counseled at least one patient who had been sexually abused by a prior therapist. It's hard to reconcile that finding with an offender rate of 10 percent or less and few repeat offenders—especially when one takes into account that many victims don't return to therapy after being abused. (One might speculate, however, that therapists who *had* counseled abused patients might be more likely to respond to a questionnaire on that subject than therapists who had never been confronted with the problem.)

The surveys, with their inherent limitations, will never yield an accurate estimate of the problem. One survey can "prove" one number, another survey a number three times as big, with about equal validity. But the sheer volume of complaints bespeaks a continuing problem. Gary Schoener, a psychologist and recognized authority on the subject, is executive director of the Walk-In Counseling Center in Minneapolis. Schoener reports that since 1974, his center has consulted in more than three thousand cases of sexual misconduct by therapists, clergy, and other mental health professionals—most of whom were therapists or counselors. Whatever its true dimensions, sex in therapy remains a major problem and a disgrace to a profession of healers.

IT DOESN'T JUST HAPPEN: BOUNDARY VIOLATIONS AND TRANSFERENCE

In T. S. Eliot's play *The Cocktail Party*, one character chides another for indulging in "the luxury of an intimate disclosure to a stranger." While harmless at cocktail parties, intimate disclosures by a therapist to his patient are one kind of boundary violation, a luxury neither can afford. Instead of keeping his emotional distance, the therapist is indulging his own needs and making emotional demands on the patient he is supposed to be single-mindedly helping. He may also be taking the first steps down the slippery slope to sex with his patient.

A 1961 English case involved some seemingly innocuous boundary violations. A London psychiatrist who took his patient to tea and visited her once in her apartment was found liable for malpractice. Somewhat bolder boundary violations—stopping short of sex—have become more prominent in malpractice cases than they were before the major health insurers excluded sex in therapy from malpractice coverage (see discussion later in this chapter). Dinner dates and trips together may be easier to prove than sex, and a series of such violations can lead to liability.

We looked at the phenomena of transference and countertransference in the story of Dr. Jonathan Fox and Joan Barkley in chapter 12. When the patient goes into transference, a strong sexual attraction may then develop, and the patient may imagine she has fallen in love with the therapist. When that happens, the patient is a virtual setup for sex with the therapist, particularly if other personality traits predispose her in that direction. One psychiatrist has called this "the sitting duck syndrome."

In addition to that syndrome, there can be a synergistic interaction between boundary violations and the kind of sexualized transference Barkley developed for Fox. A hug or a cocktail after therapy fuels transference feelings; those feelings may embolden both patient and therapist to further boundary violations, and later to sex.

Countertransference, it will be recalled, involves the therapist's projection of his feelings, including sexual feelings, onto the patient. One judge has called sexual countertransference an "occupational hazard" of psychotherapy. In any case, the therapist is supposed to control his feelings, not act on them. If he has strong sexual feelings for the patient, he should seek consultation with, and possibly ongoing supervision by, another therapist. If the feelings persist, he probably should transfer the patient to another therapist. But he should never succumb to his sexual attraction for his patient.

TYPES OF OFFENDER-THERAPISTS

Experts in the field have suggested that certain kinds of personal backgrounds and characteristics are common in therapists who become sexually involved. The evidence is largely anecdotal, coming mainly from the experience of individual clinicians, and the profiles of different types are not sharply etched.

Dr. Thomas Gutheil, codirector of Harvard's Program in Psychiatry and the Law, has been an expert witness in scores of sexual misconduct cases. Gutheil identified several types of therapists, male and female, who become involved in sex with patients. The most common type is "a middle-aged male therapist [who] begins to talk to a female patient about his marital, professional, and financial problems. These confidences may create a role reversal in which the therapist is covertly or overtly asking the patient for help. The 'help' then turns into sexual intimacy." Gutheil labeled this type the "Willie Loman syndrome" after the salesman-father in Arthur Miller's *Death of a Salesman*.

A second common type of male offender is manic or grandiose, with exhibitionist tendencies he expresses by revealing secrets to his patients or by displaying what he considers his unique qualities. The therapist considers himself a special person and thinks he can break the rules with special patients.

Gutheil's female offender types include: the therapist with hysterical character traits who becomes "emotionally flooded" and yields to sexual attraction for a male patient; the lesbian therapist whose nurturant feelings for a female patient lose their boundaries, turn into a maternal relationship, and later become sexual.

Harvard professor Alan Stone also identified several offender types, including the sexually "liberated" therapist who believes that liberation includes sex with patients, and the introverted therapist who is uncomfortable with human intimacy and succumbs to a patient who has an intense sexualized transference. According to Stone, the latter type "believes he has been seduced, but he feels very guilty nonetheless, and is very apt to confess."

The sheer number of offender types may suggest that sexual misconduct is even more widespread than it is. In fact, most therapists are ethical and competent, including some who may appear to—but don't—fit an offender type. On the other hand, the types, while they fit many offender therapists, probably don't include them all.

The public may associate a defrocked therapist with "the dirty old man" living on the fringe. In recent years, however, a few of the most distinguished members of the profession have had their sexual involvements with patients come to light. Dr. Jules Masserman, an internationally known psychiatrist, was the object of numerous sexual abuse complaints in the 1980s. Barbara Noel's best-selling book, *You Must Be Dreaming*, describes how Masserman had intercourse with her while she was sedated in his Chicago office. Masserman settled with Noel for $200,000. He surrendered his license to practice rather than face disciplinary proceedings, but continued to profess his innocence.

Dr. Edward Daniels, a Boston psychoanalyst, had been president of the Boston Psychoanalytic Society and Institute, held a faculty appointment at Harvard Medical School, and had trained many of the analysts in the Boston area. Four female former patients complained to Massachusetts licensing authorities that Daniels had abused them sexually during therapy over the preceding thirty years. Three of the four testified that Daniels had intercourse and oral sex with them repeatedly during therapy. The fourth testified that Daniels had masturbated her. Daniels was expelled from the psychoanalytic society, stripped of his license to practice, and no longer teaches at Harvard. Three of the four victims later became mental health professionals.

Attempts to compile patient-victim profiles have been unsuccessful. Victims come in a broad range of ages and diagnostic categories; they may be married or single, attractive or plain, highly educated or not. The only common characteristics are gender (female) and being considerably younger than the therapist—about fifteen years.

Just as there is no way to determine accurately how many therapists have sex with their patients, there is no way to know what percentage of the accusations of unethical sex by patients against therapists are true. On the basis of clinical and litigation experience, however, experts generally agree that the overwhelming majority of patient allegations are true. According to Dr. Thomas Gutheil, who has had extensive experience as a consultant and expert witness on both sides of sexual misconduct cases, "false accusations represent a minuscule fraction of total accusations." The relatively few false accusations tend to come from patients who are resentful about billings or seek revenge for perceived rejections, particularly termination of therapy. Some may be pathological liars.

PROVING THAT SEX OCCURRED

Assume a defendant male therapist in a malpractice case falsely denies having had sex with the female plaintiff, a former patient. How can the patient prove the act? In most cases, everything happened in the privacy of the therapist's office, and it's the patient's word against the therapist's. Sometimes the victim can testify to something only an intimate would know—such as a birthmark, a tattoo, or an uncircumcised penis.

Diaries written during the course of therapy describing sexual activity can often be admitted as evidence in court as an exception to the so-called hearsay rule. Diary entries that describe sex in detail can be persuasive evidence that sex occurred. Joan Barkley's diaries in the *Fox* case, discussed in chapter 12, were rich in detail, leading a reader to believe she couldn't have made it all up.

Sometimes the offending therapist can be trapped if the victim is equal to the task. Some patients have made tape recordings of sessions, including sex—in rare cases, with the therapist's knowledge. Much the same might be accomplished by taping an incriminating telephone conversation with the therapist. Even without an explicit admission of sex, an intimate tone might convince a jury that a sexual relationship existed. In some states, however, taping is illegal.

The offending therapist may make a damaging admission to another person, which may come back to haunt him in court. Gary Schoener of the Walk-In Counseling Center reports that in several cases, messages left on an answering machine were discovered by a spouse. Recall that Dr. Fox, the military psychiatrist in chapter 12, remarked to his commanding officer that his court martial "was a hell of a price to pay for a minor indiscretion." Linda M. Jorgenson, a Boston attorney specializing in sexual misconduct cases, reports suing therapists who have said things like, "Why should I pay for the abortion when I'm not sure it's my child."

The problems of proving sexual misconduct may be lessened when the therapist has been indiscreet—by socializing with the victim in public or by moving the sexual venue to a hotel. When the psychiatrist's lawyer learns at the victim's deposition that she can testify about the decor of his client's bedroom, it's time for him to get serious about settling the case. Telephone records may also be helpful to the plaintiff if the therapist was in the habit of calling her at home or at work.

Testimony by other patients that they, too, have been seduced by the same therapist can have a powerful impact. The therapist's lawyer would argue that sex with other patients can't be used to prove that his client had sex with the plaintiff. So-called other acts evidence is often excluded in court because it's considered not sufficiently relevant and unduly prejudicial. But other acts evidence is admitted, for example, if the defendant used a "common scheme"—for example, an unusual seduction technique—with several former patients. Barbara Noel's book, *You Must Be Dreaming*, describes a classic common scheme: a psychiatrist who sedated patients and had sex with them before they woke up.

DAMAGES

If the plaintiff can prove that sex occurred, separate questions about damages remain: in what ways, and how seriously, was the patient injured, and what are the injuries worth in dollars? Experts say that 90 percent of victims are injured, but the kind and extent of their injuries vary widely.

Twenty years ago, Julie Roy sued her therapist, Dr. Renatus Hartogs, for sexual misconduct in one of the most highly publicized cases of its day. A New York City jury awarded her $154,000—$50,000 in compensatory and $104,000 in punitive damages. (Differences between the two types of damages are explained later in this chapter.) On appeal, Roy's compensatory damage award was reduced to $25,000, and her punitive damages were disallowed altogether. The appellate court expressed the curious view that Dr. Hartogs's conduct had been "inexcusable" but not "so wanton or reckless as to permit an award for punitive damages." So Roy ended up with a pyrrhic victory. Fortunately, she also got a book deal for her story. Her book, *Betrayed*, was followed by a television movie of the same name.

Since *Roy v. Hartogs*, courts have become more hospitable to sexual misconduct cases, and awards have gone up substantially. For patients with strong cases, six-figure verdicts are now common, especially if the facts are extreme. A Florida jury awarded $474,000 to an admitted ex-prostitute who, like Barbara Noel, had been seduced by her therapist while sedated. A Virginia jury awarded $650,000 against a therapist who had become sexually involved with a teenager hospitalized for schizophrenia. The highest verdict recorded to date is $7.1 million, awarded by a Florida jury in 1994.

The 1981 case of *Walker v. Parzen* involved a San Diego woman whose sexual relationship with her La Jolla psychiatrist destroyed her marriage and damaged both her physical and mental health. The case illustrates the severity of injuries that can result from sex in therapy and the value of a good lawyer in dramatizing them.

Walker's lawyer, Marvin Lewis of San Francisco, has been called the dean of psychiatric malpractice cases. His fame rests in part on his representation of a woman against the city of San Francisco for injuries she suffered in a cable car accident. The woman claimed that the accident had made her a nymphomaniac. Lewis won the case.

When Evelyn Walker went to Dr. Zane Parzen for her recurring depressions, she was living the middle-class dream—happily married, financially secure, the mother of two children in a four-bedroom house. Early in the therapy, Parzen introduced her to addictive drugs and initiated sex, which continued for over two years. By the time the five-foot-nine-inch Walker stopped seeing Parzen, she weighed less than one hundred pounds and was borderline psychotic.

Walker lost her husband, custody of her children, even her share of community property. As her malpractice case went to trial, she was making minimum wages in a carry-out restaurant. Walker was suicidal and would need several years of hospitalization, followed by psychiatric care for the rest of her life. A jury composed of ten women and two men awarded her $4,631,666. Marvin Lewis said of the verdict, "I don't think she got enough." He had asked the jury for $6,970,557.

The most serious injuries caused by sex in therapy are psychic, not physical, and may involve long-term deterioration of the patient's mental condition. A patient's reactions may range from anger at being exploited to full-fledged post-traumatic stress disorder. Many of the typical psychic consequences were illustrated by Joan Barkley (chapter 12). Her symptoms included feelings of emptiness, bondage to the therapist, guilt, suppressed rage, fear, anxiety, and increased suicidal risk. These symptoms, collectively, would be presented to the jury under the heading "pain and suffering"—often the largest component in the jury's verdict. The same symptoms may require long-term psychiatric treatment, which could generate heavy medical expenses. Future medical expenses are a major component of damages in many sexual misconduct cases.

The patient-therapist relationship is built on trust. Inability to trust is one of the most damaging and prevalent injuries caused by sex in therapy. It takes its toll on the victim's relationships. The victim also may be unable to trust other therapists who try to undo the damage. That happened to Joan Barkley, whose therapy with another psychiatrist after Dr. Fox "went nowhere."

Dr. Phyllis Chesler, a pioneer in the field, observed that "many therapists are lousy lovers. They may not be very good doctors either." The therapist who tries to be both doctor and lover loses his objectivity. The patient is not getting what she is paying for—the undivided attention of her therapist. Furthermore, sex in therapy may well destroy whatever had been accomplished before it began. Victims should be entitled to refunds of past payments for therapy—nowadays typically over $100 per session.

These, then, are the most common categories of compensatory damages in sexual misconduct cases. Some cases might also involve recovery of lost or future earnings. Part of Bill Jackson's award against Dr. Winston (chapter 13) was for impairment of his earning power as a veterinarian. Other types of damage can arise from unusual circumstances in a particular case.

The total of all categories of compensatory damages can be dwarfed by an award of punitive damages. "Punitives" are awarded not to compensate the plaintiff for a particular loss but to punish the defendant for wrongdoing. Punitive damages can't be awarded for "mere negligence"—such as an unintentional wrong diagnosis. But they can be awarded for intentional wrongdoing. Justice Oliver Wendell Holmes captured the distinction in everyday experience: "Even a dog knows the difference between being stumbled over and being kicked."

Sexual misconduct is a classic case for punitive damages. All mental health professionals *know* that they are not supposed to have sex with their patients, and that their patients probably will be harmed by such behavior. When they go ahead and have sex anyway, they are acting in deliberate defiance of the rules and of their patient's interest. There are no set limits on amounts of punitive damages. In the *Jackson* case, the jury awarded a total of $150,000 to compensate Bill Jackson for various real injuries and $500,000 in punitive damages. Although judges have the power to reduce punitive damages when they consider them excessive, big punitive damage awards are frequently allowed to stand.

BUT IS HE INSURED?

When the number of sexual misconduct cases first became substantial in the late 1970s, the typical malpractice policy covered any claim that arose out of the therapist's practice. Since sex usually occurred in the therapist's office, most courts held that the policy covered it, even though sex with patients was condemned by the profession. Since then, many malpractice insurance companies have rewritten their policies to limit or exclude coverage of sexual misconduct. If a therapist has such a limited policy and does not appear to have substantial assets, it may not be worthwhile to go to the expense—financial and emotional—of a lawsuit.

Most psychiatrists and psychologists are covered by umbrella malpractice policies written for their national associations. Until recently, the American Psychiatric Association took an enlightened approach, reasoning that patients injured by their members deserved to be compensated. Under its umbrella policy, sexual misconduct was fully covered. That policy has been amended to exclude altogether any claim involving sexual misconduct. The American Psychological Association's group policy includes a $25,000 cap on payments in any case involving sexual misconduct. Thus the psychiatrists and psychologists, through their national associations, effectively disclaim responsibility for their rogue members.

A knowledgeable lawyer can sometimes work around insurance policy exclusions of sexual misconduct. Attorney Linda Jorgenson reports that she doesn't claim sexual misconduct in cases involving such exclusions but relies, often successfully, on boundary violations to prove malpractice.

SEX IN THERAPY—ANY WAY TO STOP IT?

No. That's the short answer. But there may be ways to lessen it. It's been estimated that less than 10 percent of victims of sexual abuse report it. The unwillingness of most victims to come forward may be the biggest barrier to further progress. But this situation appears to be improving. Concerned mental health professionals and angry consumers have done a lot in some states to focus attention on the rights and remedies of abused patients. More victims are coming forward.

Experts have differing opinions on whether educating therapists can prevent sexual misconduct. Harvard professor Alan Stone, a prominent spokesman for the profession, concluded in 1984 that "no amount of training or personal psychoanalysis seems to confer immunity on therapists." In 1995, Dr. Seymour Halleck regretfully reported that in recent years he has "helped to kick out three residents [at the University of North Carolina Medical School] who were involved in sex with patients. They really had no remorse." However, Gary Schoener, executive director of the Walk-In Counseling Center, believes that education of therapists hasn't really been tried. According to Schoener, "Religious communities have created more preventive educational aids in five years than all the psychotherapy professions have in twenty."

Educating therapists to report their offending colleagues may be a more promising approach. About half of all psychiatrists have treated patients who have been sexually abused by a prior therapist. When prior abuse comes out in therapy, the psychiatrist may feel an ethical conflict between a duty of confidentiality to the client and a duty to report the offense. Schoener believes that this conflict should be resolved through mandatory reporting—the "snitch laws" already on the books in several states. Professor Stone points out that "the psychiatrist typically has only hearsay knowledge of wrongdoing," and that "even when one does recognize the often ignored affirmative duty to 'expose' such a colleague, one often feels helpless to do anything. Doing nothing, then, can become the accepted norm of professional behavior." There may also be a feeling that snitching on a colleague is as bad as seducing a patient, or, worse, that professional retribution will be visited on the snitch.

Enforcement by state licensing boards has been uneven. These boards are typically underfunded, slow to investigate, and slower to act. Their mounting caseloads have made increased personnel and funding priority needs. In the past, lack of coordination between state boards sometimes rendered them ineffective. However, the computerized National Practitioner Data Bank has now been implemented, providing all the boards with information about any disciplinary action against a therapist.

Professional associations are not structured to discipline their own members, even if they had the will to do so. When they do take action, their strongest sanction—expulsion—doesn't keep the former member from practicing because membership is not a requirement for practice. Expulsion can have some significant negative consequences, however. For example, it may be reported to the state licensing board, which may bring a disciplinary action based on the same conduct. Or it may make malpractice insurance more expensive or even unobtainable.

In 1975, Masters and Johnson—appalled by the number of their research subjects reporting sex with therapists—called for criminal sanctions. During the last decade, fourteen states have made it a crime, usually a felony, for a therapist to have sex with a patient, typically without regard to the patient's consent. It's too early to say whether criminal statutes will prove effective. They may be the only practical sanction against the unlicensed therapist. On the other hand, there have been concerns that they could be counterproductive, causing sex in therapy to be reported less frequently because colleagues and patients might be reluctant to expose the offender to criminal prosecution.

Mandatory liability insurance that covers sexual misconduct would be a helpful reform. Most therapists choose to carry insurance, but it's not legally required. Society can require people who engage in a hazardous activity to carry insurance. Every motor vehicle driver, for example, must be insured as a condition of holding a driver's license. By analogy, state legislatures could require therapists to carry comprehensive liability insurance. If that were done in several populous states, the group insurers for the American Psychiatric and Psychological Associations would have to drop their exclusion of sexual misconduct or lose many customers. Resentment over the higher premiums might make ethical therapists more willing to turn in their errant colleagues.

A civil suit for malpractice may be the best remedy for some victims of sex in therapy. It's the only remedy over which the victim has a degree of control. She can file suit and set in motion judicial machinery that will move forward to a decision, however slowly. Assuming the therapist is insured or has substantial means, a malpractice suit is the surest way a victim can be compensated for her injuries.

But there are disadvantages to the civil remedy which make it unsuitable for some. A civil suit can be hard on the former patient. The defense has wide latitude in probing her personal history, including her sexual history. By contrast, in many states, complaints to licensing boards are kept confidential, even from a spouse—perhaps especially from a spouse. It may be hard to hire a lawyer unless the patient has a strong case and the prospect of big (six-figure) damages. Expert witnesses may cost, say, $300 per hour. The patient may have to come up with large amounts (upwards of $25,000) for expenses, chiefly for expert witnesses, if the lawyer is unwilling to "front" expenses.

No one remedy is necessarily best for, or even available to, every victim of sexual abuse. Victims should discuss their situations, goals, and fears with a knowledgeable professional—perhaps both a lawyer and a therapist—before deciding what action to take.

CHAPTER 15
▼ ▼ ▼
Afterword

One purpose of this book is to tell stories about people that capture the reader's attention and sympathies. If I have succeeded in that, the stories could perhaps stand by themselves. But they have broader implications for patients, psychiatrists, and the lawyers and judges who run the system.

Many people who go to psychiatrists expect them, like other doctors, to be able to diagnose their problem and administer the right treatment. Patients and their families need to know that psychiatry is an uncertain branch of medicine, that well-qualified psychiatrists frequently disagree, that they deal more in judgment calls than in answers, and that the risk of a bad outcome is sometimes high. People considering psychotherapy should be aware that it's more art than science, that treatment can take a long time and be very expensive, and that rapport may be more important than the therapist's theoretical orientation.

Malpractice happens. Patients need to know their rights and have the courage to enforce them when they are violated, but to accept that a bad outcome in therapy doesn't necessarily mean that malpractice has occurred. Sexual misconduct—the most blatant and common malpractice—too often goes unreported and unpunished, partly because victims are ignorant of their rights. But the rage and anguish of the survivors of patients who commit suicide often lead them to mistake a bad outcome for malpractice.

The specter of a malpractice suit undoubtedly influences psychiatrists to practice defensive medicine. As noted earlier, Dr. Seymour Halleck reports that he practiced better with suicidal patients twenty years ago because he's "doing it by the book now, and thinking about what's going to get me sued." Defensive medicine can take various forms, including hospitalizing or refusing to discharge suicidal or violent patients, prescribing unnecessary medications, or spending too much time making self-protective chart notes when the patients need attention. There is no way to measure the social and economic costs of defensive medicine. They may be high, but not, I think, as high as the costs of abolishing the malpractice lawsuit—sometimes the only effective remedy for a patient who has been injured by substandard treatment.

Uncertainty is the hallmark of psychiatric malpractice litigation. As one forensic psychiatrist put it, "It's a crap shoot." The jury is probably the greatest source of uncertainty. Jurors may not understand the expert testimony and may not follow the judge's instructions even if they do. But many legal observers believe that jurors somehow "get it right" most of the time.

There is no demonstrably correct number of dollars to award a plaintiff for intangible injuries like pain and suffering. In the cases I discussed in detail—with one exception—the juries seemed to reach a fair verdict, whatever their reasoning may have been. The jury awarded Bill Jackson (chapter 13) $152,670 for injuries caused by his psychiatrist's sexual relationship with his wife. The jury gave the parents of Johnny Moore (chapter 3) $1 million for intangible injuries in the suicide death of their son. The jury awarded Shelley Rotman's parents (chapter 6) $4.5 million for pain and suffering associated with their daughter's brutal stabbing death.

The jury awards to Bill Jackson and the Moores, while obviously not the product of logical analysis, nevertheless seem reasonable. The Rotman award of $4.5 million may seem very high, yet understandable given the horrifying circumstances of Shelley Rotman's slaying. Arriving at the "right" award for intangible injuries is a matter of judgment, empathy for the human elements, and the unique facts of the case. Who better to make those judgments than twelve men and women chosen at random from the community?

In my opinion, *Paddock v. Chacko* (chapter 4) was the only case in which the jury went seriously wrong. Despite Dr. Chacko's strong case, they awarded Linda Paddock more than $2 million for injuries growing out of her unsuccessful suicide attempt. In that case, however, the trial judge exercised his corrective power to set aside a verdict that was lacking in substantial evidentiary support—illustrating one of the procedural safeguards built into the system to promote just results. Excessive jury verdicts can also be reduced on appeal. The Rotmans' verdict of $4.5 million for their daughter's death was reduced to an undisclosed amount in a settlement reached while an appeal was pending.

There are other reasons to give a major role in the process to lay juries. The uncertainty factor they represent can put a healthy pressure on the parties to settle before trial. In a close case, both sides will be reluctant to roll the dice with a jury. Beyond that, there is much to be said for preserving the jury as the average citizen's only opportunity to participate in the civil justice system.

In any event, debates about the merits of juries are largely academic. As a practical matter, it would be impossible to eliminate juries from malpractice and other civil cases. The right to a jury trial is embedded in the Seventh Amendment to the United States Constitution and in the constitutions of virtually every state. Constitutional rights aside, juries are widely perceived as a strength of American democracy.

Some critics of malpractice litigation point to long delays between the alleged malpractice and the trial. For example, the complaint in the *Rotman* case was filed in 1980, but the trial didn't get under way until 1988, eight years later. Delays postpone relief for some plaintiffs and vindication for some psychiatrists; they also dim the memories of witnesses and make some potential witnesses unavailable. Often, however, delay isn't the fault of the court system. Plaintiffs may file suits late because they aren't aware of their claims until years after treatment. Once the suits are filed, lawyers on both sides need time to prepare their cases, primarily by taking depositions of experts. That process can take a year or longer. To be sure, congested court dockets in metropolitan areas have been the cause of long delays in some cases. But those delays affect virtually all civil litigation, not just medical malpractice cases. In recent years, judges and court administrators have been paying increased attention to calendar congestion problems, and cases are going to trial more rapidly.

Attempts to simplify and expedite the medical malpractice process haven't been notably successful in the past. Arbitration is the prime example of a failed experiment. Under a typical medical malpractice arbitration statute like Maryland's, plaintiffs are required to resort first to arbitration (unless both parties agree to waive it). However, both parties have the right to appeal and receive a full court trial if they are dissatisfied with the arbitrator's decision.

Arbitration was initially viewed as quicker, less formal, and cheaper than conventional litigation—a helpful reform, if not a panacea. In practice, none of these virtues has been fully realized. Most of the time, one or both parties appeal the arbitrator's decision to court, making the process longer and more expensive than before. Or both parties will allow the case to proceed partway through the arbitration process and then waive arbitration before that process is completed. My experience as an arbitrator in medical malpractice cases in Maryland indicates that that process is occasionally successful; that is, the case is resolved while in arbitration, keeping it off crowded court dockets. But for the most part, arbitration in Maryland does not proceed to a decision, or it ends up causing additional delay and expense. There is growing sentiment to repeal that state's malpractice arbitration statute.

So-called tort reform (a euphemism for any proposed change, good or bad) has aroused lively interest in the Congress and in some state legislatures. Caps on awards for pain and suffering of, say, $350,000 are a frequent feature of reform proposals. That amount may be adequate in some cases but seems grossly inadequate in others—for example, for Shelley Rotman's murder. The problem with caps is that they're either too high, defeating their purpose, or too low, defeating deserved relief. As typically drafted, they don't keep pace with inflation. A cap might be workable if it incorporated a measure of flexibility—perhaps a certification by the judge that the facts warranted the jury's exceeding the cap.

One strong candidate for change is the general rule allowing punitive damages where the psychiatrist or hospital has acted with "malice" or in "reckless disregard" of the patient's welfare. In the *Moore* case, the jury awarded $6 million in punitive damages on top of $1 million in compensatory damages. Those millions in punitive damages would represent a windfall to the parents of Johnny Moore, who were already being compensated for injuries associated with their son's death. In any case, punitive damages would be paid by insurance companies—assuming they were within policy limits—not from the offenders' pockets. As a result, any deterrent effect they may have would be indirect. License revocation or suspension would be more effective ways to punish the few errant psychiatrists or hospitals who exhibit a reckless disregard for their patients' welfare.

On the whole, I think the present system works about as well as can be expected. Its disadvantages—delay, expense, uncertainty—are to some extent inherent in any system designed to address an alleged malfeasance by a doctor against his patient. Except for abolishing punitive damages, other possibly useful changes in the system would involve tinkering, not major change.

Psychiatrists have a phrase for people who try to cope with an unpleasant reality—such as losing a job—by pretending it hasn't happened; they're said to be "in denial." Some psychiatrists are into something resembling denial when it comes to malpractice litigation. They see it as an unfair and unwarranted threat to their professional lives, something that should be cut back or abolished entirely. The trouble with that approach, of course, is that it would deprive victims of malpractice of an often effective remedy against the small minority of psychiatrists who commit it and take away the deterrent effect of the present law. Psychiatrists should accept that malpractice suits come with the territory.

If a prospective client were to come to my office thinking he had a malpractice case against his psychiatrist, in addition to the when, where, and how, I would ask the following questions: What harm do you think has been done? Are you prepared to reveal in public embarrassing conduct and painful feelings? Would money in itself give you emotional satisfaction and real help, or are you more interested in vindication or revenge? Why don't you go to another psychiatrist instead of suing this one? Or file a complaint with the state licensing authorities? Are you prepared to spend a lot of money on experts' fees, realizing that you may lose your case and end up with a big net loss? Questions like these can create healthy second thoughts about litigation.

People we have seen struggling in this book went through those difficult questions and decided that they had to take their psychiatrists to court. Their decisions deserve our respect and fellow feeling. Joan Barkley, with her dependencies on sex, drugs, and father figures, may seem pathetic, but she cared about her children and worked a night job to help pay the bills. Johnny Moore killed himself at sixteen partly because he took on the impossible job of holding a dysfunctional family together. Their psychiatric problems were not of their own making, and they—and society as a whole—had a right to call on the law for help when psychiatrists failed them.

Perhaps it's hardest to relate to someone like Dennis Gould who killed young Shelley Rotman in cold blood. But Gould had once been a college student with a pretty girlfriend, until a demon took over his mind and his life.

SOURCES

Where a list of published sources is provided, citations of books, articles, and other source materials appear first, followed by judicial decisions of principal interest.

CHAPTER 1. INTRODUCTION

Boodman, Sandra. "A Horrible Place & a Wonderful Place." *Washington Post Magazine*, October 8, 1989.

Charles, Sara C. *Defendant*. Free Press, 1985.

Fieve, Ronald R. *Moodswing: The Third Revolution in Psychiatry*. Morrow, 1995.

Goodwin, Frederick K., and Kay R. Jamison. *Manic Depressive Illness*. Oxford University Press, 1990.

Grob, Gerald N. Letter to Karen Reeds, science editor, Rutgers University Press, July 18, 1995.

Rogers, Patrick. "Mental Health Malpractice Lawsuits, Insurance Costs Rising." *Mental Health Law Reporter*, February 1985, 3–4.

Slawson, Paul F., and Frederick G. Guggenheim. "Psychiatric Malpractice: A Review of the National Loss Experience." *American Journal of Psychiatry* 141 (1984): 979–981.

Slovenko, Ralph. "Malpractice in Psychiatry and Related Fields." *Journal of Psychiatry and Law* 9 (1981): 5–63.

———. "On the Need for Recordkeeping in the Practice of Psychiatry." *Journal of Psychiatry and Law* 7 (1979): 399–439.

Task Force on DSM-IV. *Diagnostic and Statistical Manual of Mental Disorders*. 4th ed. American Psychiatric Association, 1994.

Wahl, Otto. *Media Madness*. Rutgers University Press, 1995.

CHAPTER 2. THE LAW OF PSYCHIATRIC MALPRACTICE

American Psychiatric Association. *Principles of Medical Ethics with Annotations Especially Applicable to Psychiatry*. 1992.

Code of Maryland. Courts and Judicial Proceedings Article, Section 11-108 (b) (non-economic damages limited to $350,000).

Dawidoff, Donald J. "The Malpractice of Psychiatrists." *Duke Law Journal* 1966 (1966): 696–716.

Freiberg, Judy. "The Song Is Ended but the Malady Lingers On: Legal Regulation of Psychotherapy." *St. Louis University Law Journal* 22 (1978): 519–533.

Giesen, Dieter. *International Medical Malpractice Law.* Martinus Nijhoff, 1988.

Simon, Robert I., ed. *Review of Clinical Psychiatry and the Law.* Vols. 1–3. American Psychiatric Press, 1990–1992.

Simon, Robert I., and Robert L. Sadoff. *Psychiatric Malpractice: Cases and Comments for Clinicians.* American Psychiatric Press, 1992.

Smith, Joseph T. "The Expert Witness: Maximizing Damages for Psychic Injury." *Trial,* April 1982, 51–55.

Stone, Alan A. *Law, Psychiatry, and Morality.* American Psychiatric Press, 1984.

Brady v. Hopper, 570 F. Supp. 1333 (D. Colo. 1983), affirmed, 751 F.2d 329 (10th Circuit 1984).

Dr. Groenvelt's Case, 1 Lord Raymond 213 (1694).

Naidu v. Laird, 539 A.2d 1064 (Delaware 1988).

Riley v. Presnell, 409 Mass. 239 (1991).

CHAPTER 3. THE WALKING SUICIDE TIME BOMB

Chapter 3 is based on the trial record in *M. v. Charter Hospital of Winston-Salem, Inc.,* Guilford County, N.C., General Court of Justice, Superior Court Division, Case No. 88 CvS 7329. The names of the plaintiffs have been changed in the chapter and omitted here to respect their privacy.

CHAPTER 4. BUM RAP IN ORLANDO

Chapter 4 is based on the trial record in *Paddock v. Chacko,* 522 S.E.2d 410 (Florida 1988), except for certain background information from Sydney P. Freedberg, "Weird Antics Enliven Burn Trial," *Miami Herald,* May 27, 1986.

CHAPTER 5. SUICIDE: THE THERAPIST AS SCAPEGOAT

Bursztajn, Harold, Thomas G. Gutheil, Archie Brodsky, and Evelynn L. Swagerty. "Magical Thinking, Suicide, and Malpractice Litigation." *Bulletin of the American Academy of Psychiatry and Law* 16 (1988): 369–377.

Bursztajn, Harold, Thomas G. Gutheil, Robert M. Hamm, and Archie Brodsky. "Subjective Data and Suicide Assessment in the Light of Recent Legal Developments." *International Journal of Law and Psychiatry* 6 (1983): 317–350.

Bursztajn, Harold, Thomas G. Gutheil, Mark J. Warren, and Archie Brodsky. "Depression, Self-Love, Time, and the 'Right' to Suicide." *General Hospital Psychiatry* 8 (1986): 91–95.

Fawcett, Jan, William Scheftner, David Clark, Don Hedeker, Robert Gibbons, and William Coryell. "Clinical Predictors of Suicide in Patients with Major Affective Disorders." *American Journal of Psychiatry* 144 (1987): 35–40.

Gutheil, Thomas G. Interview with the author. 1995.

———. "Malpractice Liability in Suicide." *Legal Aspects of Psychiatric Practice* 1 (1984): 1–3.

Halleck, Seymour L. Interview with the author. 1995.

Halleck, Seymour L., and Nancy H. Halleck. *Law in the Practice of Psychiatry: A Handbook for Clinicians*. Plenum, 1980.

Pokorny, Alex D. "Prediction of Suicide in Psychiatric Patients." *Archives of General Psychiatry* 40 (1983): 249–257.

Sadoff, Robert L. Interview with the author. 1995.

Simon, Robert I. *Clinical Psychiatry and the Law*. American Psychiatric Press, 1992.

Styron, William. *Darkness Visible: A Memoir of Madness*. Random House, 1990.

Pisel v. Stamford Hospital, 180 Conn. 314 (1980).

Schuster v. Altenberg, 424 N.W.2d 159 (Wisconsin 1988).

Stepakoff v. Kantar, 473 N.E.2d 1131 (Massachusetts 1988).

CHAPTER 6. MAN WITH A MISSION

Chapter 6 is based on the trial record in *Rotman v. Mirin*, Civil Case No. 88-1562, Middlesex Superior Court, Commonwealth of Massachusetts. The decision is not published.

CHAPTER 7. SEARCH AND DESTROY

Chapter 7 is based on the trial record of the criminal prosecution of Leonard Avery for murder, *State v. Avery*, Durham County, N.C., General Court of Justice, Superior Court Division, Case No. 82 CRS 19151, on the decision of the United States District Court in *Currie v. United States*, 644 F. Supp. 1074 (1986), and on the decision of the Court of Appeals for the Fourth Circuit in *Currie v. United States*, 836 F.2d 209 (1987).

CHAPTER 8. A DANGER TO OTHERS

Ablow, Keith R. "Emotions on Ice: Imperfect Treatment for Violent Patients." *Washington Post Health Magazine*, March 2, 1993.

American Psychiatric Association Council on Psychiatry and Law. "The Physician's Duty to Take Precautions against Patient Violence." Guidance document approved by the Board of Trustees, June 1987.

American Psychiatric Association Task Force on Violence. 1974.

Geske, Michael R. "Statutes Limiting Liability for Violent Acts of Patients." *Indiana Law Journal* 64 (1989): 391–422.

Gutheil, Thomas G. Interview with the author. 1995.

Gutheil, Thomas G., Harold Bursztajn, and Archie Brodsky. "The Multidimensional Assessment of Dangerousness." *Bulletin of the American Academy of Psychiatry and Law* 14 (1986): 123–129.

Halleck, Seymour L. Interview with the author. 1995.

Klein, Joel I., and Peter E. Scheer. Amicus Curiae Brief for the American Psychiatric Association in *Barefoot v. Estelle*, 463 U.S. 880 (1983).

McCarty, Charles B. "Patient Threats against Third Parties: The Psychotherapist's Duty of Reasonable Care." *Journal of Contemporary Health Law and Policy* 5 (1989): 119–140.

Pettis, Roderick W., and Thomas G. Gutheil. "Misapplication of the Tarasoff Duty to Driving Cases: A Call for a Reframing of Theory." *Bulletin of the American Academy of Psychiatry and Law* 21 (1993): 263–275.

Sadoff, Robert L. Interview with the author. 1995.

Slovenko, Ralph. "The Hospitalization of the Mentally Ill Revisited." *Pacific Law Journal* 24 (1993): 1107–1123.

Stone, Alan A. "The Tarasoff Decisions: Suing Psychiatrists to Safeguard Society." *Harvard Law Review* 90 (1976): 358–378.

Torrey, E. Fuller. *Nowhere to Go: The Tragic Odyssey of the Homeless Mentally Ill.* Harper & Row, 1988.

Barefoot v. Estelle, 463 U.S. 880 (1983).

Peck v. Counseling Service of Addison County, 499 A.2d 422 (Vermont 1985).

People v. Poddar, 518 P.2d 342 (California 1974).

Tarasoff v. Regents of the University of California, 551 P.2d 334 (California 1976).

White v. United States, 780 F.2d 97 (D.C. Circuit, 1986).

CHAPTER 9. DR. OSHEROFF'S CASE

Chapter 9 is based primarily on depositions taken in the case of *Osheroff v. Chestnut Lodge Hospital, Inc.*, Claim No. 82-262 before the Health Claims Arbitration Office of the state of Maryland, and on hospital records. The trial before an arbitration panel was videotaped but never transcribed because the case was settled before a transcribed record was needed. As a result, there is no written record of the trial testimony. However, the deposition and trial testimony of the expert witnesses can be expected to be virtually identical in substance.

Other sources for this chapter include an unpublished manuscript by Dr. Raphael Osheroff, "A Symbolic Death," which was included in the trial record, and an article about Chestnut Lodge by Sandra Boodman, "A Horrible Place & a Wonderful Place," *Washington Post Magazine,* October 8, 1989. *I Never Promised You a Rose Garden* (Holt, Rinehart and Winston, 1964) by Joanne Greenberg, a former patient at Chestnut Lodge, provides further background information.

CHAPTER 10. DR. BEAN-BAYOG: THE THERAPIST AS MOM

Chapter 10 is the only chapter not based on the record of a formal judicial proceeding. The chapter is based primarily on extensive media coverage during the spring of 1992 concerning Dr. Margaret Bean-Bayog's treatment of Paul Lozano and the malpractice case and disciplinary proceeding against her arising out of that treatment.

Newspaper coverage included articles from the *Boston Globe* during the period March 27–April 23, 1992; the *Boston Herald* during the period March 28–April 15, 1992; Fox Butterfield, "Paths of Patient and His Therapist Cross on Dark Journey Leading to Death," *New York Times,* April 12, 1992; and Megan Rosenfeld, "The Fatal Attraction of Psychiatrist and Patient," *Washington Post,* April 17, 1992.

Other sources include:

Amended Complaint, *Lozano v. Bean-Bayog*, Commonwealth of Massachusetts, Middlesex Superior Court, Civil Action No. 91-6306.

Chafetz, Gary S., and Morris E. Chafetz. *Obsession*. Crown, 1994.

"Dr. Bean and Her Little Boy." *Newsweek*, April 13, 1992.

Gutheil, Thomas G. Interview with the author. 1995.

Statement of Allegations and Respondent's Evidentiary Submission. *In the Matter of Margaret Bean-Bayog*, Adjudicatory Case No. 92-12-DALA, Board of Registration in Medicine, Commonwealth of Massachusetts.

CHAPTER 11. IN SEARCH OF A STANDARD OF CARE

Chodoff, Paul. "Assessment of Psychotherapy: Reflections of a Practitioner." *Archives of General Psychiatry* 39 (1982): 1097–1103.

———. Interview with the author. 1995.

Commonwealth of Massachusetts, Board of Registration in Medicine. Policy No. 94-001, "General Guidelines Related to the Maintenance of Boundaries in the Practice of Psychotherapy by Physicians (Adult Patients)," January 12, 1994.

Elkin, Irene. "The NIMH Treatment of Depression Collaborative Research Program: Where We Began and Where We Are." Chap. 4 in *Handbook of Psychotherapy and Behavioral Change,* ed. Allen E. Bergin, and Sol L. Garfield. Wiley, 1994.

Gutheil, Thomas G. Interview with the author. 1995.

———. "True or False Memories of Sexual Abuse? A Forensic Psychiatric View." *Psychiatric Annals* 23 (1993): 527–531.

———. "True Recollections of a False Memory Case: *Ramona* Has Ominous Implications for Psychiatrists." *Psychiatric Times*, July 28, 1994.

Halleck, Seymour L. Interview with the author. 1995.

Karel, Richard. "Bean-Bayog Case Leaves Multitude of Unanswered Questions." *Psychiatric News*, February 5, 1993.

Klerman, Gerald L. "The Patient's Right to Effective Treatment: Implications of Osheroff v. Chestnut Lodge." *American Journal of Psychiatry* 147 (1990): 409–418.

Krauthammer, Charles. "The Twilight of Psychotherapy." *Washington Post*, December 27, 1985.

Rubenstein, Leonard. Interview with the author. 1992.

Sadoff, Robert L. Interview with the author. 1995.

Stone, Alan A. "Law, Science, and Psychiatric Malpractice: A Response to Klerman's Indictment of Psychoanalytic Pshchotherapy." *American Journal of Psychiatry* 147 (1990): 419–427.

———. "The New Paradox of Psychiatric Malpractice." *New England Journal of Medicine* 314 (1984): 1384–1387.

Tarantolo, Joseph. Interview with the author. 1995.

CHAPTER 12. MRS. BARKLEY, TWICE A WEEK

Chapter 12 is based on the court martial trial record in *United States v. R.*———. The court martial decision was affirmed by the United States Court of Military Appeals, as reported in 26 Mil. Justice Rep. 638 (1988). Names and places have been changed in the chapter and omitted from this reference due to the decision to respect the privacy of the psychiatrist and his former patient.

CHAPTER 13. ONE DOESN'T JUST SAY GOODBYE

Chapter 13 is based on the trial record in *M.*——— *v. H.*———, Wake County, N.C., General Court of Justice, Superior Court Division, Case No. 79 CvS 653, except for the shooting incident involving Dr. Winston, which is based on a newspaper article in the *Denver Post* of May 5, 1987. Names and places have been changed in the chapter and omitted from this reference to the decision to respect the privacy of the psychiatrist and his former patient.

CHAPTER 14. SEX AS "PART OF THE THERAPY"

American Psychiatric Association. *Fact Sheet—Patient/Therapist Sexual Contact.* 1992.

Appelbaum, Paul, and Linda Jorgenson. "Psychotherapist-Patient Sexual Contact." *American Journal of Psychiatry* 148 (1991): 1466–1473.

Bass, Alison, and Luz Delgado. "Board Votes to Strip Psychiatrist of License." *Boston Globe*, June 25, 1992.

Chesler, Phyllis. *Women and Madness.* Doubleday, 1972.

Coleman, Phyllis. "Sex between Psychiatrist and Former Patient: A Proposal for a 'No Harm, No Foul' Rule." *Oklahoma Law Review* 41 (1988): 1–52.

Forster, Mark. "California Woman Who Sued Psychiatrist for Seducing Her Is Awarded $4.6 Million." *Boston Globe*, July 8, 1981.

Gartrell, Nanette, Judith Herman, Sylvia Olarte, Michael Feldstein, and Russell Localio. "Psychiatrist-Patient Sexual Contact: Results of a National Survey." *American Journal of Psychiatry* 143 (1986): 1126–1131; 144 (1987): 164–169.

Grosskurth, Phyllis. *The Secret Ring: Freud's Inner Circle and the Politics of Psychoanalysis.* Addison-Wesley, 1991.

Gutheil, Thomas G. "Borderline Personality Disorder, Boundary Violations, and Patient-Therapist Sex: Medicolegal Pitfalls." *American Journal of Psychiatry* 146 (1989): 597–602.

——. Interview with author. 1995.

——. "Patients Involved in Sexual Misconduct with Therapists: Is a Victim Profile Possible?" *Psychoanalytic Annals* 21 (1991): 661–667.

——. "Patient-Therapist Sexual Relations." *Harvard Medical School Mental Health Letter* 6 (1989): 4–6.

——. "Therapist-Patient Sex Syndrome: The Perils of Nomenclature for the Forensic Psychiatrist." *Bulletin of the American Academy of Psychiatry and Law* 20 (1992): 185–190.

Gutheil, Thomas G. and Glen O. Gabbard. "The Concept of Boundaries in Clinical Practice: Theoretical and Risk-Management Dimensions." *American Journal of Psychiatry* 150 (1993): 188–196.

——. "Obstacles to the Dynamic Understanding of Therapist-Patient Sexual Relations." *American Journal of Psychotherapy* 46 (1992): 515–525.

Halleck, Seymour L. Interview with the author. 1995.

Jorgenson, Linda. "For Whom the Statute Tolls: Extending the Time during which Patients Can Sue." *Hospital and Community Psychiatry* 42 (1991): 683–684.

——. "The Furor over Psychotherapist-Patient Sexual Contact: New Solutions for an Old Problem." *William and Mary Law Review* 32 (1991): 645–732.

——. Interview with the author. 1995.

——. "Psychotherapist Liability: What's Sex Got to Do with It?" *Trial*, May 1993.

——. "Sexual Exploitation and Insurance Liability." *Tort and Insurance Law Journal* 27 (1992): 595–614.

——. "Time Out: The Statute of Limitations and Fiduciary Theory in Psychotherapist Sexual Misconduct Cases." *Oklahoma Law Review* 44 (1991): 181–223.

Noel, Barbara, with Kathryn Watterson. *You Must Be Dreaming.* Poseidon, 1992.

Sadoff, Robert L. Interview with the author. 1995.

Schoener, Gary. Letter to the author. February 24, 1995.

——. *Psychotherapists' Sexual Involvement with Clients: Intervention and Prevention.* Walk-In Counseling Center, 1989.

Slovenko, Ralph. "Liability Insurance Coverage in Cases of Psychotherapy Sexual Abuse." *Journal of Psychiatry and Law* 11 (1993): 277–288.

Strasburger, Larry, Linda Jorgenson, and Rebecca Randles. "Criminalization of Psychotherapist-Patient Sex." *American Journal of Psychiatry* 148 (1991): 859–863.

Strasburger, Larry, Linda Jorgenson, and Pamela Sutherland. "Avoiding the Slippery Slope." *American Journal of Psychotherapy* 46 (1992): 544–555.

Landau v. Werner, 105 Solicitors Journal 1008 (1961).

Roy v. Hartogs, 381 N.Y. Supp.2d 587 (1976).

Vigilant Ins. Co. v. Employers Ins. of Wausau, 626 F. Supp. 262 (New York 1986).

Walker v. Parzen, 24 Los Angeles Law Reporter 295 (1981).

INDEX

ABOUT THE AUTHOR
▼ ▼ ▼

James L. Kelley received a B.A. in humanities and a J.D. in law from the University of Iowa. He worked as a lawyer for thirty years in private practice, in teaching, with the United States Department of Justice, and with the Nuclear Regulatory Commission. He turned to full-time writing in 1993. Kelley has a long-standing interest in psychiatric malpractice and other mental health issues; he has published articles and made presentations on those subjects at mental health conferences. He lives in Takoma Park, Maryland.